PROLOGUE

PRESENT DAY
NW PENNSYLVANIA

Old Man scanned the crisp morning sky, smiled, breathed in a big gulp of excitement, and exhaled fifty years of waiting. He had almost not made it to this revered place, if "almost" was defined as "defied all earthly odds." There had been a boatload of help—doctors and surgeons, an amazing wife, an ever-supportive family, all-in friends, and a little fox. Yes, a wild red fox.

The first tee at Latrobe is an apogee in many respects as it crowns a bucolic setting in western Pennsylvania. The course is a pinnacle in another sense. If golf was born in St. Andrews, then the man, Arnold Palmer, who made it popular, had been born here. The golf club's immaculately coiffed, spongy-soft first tee is positioned at an elevation of 1,014 feet—a high point, an apogee. The tee box is an extension of the luxuriant putting green, which sits in the shadows of the history-rich clubhouse's veranda. Roll in a few three-foot practice putts, exchange the putter for the driver, and you are at the opening tee.

Old Man walked onto it.

The September morning broke beautifully—a mixture of three-quarters warm and one-quarter chill in the air. Football game temperatures, he thought. The first day of sweater weather, no, not quite. The sky overhead was blazed blue and cottontail clouds dotting the heavens here and there. The scent of pinecones, the best of potpourri smells, hung in the air. This place was not only his Holy Grail of golf; it smelled like Christmas, too, he thought.

Old Man teed up a forty-year-old Top Flite golf ball. His bond to the brand began decades ago, when he struck a low hooking eight-iron into the cup for a hole-in-one in a Virginia Commonwealth University team practice round. When he plucked the golf ball out of the cup way back then, he had no way of knowing that he would tee a similar ball in the hallowed ground of Latrobe many years later. Old Man could afford a so-called tour quality ball now; back then, a sleeve of new Top Flites and a buck for a hot dog were the high life.

The ball atop the wooden tee was a gift from an old buddy, an aging red fox. The fox, named Mr. Fox, had left the ancient golf ball by a log where Old Man and he sat to eat cherry pie and muse about life. Old Man appreciated the longevity of the golf ball on the peg, sold long ago either in a municipal course pro shop or off the shelf at discount sporting goods store. The yellowed ball had been in the forest of Fox World for decades, likely lost in a backyard chipping contest and found by a playful fox pup. It was the ideal gift for Old Man's sixtieth birthday, Mr. Fox thought. The polite canine brought gifts often—rubber balls, hawk feathers, sunglasses, missing gloves, a lost cigar lighter, and sixty-six dollars in US currency.

Old Man took in the western Pennsylvania vista a second time, breathed in another lungful of air, and sighed. He remembered a morning two years ago on the tenth tee at St. Andrews Old Course. There had been slight heart pain, shortness of breath, and stomach nausea. Old Man had blamed the incident on acid reflux from late pub nights on a Scotland golf trip and his daily consumption of a spicy meat pie and an Irn-Bru soda combo platter from a food truck parked behind the Old Course's ninth green. But he knew better. The meat pie was delicious and high quality—like everything at the Old Course. As for the soda, Old Man had consumed dozens before without effect. The source of the chest pain felt deeper, Old Man had thought back then, but he concocted a plausible excuse by blaming the pie and blaspheming the soda gods of Scotland. Do anything but own it, Old Man had said silently back then. Denial is a cheap, temporary solution for those in a hurry.

After the Scotland incident, the bell of change rang loud a few months later. Old Man's world cratered with illness, career disruption, and near death. Patches and fixes followed. Four heart operations spawned a pulmonary embolism and upper-arm blood clots, necessitating a dozen hospital bracelets and months of cardiac rehabilitation. Cures, with a long list of side effects, arrived in pill bottles; others dripped in from IV bags. Every pill or therapy was chased down with one thing—a healing swig of hope. The doctors were clear and united in their prognosis: find a way to relax or the arrythmia would take him. So, after forty plus years of "work hard, run fast, do more," he was left alone to figure it out.

The universe had sent a guide from the oddest of provenances. A red fox, an aging fox from a magical forest called Fox World, stepped up to help. Old Man had laughed quietly back then. Even in his animal-loving depths, Old Man felt the universe's offering was disappointedly short of the mark. A fox? Really? That's it? No calvary coming over the hill? Apparently not. The cash out after a life of hard work was a one-fox Praetorian Guard brigade.

Old Man looked down the first fairway at Latrobe and saw the umbrella-logoed flag far away on the first green. He laughed under his breath. Wow, had he underestimated that old fox or what. "Or what" was the answer, because the fox was Mr. Fox, and Old Man would discover that Mr. Fox was an often challenged, but never defeated, leader.

Old Man looked at the Top Flite on the tee and inhaled deeply a third time. Enough commiserating about the ills of days gone by; it was go-time, and he formed a "V" with his right thumb and index finger on the club's grip. His grip was strong, too strong golf instructors often said, so the "V" pointed a bit right of his right shoulder. He looked down at the aged-yellow ball, waggled the driver once, and started his backswing with a non-textbook fast jerk. The transition at the top of Old Man's golf swing was a mere nanosecond; the downswing chopped down and sped forward erratically.

This is where the engineering problems ensued. Old Man had forgotten to insert a half-inch heel lift in his left golf shoe. Needed to correct a leg-length discrepancy, the missing heel wedge was the first falling domino in an ill-fated swing. The left heel dropped quick—and too far—and the mechanical flaw shot the right hip forward and then into a hard roll to the left. If Old Man had one speck of athleticism (and that was doubtful), it was hand-eye coordination. More than once, he had caught tipped wineglasses at business dinners before the white linen was stained cabernet red. Not today. The brain's neurons fired an alert to slow down the roll of the wrists, anchored in their path by his overspun hips. His fascia-bound shoulders and scarred chest muscles would not process the change order. The toe of the club outraced the heel to the ball and the ball's destiny was locked in.

The ball shot left—about fence post high. The left curving side-spin bled off the altitude of the golf ball in a blink. It dove into the pine needles like a scared quail seeking cover. It was a masterpiece duck hook with no brushstrokes missed in its perfection. Yet, it was the sweetest duck hook that he had ever hit, because he was here at the storied Latrobe to hit it. *If you're alive, you've won*, the old fox would say.

Old Man locked eyes with Smiling Wife sitting patiently in the golf cart. His heart fluttered in a healthy, right kind of way. What a rock this lady had been for two years—loving, omnipresent, and always smiling. He ambled stiffly back to the cart and inserted the Callaway driver into his golf bag. He double-checked the adjustment setting on the back of the club. There was a fade adjustment screw, but there was no setting for "anti-screaming duck hook." With a smile, he slid the fox-themed headcover onto the club and whispered Mr. Fox's mantra again.

Smiling Wife asked innocently, "Do you think that we can find your Mr. Fox golf ball?" Coming from a golfing buddy, the comment would have been a sarcastic dig. From her, it was well-meaning, and they laughed and began the search. She rolled forward in the golf cart; he walked the one hundred forty yards to his ball. His health would not allow an eighteen-hole walk, but he was determined to walk downhill to the first green and later to tackle the steep ascension of the eighteenth fairway on this storied course. Old Man hitched up his pants and began walking. He had waited fifty years for this day. His gazed southeast to Fox World, two hundred and seventeen miles away in Virginia. Old Man thought of the oasis where he had healed and of his devoted hiking mate with whom he had walked. With sign language, he relayed their signature "one-two-three-for-you-and-me" greeting to the southeast compass point and mouthed the words, "Thank you, old friend. I'm here because of you!"

Back in Virginia, Mr. Fox looked northwest, pricked his ears, and picked up the telegraphed message. He looked up to the sky with a toothy grin and fox-texted back, *we are alive, we won; now bring home some of that Latrobe cherry pie.*

Hours later at Old Man's sixtieth birthday lunch, there was a succulent surprise—a slice of the golfing legend's favorite dessert, Latrobe Country Club cherry pie. Old Man forked a generous bite, passed on the side dollop of whipped cream, and savored the pie's sweetness. Only one thing would have made it sweeter—if the pie-loving Mr. Fox had been there on the veranda to share the fruity treat. With that thought, Old Man wrapped half of the pie slice in a napkin and placed it inside his golf hat on the chair beside him. Mr. Fox would have his cherry pie, and as he relaxed and ate it, Old Man would tell the story of their five hundred mile walk in Fox World.

TWO YEARS EARLIER

SAN DIEGO, CALIFORNIA
TO WASHINGTON, DC

United 232 backed out of the gate at 8:15 a.m. and slow rolled to the edge of Runway 927. With engines spooling and air brakes on, the plane shook gently until there was a soft lurch forward. The plane climbed steadily, piercing the marine layer hunched over San Diego, until robin egg blue skies popped. The metal bird turned right and set an east-northeast heading to Ronald Reagan National Airport in Washington, DC. The tired business executive buckled into seat 2-A. Years gone by, there may have been a free upgrade to first class. In a waning career, perks dry up and get redistributed. Old Man, as he often referred to his tired self these days, had bought the first-class bump out of his own pocket. He wanted to stretch out his legs, sore from walking the thinly carpeted concrete floor of the San Diego convention center, all 615,700 square feet of it and he also desired a quiet refuge to think, to examine, to analyze. The seat upgrade was a much-needed alone zone. That said, there is never a more efficient torture chamber than one of a tired, confused man alone in his thoughts, so maybe the alone zone was a bad idea. His grimace turned to a grin with that mental gem. Might as well laugh (at himself), Old Man thought.

San Diego was an optimal mix of good weather and great people. The business trip to his favorite city in America had been filled with promising prospect meetings and relationship-enhancing luncheons with colleagues. There was even a lovely chance meeting with a close-as-a-brother friend of twenty years, Jeff, and his fiancée. The three compressed two years of catch-up into a single cocktail at an outdoor bistro. As he walked away from the impromptu libation, Old Man knew that the sand grains of these delightful serendipities ran low in the hourglass.

There had been time for a speed walk through the San Diego Zoo where the meerkats monopolized his fast-moving visit. Meerkats had first captured his eye at the Cheyenne Mountain Zoo in Colorado Springs during a symposium junket years ago. Diligent sentries, pack loyal, observant to an obsessive degree, meerkats scan the sky constantly—not in search of an esoteric higher meaning of life. No, meerkats know that threats come from everywhere, from every direction. They sure as hell do, Old Man agreed. Meerkats watch the sky; business executives look over their shoulders. Meerkats lock their long-nailed paws into the dirt—grounded in their environs but poised to move, bolt, evade. Was Corporate World really any different, Old Man asked himself. Stay grounded, trust few, and be ready to roll with change—thank you meerkat brothers for the reminder. Over the span of consuming a zoo creamery ice cream cone, Old Man decided that he wanted to be reincarnated as a meerkat.

Hundreds of business trips had totaled to little more than endless plane walking and plain talking in the hollow life of a salesperson. The San Diego trip ranked with the best—for a different reason than normal, he suspected. Yes, the pulchritude of this waterfront city was second to none. But melancholy rose and ruled the mood in his mind for a moment. Could this trip or one soon in the future be his last? Old Man had read many stories about sudden endings and premature retirements. Athletes, CEOs, salespersons, etc., regardless of rank or slot, never know when the end will come. An injury, an illness, a regime change, four rough quarters on the NYSE and you are gone in a New York minute.

The end—was it here? The acrid taste in his mouth was not from the fresh brewed coffee in the United Airlines waxed paper cup. Like any confident sales executive, his ego reared a little. If this was indeed the last lap, he would accept it, but he would run faster than ever before. *Run fast, work hard, win.* It was a game plan that had worked for thirty-five years. Yet he admitted silently that the same play from the same playbook had led to one place—being aching tired. So why on earth run the same play in the future and try to run it better and faster and stronger? Ignorance and limited repertoire were the answers. If there was a blessing in his self-flagellation, it was that a speck of self-awareness emerged. Old Man tilted the coffee cup to his lips and swallowed the coffee and the sour taste of acceptance.

Old Man centered his racing mind, tapped on email links, and confirmed a physician appointment and vitamin refills from Amazon. Discarding the caffeine-laced airline coffee, he pulled a Ph-balanced Icelandic water and a plump navel orange from his backpack, reclined his seat for a twenty-minute nap and just that quickly he imagined he was back in control.

Except he was not. A better plan (he would learn later) would be to let go. Let it all go, but that felt vulnerable and mentally lazy, Old Man agonized. Old lions could not expose their underbelly to predators. Old Man dropped the self-tormenting and opted for the solitude of meditation on the cross-country flight. Never proficient at meditation, he tried anyway and relaxed and breathed in and out rhythmically for a few minutes. Random positive thoughts scrolled in his fogged brain. Think of something or a situation that relaxes you, he commanded himself. Old Man centered his mind on an autumn afternoon walk in the woods and hearing the owls and the hawks and maybe, hopefully, a chance sighting of his friend, a wild red fox. The old fox always seemed calm and in charge, but not flaunting it. Soothing yellow light enveloped the tired salesman's thoughts, and sleep followed quickly and deeply.

Four hours later, Flight 232 lowered its landing gear. The jet made a low-altitude wide arc and lined up for approach into Ronald Reagan National Airport. In the sharp turn, the wings tilted. Bright orange light from the afternoon sun danced off the surface of Beaver Lake and reflected into seat 2-A's window. The refreshed (at least for the moment) business executive awoke and craned his neck to see the pond's golden surface. Below, he saw his neighborhood and his house on the border of Fox World, the green canopy speckled with dots of autumn's orange and yellow. A short cab ride home and there would be enough daylight for a forest walk tonight. He looked closer at Beaver Lake and focused his eyes keenly. Was that an orange fox on top of the old beaver dam? Old Man's spirits lifted.

From the hillside near Beaver Lake, the old fox looked up and squinted. The sun bounced off the shiny silver body of Flight 232. Mr. Fox liked the giant metal dragonflies that flew over the forest in the morning and afternoon. Often, he tracked them across the sky. The plane caught and held his fox eye. *Was that his friend looking out the window of the metal dragonfly?* Maybe and the hope lifted Mr. Fox's spirits.

With a bracing jolt and a bark of rubber on Runway 12-30, United 232 settled into Virginia. The tired old guy gathered his backpack, left his seat, and walked the plane's departure ramp in paralyzing thought. He longed to walk a new path— even if for just a little while. In thirty days, Old Man would get his wish; the gateway would be unusual, and the ticket would be stamped with the highest price ever.

FOX WORLD, VIRGINIA

In Fox World, 2,732 miles from San Diego, the aging red fox sat atop the long-abandoned fox den overlooking Beaver Lake. Virginia's autumn afternoon sun warmed his creaky bones as he watched the sun shimmer on the glass-still surface of Beaver Lake. He considered fishing or frogging, but he had not walked here to hunt. This was not his territory and there could be scraps initiated by stronger foxes because of Mr. Fox's stealthy intrusion. Mr. Fox risked a fox fight just by being here. Food was scarce, new home construction had taken acres of pristine hunting fields. There had been a lot of small game here in the tall, wild grasses in the old days. His habitat was mostly gone now, replaced by driveways and swing sets.

Mr. Fox walked the two-mile length of Fox Forest; his thoughts crevassed in conflict. He had not been back to his birth home in the forest's west end in many years. *Something had driven him to come here on this day. What? Why? Was it for closure?* He had lived much longer than most wild red foxes. An average lifespan of a red fox in the wild is five years. He was almost nine. *Was his life winding down? Had this long trek today been born of silver-aged nostalgia?*

Mr. Fox was born at Beaver Lake during the most horrific winter storm in Virginia history. During a three-day period that February, it had snowed fifty-one inches. His mom, Buttercup, had sculpted the top of an ancient beaver dam into a fox burrow. And there, he and his brother were born in the snowstorm. He remembered how he and Favre, as kits, had competed for the highest vantage point on the dam. The apogee provided the best views—a theme to a good life.

A train track was erected near the spot where he sat now. It had taken five years (or sixty full moons in fox time) to build. The crumpled *Washington Post* newspapers (near the dumpster he had eaten out of when he was young) had stated that the train track cost over $46,000 per foot. As a fox with a long tail, he was three feet in length. As a train track, he would be worth almost $150,000—but he was just a little fox, one forgotten by modern progress. It would have made his hardscrabble life easier if the train budget had included a few dollars for new habitat grasses, milk weed, fruit trees, and thistle to help butterflies and birds and small animals. There had not been apparently.

Once built, the commuter train changed everything in Fox World. The screeching brakes pierced the air during daylight hours, waking nocturnal creatures like foxes. The heavy metal train cars shook their fox den walls as they rolled by and as a result, Mr. Fox had moved into another part of the forest. Near his new home, there were challenges as well. High-rise condominiums arched to the sky on the edge of Fox Forest. The skyscrapers were much taller than The Great Oak, the largest tree in Fox Forest. Built on the east end of Fox World, the condominiums blocked the sunrise. This made Mr. Fox sad; he liked sunrises. Obstructed morning sunlight, diminished hunting grounds, road noise—these were the things that challenged the aging fox and his fiefdom, Fox World. Yet he had survived a hundred full moons here. It was his home, and he accepted its flaws and shortcomings.

He thought of his mother, Buttercup. A twinge of sadness gripped his heart. She had passed away suddenly in a windy thunderstorm six months after he and his brother, Favre, were born. His mother was four years old when she left Fox World to join The Great Fox upstairs. She had been the most caring mother ever, and Mr. Fox missed her sweetness, her wisdom, her gentle teaching lessons. Buttercup had taught him a life of lessons in their brief months together.

Orphaned, he and his brother survived on grasshoppers their first summer. He remembered the bond that he and Favre had formed as they stalked insects. Favre was bigger, so he took most of the catch. They scratched out a living—barely. They missed their mother, but the hardship of hunger drove them forward. *Try harder, do more, run faster* was their motivation for survival heading into winter, yet they were fearful. If the winter brought another fifty inches of snow in a Virginia climate accustomed to one-fifth that, they were in jeopardy. Their chances of survival would be better if they split. Nature drove that decision too as foxes are lone wolves when they are not raising a family. The golden days of the grasshopper-hunting buddies ended far too soon. One morning in October, Mr. Fox walked east; Favre walked southwest. And to this day, Mr. Fox had not seen his brother.

His first winter alone was fortunately mild, but as a juvenile fox with ill-developed hunting skills and low body weight, he was in peril daily. The young Mr. Fox had been without food for days (except for spillage from bird feeders or licking ketchup packets from the trash cans) when the coldest temperatures hit. The hunger made him lethargic, and he napped in a curl under his fluffy tail to preserve body heat. With winter on top of him, he needed calories, lots of calories. His brother, Favre, had headed towards the six-lane highway when he left. There was a fast-food restaurant there that threw away unsold cheeseburgers at night. With the right wind conditions, the odor wafted over to Fox World on occasion. Mr. Fox was tempted. He was starving and he was afraid. His fear exceeded his hunger, though. Foxes who crossed the big highway often did not return.

Mr. Fox continued to reminisce about his youth as the September sunbeams warmed his graying orange forehead. A wide fox smile spread across his face, triggered by the thought of the good fortune that had come when he was a starving pup nine years ago. It was like yesterday when N. Oldman and Beacon had entered his life and saved him.

On that fateful day, Mr. Fox had been napping under a five-foot tall American holly tree, its waxy bushy green leaves sheltering him from the December snow dusting. Mr. Fox saw the human walk close. His mom, Buttercup, had said humans were to be feared; humans thought foxes were bad and dangerous. He thought, *I'm just a little fox. I only weigh eleven pounds. I do not want to hurt anyone. I'm just cold and hungry.* Buttercup had said one other thing. *There are good humans that you can trust. You will know them. Trust your fox heart,* she said.

The dog spotted the adolescent Mr. Fox first and the terrier whirled and whined, which caught the human's attention. Terrified, the young Mr. Fox flattened his body to the ground and tried to disappear. He peered through the bush's thick green leaves to assess if the danger would pass. He heard his mom's voice again: *You will know, son; trust your fox heart.* The man pulled a clear plastic zippered bag out of his pocket, leaned down and gave the puppy a piece of meat. The puppy wagged his tail, spun around with yipping joy, and jumped into the man's fleece-covered arms. *That looks like a warm spot,* thought the young, shivering Mr. Fox. Under a nearby holly tree, the man scraped a pile of leaves into a warm, sheltered bed. As Mr. Fox watched, the man did the most exquisite of things—he opened the plastic baggy and poured all the meat morsels onto the leaf-lined bed. There were several mouthfuls, the little fox counted. The kind man and the energetic terrier puppy walked away.

Years later, the memory of that day was still snapshot vivid in Mr. Fox's mind. He was sure that the food sustenance had saved his young life. He slept in his leaf bed that night, his body safe from snow and warmed inside by the delicious protein calories. When he awoke the next morning, it was a charcoal-gray day and snowflakes were piling up beyond the radius of his tiny tree. Surprisingly, there were human shoe tracks in the fresh-fallen snow. Down the trail under a second American holly tree was a fleece blanket, a steamed Cornish hen, and a bright-orange, spiky, rubber-ball chew toy coated in honey and peanut butter. It was Christmas Day, Mr. Fox's first one. His mom had been right. *If you trust your fox heart, you can make special friends.*

Mr. Fox's reminiscing about his childhood faded, and his mind clock readjusted to the present day. He was happy that he had come to his birthplace and spent time thinking about his mom and his brother. *Was Favre still alive? What a joy it would be to see him,* Mr. Fox thought. He rose from his curled position atop the crumbling beaver dam and stretched his old creaky bones to their rigid limits. Downward dog ... whoaaaa!!! Upward facing dog ... stretttccchhh!!!

Before leaving Beaver Lake, Mr. Fox decided that this would be his "die spot" someday. It was a splendid spiritual hideaway where he could draw one last breath in Fox World and accept the golden light of the next world. He felt connected to this spot—the last spot where he had seen his mother and his brother. Today had been a special day, an afternoon to remember his heritage.

With a poignant parting glance at Beaver Lake, he turned for the walk home to his den in Foxville. A giant metal dragonfly, aka United 232, cast a large shadow on Beaver Lake as it crossed under the sun. Mr. Fox looked up with a hopeful glance and tracked it. He saw (or imagined) a face in the airplane's window. His spirits lifted; the human that he trusted was home. One ancient paw in front of another, he walked home to meet his friend from Human World.

 # FOX NIRVANA

Mr. Fox, as hard as his life was, viewed his forest as a nirvana. He cherished every morning and every sunset in Fox World. Here, he lived a simple grateful life, aimed for the best, and mustered enough grace to accept the rest.

Old Man was notably different—disappointingly. He did not know, or admit it if he did, that he needed a nirvana, too, along with a darn good measure of time immersed in it. The human had one gear and it was the bull-in-a-china-shop variety. Old Man aimed for the best, and if less came, he broke a lot of china. One, a creature of finesse, and the other, a human of dogged determination, Mr. Fox and Old Man were an odd couple. The fox saw beauty in everything, and the man could not see nirvana right in front of his face.

An oasis is defined simply in the dictionary as "a fertile spot in a desert where water is found," and by this definition, Fox World was a blissful pocket of nature's serenity, and it most certainly watered one's soul. It was an oasis surrounded, engulfed, and dominated by a desert—aka the sprawling Washington, DC suburbia. Some would say that Washington, DC is a wasteland, not a desert. Mr. Fox would be too diplomatic to criticize; he liked to see the best in all things.

Fox World, oasis or not, was shrinking—visibly. Boxed in on three sides by a six-lane highway, a subway train track, and expansive concrete office parks filled with Fortune 1000 companies, the greenness of Fox World was an anachronism to the gray hardness of the suburbs. Newly constructed homes on the fourth boundary of Fox World hasten the shrinkage, as Human World's mantra was "everyone needs a big grass-mowed-short yard."

And yet, there in the middle of the urban sprawl's macadam parking lots are the sixty bucolic acres of Fox World. The land is shaped oddly—a long and skinny piece of forest running east to west. It is 2,900 yards long end to end—longer if one walks to the top of Fox Mountain in the east and the western edge of Beaver Lake. Fox River runs the entire expanse. Fox Creek branches into the river midway through the forest. Beaver Lake, until recently home to actual beavers, is an end point in the west, *the land of the setting sun*, the foxes would say. The "lake" is two acres large. Sediment from parking lot run-off has reduced the depth noticeably. Elevation of Fox World is 495 feet above sea level. Fox Mountain, at the eastern end of Fox World, rises a bit higher.

The forest is replete with mighty oaks and other deciduous trees, many are two centuries old, and build the forest's apex to sixty-five feet tall. There are sparse patches of evergreens—fortunately enough to provide pine needles for bluebird nests and deer bedding. Plentiful stands of American holly, one of the best outcroppings in Virginia, line the forest and provide rain and snow cover for Fox World's citizens. The holly trees vary in height from five-foot-tall bushes to trees that stretch to thirty feet high and their dark green leaves frame bright red berries in a classic Christmas image. The bitter red berries are consumed by songbirds as a last resort when winter hunger sets in.

A casual observer might think that the forest, threatened by massive urban encroachment, would be bereft of wildlife. In fact, development and progress had concentrated wildlife as other nearby forests fell. The forest citizens are diverse—squirrels, raccoons, opossums, beaver, chipmunks, heron (great blue and little green), owls (barred and great horned), hawks (various, including red shouldered, red tailed, broad), woodpeckers (red belly, pileated, downy, and hairy), foxes (red and gray), deer, and dozens of songbirds. Rabbits are spotted rarely because the tightly mown fringe grasses impinge their habitat. A bobcat and a coyote mosey through on rare occasions.

Mr. Fox, Bucky the deer, Professor Owl, Colonel Hawk, Russell Raccoon, and Deja Blue the heron are the kingdom elders. They hold high hope for Fox World, and when worry is merited, they do so silently. After all, leaders must be stoic and sanguine when challenged. These animal sentries answer the clarion call to lead, and they do so gently and fairly.

Human World and Corporate World squeeze Fox World. Car parks. Office buildings. Train tracks. Bulldozers. Pollution in Fox River. Skyrises. Mostly, though, people ignore the forest. Human visitors include an occasional dogwalker or a coder on a cigarette break seeking cool shade at the forest's edge. All are in a hurry; thus, they see no stake in the ground with which to gauge the forest's shrinkage. It is hard to grasp the tree canopy's plight in the duration of a break-time cigarette. And even if one did, they would likely shrug it off. After all, the animals can always go somewhere else, they would say.

Until they can't.

FOX BITS

The next morning, Old Man unpacked from the sales convention trip. September was convention season, so he did not carry the roller suitcase to his home's fourth story loft. The roller bag took up its secondary (and ready to go) position against the master bedroom wall. His interest piqued by the plane-ride thoughts of Mr. Fox, he sat with a coffee in the den and surfed the web about foxes. Friends were always asking him questions about foxes because "he knew one," so he decided to build a conversational knowledge for the next colleague's inquiry.

Vulpes vulpes, part of the Candidae genealogical branch, is a worldly citizen. The red fox roams North and Central America, Europe, Asia, Australia, and North Africa. There are none in Iceland or New Zealand. The Fox World version is thirty-two to thirty-six inches long and weighs eleven to fourteen pounds. The male is called a "dog"; the female is a "vixen." Baby foxes are affectionately titled "pups" or "kits". A group or family of foxes is a "skulk" or "leash." Red foxes choose a mate for life, and both male and female hunt food for their growing pups. When not raising their young, foxes enjoy being loners. Old Man nodded in agreement, solitude is good,ll—as he read this fox characteristic on the internet.

Foxes are omnivores—combining their hunting and scavenging skills to assemble meals. They hunt small animals (rabbits, chipmunks, field mice, moles), ground birds and their eggs, fish, crawfish, and amphibians (frogs, small snakes, lizards). They snack on grasshoppers, worms, and grubs. They equally enjoy strawberries, blackberries, blueberries, plums, carrots, and wild grasses. Red foxes live along the forest's edge. Their homes are in hollow logs, rock overhangs, or in burrows they dig. Dens always include multiple egresses in the event of danger. In urban areas, they rear their young in temporary shelter under sheds, porches, or decks. Foxes are afraid of humans but often seek to be close to them. The reason is simple—their nemesis, the coyote, avoids humans, thus, the fox sees humans as de facto protectors.

Mating season is December and January. The relationship is woman-led; the vixen calls the male to mate with a loud squall. Kits are born fifty days later. Kits remain in the den for four weeks and are weaned from their mother's milk within six weeks. They remain near mom or dad until autumn. Four out of five foxes perish in their first year due to automobiles, starvation, or cold. Predators include wolves, coyotes, and eagles. Humans hunt them for fun and trap them for fur. In the wild, five years is a normal life span for a red fox. In sanctuaries, foxes may live ten to twelve years.

The red fox vehicle is equipped with excellent accessories. Vertical eye slits refract double the amount of light, giving them reasonable night vision. Their hearing is acutely tuned and they can hear moles tunneling several feet underground. Their back legs are powerful, capable of a vertical leap of six feet and propelling their light frame to thirty-five mph. Their pawprints are an odd set—five plus four. The front foot shows a five-toed print in the snow; the rear foot, though, has only four toes. Foxes, quiet and stealthy, are also quite vocal. From barks, grunts, yips, and primal screams, the red fox has over a dozen vocalizations. The most interesting one is made when one fox is approaching an acquaintance. Called gekkering, it is a high-pitched happy-sounding song that sounds like chimpanzees playing together at the zoo.

THE PORTAL TO
MAGICAL FOX WORLD

For years, Mr. Fox had been friends with Old Man's terrier, Beacon. If Beacon had not spotted Mr. Fox half-frozen under a holly bush nine years ago, Mr. Fox would have likely perished. Beacon had saved Mr. Fox, and the fox was always thrilled to see the feisty pup. Beacon had a purposeful walk, Mr. Fox noted. His short legs were little pistons that went up and down with great efficiency and drove him forward. His eyes were keen; they missed nothing. He was bold and confident and he explored and sniffed things assertively—yet he was kind. *Beacon's big button eyes were his old soul mark*, thought Mr. Fox. The Jack Russell terrier wore a jingly bell on his collar, and when it rang in his fox ear, he would run through the forest to see his friend. He liked Beacon's white fur and tri-color markings, punctuated by a quarter-sized, milk-chocolate brown spot centered on top of his head.

Stressed after the San Diego conference, Old Man self-prescribed a Saturday morning walk with Beacon in Fox World as the right tonic. The pleasant thought had calmed his mind on the plane yesterday. It would be a long hike, he hoped, and as such, a hiking supplies list was called for. The avocado-green backpack had been purchased impulsively at a Tumi kiosk during Corporate World's great harvest bonus days. Stylistically speaking, it was incredibly cool then; in fact, it was cool now—many years later. It was the "old man" who carried it who was no longer cool. Carrying the avocado Tumi bag on the morning train commute looked like Old Man was "trying too hard to be hip," aka "too cool for school." Better put, Old Man had simply become "teacher old" at the school. He laughed at his own joke. Cool bag, not so hip old guy.

The laptop shoulder bag had been converted to a day-hiker back-pack and "dash bag." Grab it and go. Stocked for a fast exit, it had everything for a half-day hike and photo safari: Nikon P1000 for nature shots, two extra Nikon batteries, a pair of lightweight 12x25 Nikon birder binoculars, laminated Virginia bird and butterfly guidebooks, smartphone and back-up battery (after all, Old Man did not want to lose power while listening to biohacking tips or paranormal Bigfoot podcasts); Bose noise-cancellation ear buds, Boker utility knife, dog/fox whistle, gray Guinness Brewery fleece in case the weather kicked up, Green Bay Packers hat (the green was good camo color for birding), dry wool socks, sunglasses, aluminum water bottle and Liquid IV hydration-powder packets, instant coffee, dehydrated chicken noodle soup, a banana or an apple, a Snickers candy bar, fresh blueberries and a bison bar for Mr. Fox's snack, dried cherries for Mr. Fox's dessert, bison dog biscuits for Beacon, and a folded 6' x 8' plastic tarp for sudden rainstorms. Last into the backpack went the Opus X torch lighter/cutter and an emergency cigar—there were always emergencies in Fox World … wink, wink. Orchestrated emergencies reminded Old Man of the W.C. Fields joke: "I always carry a small flask of gin in case of snake bites. I also carry a small snake." Aaahh yes, be prepared.

His memory scrolled back to years ago when a fierce spring rain-storm hit Fox Mountain. Two miles from home and three inches of rain coming, according to AccuWeather radar; the only choice was to bed down. The plastic tarp had saved the day. The heavy-gauge plastic tarp spread over the top of a six-foot holly tree had created a rain shelter and a toasty gray fleece had countered the dropping thermometer. A portable Bunsen burner, a bottle of water, and a soup packet had rendered a hot meal. A pocket radio tuned to the Jim Rome sports-talk station had added a lively spark to the rainy after-noon. The emergency cigar had been tapped and soothed the tension of being trapped in a rainstorm in the woods. Beacon had nibbled biscuits and meat treats on Old Man's lap, and both had succumbed to a raindrop-rhythm-induced nap.

What unfolded was one of the best afternoons of his life—unex-pected and totally unblemished solitude in a portable man cave with his devoted terrier. Old Man cherished that memory. Maybe again someday, he hoped. He shouldered the laptop-bag-turned-hiking-backpack and headed out with Beacon for the one-mile walk to the entrance of Fox World, the autumn sun warming the back of his neck as he walked the trail.

Blue jays and crows sent piercing warnings through the forest. *Human is coming! Beware! No, wait a minute, cancel the warning; it is the human who brings peanuts in a shell to us in his ever-fashionable green backpack. Meet us at the trail head for a peanut picnic.* Old Man laughed, spread the peanuts, and kept walking. Autumn's warmth dimmed a notch as he entered the forest's yellow-orange-red speckled canopy and so did Old Man's edginess. Corporate World's stress never disappears, he thought, but it does dissipate sometimes—little by little.

Up ahead, Professor Owl sang her barred owl serenade: *"Who, who, who cooks for you?"* from her sky-high seat atop the sixty-five-foot Great Mighty Oak. Deja Blue the heron walked Fox Creek on tall spindly legs and fished for dinner. From a fish's perspective, her manatee-blue feathers blended with the sky above, making her invisible. She froze, her four-inch yellow bill cocked like a hunter's crossbow. With a blur, it snapped forward and pierced the water's surface and her reward was a juicy bluntnose minnow, digested alive. Sushi as fresh as it can be served. Five more and dinner would be done.

Rustling leaves and snapping branches signaled the upstream arrival of nine-year-old Bucky the deer. Years before, Old Man had chased off a poacher who had drawn an arrow at Bucky and since then, Bucky never missed an opportunity to greet Old Man. Bucky walked with the confident gait of a hulking athlete. Not in a rush, the bulk of his mocha frame and twelve-point antlers parted the brush brusquely and noisily. Rainfall two days previous had added weight to the acorn crop hanging in the trees, and the succulent treats had begun to fall. Bucky craved the calories, and he could not wait to gobble up the new crop. He preferred the white oak acorns—they contained less tannic acid, making them buttery and smooth. Unlike chardonnay that could wait longer in the barrel for its day, acorns could not. Eat them quick before they perish was Bucky's plan.

From atop his comfortable log in the Lincoln Logs section of Fox World, Mr. Fox took it all in—the owl serenade, the heron hunter, his buddy Bucky, and the approaching human. *He was so lucky,* the fox thought. He had a circle of good friends for life.

Old Man was less cheerful and more monotone, a pale emotional palette inherited from the rigors of Corporate World. Sure, he saw the fox, the deer, the heron, and the owl. Colonel Hawk flew tight protective circles of air cover. She was majestic, Old Man observed admiringly. To him, though, at this point in his life, these majestic wild animals were merely cardboard cut-outs pasted in an idyllic postcard—2-D, not 3-D. Old Man was more relaxed here in Fox World, for sure, but he was not immersed in its hidden magic. He had not yet found the portal, the escape hatch. His mind was still elsewhere in the trials and throes of Corporate World. A career comeback was still possible, he fantasized. Work longer, try harder, run faster. An addict's sad song. The back of his head tingle. It hurt, but Old Man shook if off.

He waved to Mr. Fox, left some meat and berries, stayed awhile, shuffled his feet, and with his mind racing about work, he turned promptly for home. He did not stay, relax, talk to his fox friend, and breathe in the serenity. Halfway back home, he was twisted up in Human World and Corporate World conflicts and regretted that he had not lingered in Fox World. He had gone there to relax. Instead, he had obsessed about Corporate World and abandoned his animal friend. Even Beacon felt rushed and shortchanged. He barked and tugged at Old Man's khaki pants. Old Man reached down and lifted the terrier in his arms, kissed the quarter-sized circle on his head, and spoke: "Time to go home, boy." The little terrier tike pouted. *Not yet, Dad, there is magic here. Healing magic.*

Mr. Fox watched his human friend turn and walk away and his heart sank. He did not care about the food; he just wanted to talk and listen to his friend's stories about the world outside Fox World. *Come back soon, N. Oldman,* he sighed.

THE SMELL OF DANGER

Days after the San Diego sales conference and the perfunctory walk in Fox World with Beacon, Old Man visited his physician for an annual check-up. He expected no problems and he received none.

Old Man walked through the clinic's parking lot, gait brisk and chin up. He was in sound health, according to his physician, who issued an "A+" health report (for a man in his late fifties, he added). Old Man felt proud to be in his fifties—not. With 115/70 blood pressure, flawless EKG, lowest body weight in fifteen years, and excellent blood enzymes, Old Man was thankful for the clean report, and it was a clear sign that he had overthought his prior worries. Forget the occasional indigestion and the episodes of mild fatigue. Vitamins and a cleaner diet would punch up his energy level. He planned to go to work on Monday and get his career on a higher arc. An upcoming exciting new product launch assignment was just the ticket and Old Man had lots of sales ideas for the new product. The doctor suggested one additional test—a cardiac stress test. Old Man jotted the date and rolled his eyes. Time to go to work; there were sales goals to meet. Hidden though in the doctor's perfect annual examination report was a time bomb.

Massive heart failure (heart attack) and sudden cardiac arrest (SCA) are two phrases used interchangeably in laymen's language. They are not the same. They are two different conditions—both potentially fatal. The first is simply a plumbing problem, i.e., an artery blockage occurs. There are symptoms in advance—pain (often severe), breathing becomes difficult, pressure in the chest, extreme fatigue. The latter, a SCA, is an electrical issue in the heart. The heart's electrical system is disrupted somehow, arrythmia sets in, and the heart stops or flutters. Blood flow to the brain ceases, and the death process begins. With sudden cardiac arrest, there are few or no advance symptoms other than heart palpitations or slight fatigue. Most heart attack victims recover if the coronary incident occurs near a hospital. The odds are far less fortunate to sudden cardiac arrest victims; many do not survive if the condition strikes outside an emergency facility.

Somewhere deep in Fox Forest, Mr. Fox looked to the sky. The light breeze rippled his nose whiskers. Danger was near; he smelled it, and a canine's nose is never wrong. Soon, Old Man's heart, driven by stress, fatigue and dehydration, would fail and Fox World, the oasis, would become healing ground.

THE FIGHT WITH BIG RED

Big Red was a rogue fox, the kind that wanders through an established territory looking for a weak point. He was also a big fox physically, the largest ever in Fox World. He was different than the other gentle fox citizens of Fox World, for he appeared to have no sense of fairness or any care for right or wrong. He was young, impetuous, aggressive, and territory hungry. Big Red was, put simply, twenty pounds of nasty. He took what he wanted when he wanted it, and if the old, the weak, or the infirm had to pony up the price, they had best do it.

In the 1984 movie *Red Dawn,* the actor, Powers Boothe, plays a downed Air Force pilot and is asked by the patriot group, Wolverines, why Russia has attacked the United States. He studies the question for a moment and then replies, "I dunno. Two toughest kids on the block, I guess, sooner or later, they gonna fight."

This was the day.

Backpack on shoulder, Old Man was back on the path to Fox World. He was determined to find Mr. Fox, pull up a stump as a chair, and talk to his canine friend. Old Man was neglectful in his previous Fox World visit. Today, he had unlimited time for Mr. Fox. He added his thousand-lumens flashlight and a small box of CR123 batteries to his backpack in case their visit stretched into dark. Old Man planned to spend a lot of time with Mr. Fox, enjoy a coffee or two, and relax and think. No, scratch the concept of thinking. How about just sitting and relaxing? Perfect, but fortune did not have relaxation in store. This was not the day for either man or fox to take it easy.

Big Red got the surprise drop on Mr. Fox with an underhanded sneak attack. At Mr. Fox's age, he relied on advance battle strategy planning, i.e., fight immediately, delay for better position, or run. Strategy went out the fox den window when Big Red jumped him from behind. The initial lunge knocked the wind out of Mr. Fox, and he grunted painfully. Weakened immediately, his quiver of tactics narrowed to one—he could not let Big Red flip him. If he did, Big Red would deliver a fatal incision with his long canine fangs. Screams and growls filled the air—the sounds that crystallize physical hurt in one's brain and portend escaping hope. The old fox was in trouble, Old Man knew it immediately.

Deja Blue, the heron also saw that Mr. Fox was hurting and walked as fast as her wobbly, stick-thin legs would carry her. She flapped her big blue wings to distract Big Red. Professor Owl screeched, *Where's Bucky? Run and get Bucky! Mr. Fox needs urgent help.* Colonel Hawk circled the forest in flight to look for Bucky the deer. She found Bucky down by Beaver Lake and sounded an all-animal emergency signal. Bucky responded like a firefighter; he rose and rushed towards the trouble. Too far away to help Mr. Fox, Bucky ran hard anyway, digging his hooves into the dried fallen leaves on the forest floor. He was no Man O' War or Secretariat, but his arthritic legs propelled him faster than he thought possible at his advanced age. Clomp! Clomp! Clomp! *Mr. Fox was his buddy. He had to get there. He had to.*

Two kings in a battle: one aging and fair, the other strong and menacing. One embraced the concept of good in its truest sense, the other embodied the nastiness of everything else. On they fought. Mr. Fox screeched in pain but managed to stay off his back. Fighting valiantly, he was running out of time and was certain to succumb to the bulk and youth of Big Red.

Old Man ripped off the backpack, grabbed his camera monopod to serve as a weapon, and ran into the fray. He had no time to regret an act that nature would frown upon. Nature's rule was grounded in the concept of the survival of the fittest. But Old Man screamed inwardly, surely being fit includes being just, fair, and of gentle nature. Old Man decided to put his thumb on the scale and disrupt and alter the natural order of things. Without hesitation, he rushed forward. With guttural screams and a camera monopod serving as a fixed bayonet, Old Man charged across the shin-deep waters of Fox Creek. He was unrestricted by equivocal thinking or paralyzing rationalization. No, this was just dead on, leave-my-friend-alone motivation. N. Oldman (as the foxes called him) was plain darn tired of seeing the wicked thrive in this world—whether the world be Fox, Human, or Corporate. Old Man's belly was full of cocky youthful interlopers at this point in his life. Proudly, he claimed the score-settling emotions that welled up inside him. It was high time that the good, the innocent, and the hard working won one.

Like any bully when confronted, Big Red ran. He never picked fights on a level canvas. *Fighting fair was for wimps*, Big Red thought arrogantly. Big Red had made one miscalculation; Mr. Fox was well liked and embraced by a network of loyal friends. The evidence surrounded Big Red. The deranged corporate executive with a bayonet and the thunder of Bucky's hooves approaching were Mr. Fox's pocket aces. Big Red tucked fox tail and ran.

Wounded and whining in pain, Mr. Fox crawled deep into the thick brush where Old Man could not reach him. The fox curled into a defensive ball and licked his bleeding paws. Human, deer, heron, hawk, and owl circled Mr. Fox and stood guard. Other than filtered water and berries, there was nothing to offer Mr. Fox but prayers and words of encouragement. Hang tough, little buddy, we still have more sunsets to see, Old Man channeled. Old Man stayed by his side until a panicked are-you-ok cell call from his wife. Old Man left more supplies for Mr. Fox and whispered encouragement. The flashlight cast a headlight-shaped glow on the forest path on the return walk to Human World. Sadness permeated Old Man's heart.

Old Man punched in the security code to his home garage, hung up his backpack on a hook in the garage's slot wall, and walked through the small mudroom. The adrenaline was draining – finally. He unlaced his soaked hiking boots and exhaled a "wow that was wild" breath. He petted the doting Jack Russell terriers at his feet and gave both a meat treat. They smelled the forest on his boots with keen interest and both danced with excitement, knowing that soon they would sit on dad's lap by the firepit. He gathered both dogs in his arms and as he straightened up, dizziness struck and there was a buzzy feeling in the back of his neck. That was the second time in three days—what was that? He was thirsty. The autumn weather had been hot and dry today, and because of the fox clash, he had not drunk his Liquid IV hydration fluids. Was the buzzy feeling in his head a dehydration warning? He walked across the brownstone's deck to hug his wife. It was Saturday night. Pizza? Movie? Dessert and coffee by the firepit? Two days off with his family was always a cherished gift; yet he was sad. Mr. Fox was a mile away in Fox Forest, under the bushes, alone and hurt. Worried about the old lion, Old Man abandoned his attempt to sleep and arose stealthily so as not to awake Smiling Wife. Downstairs, he boiled hot honey-laced tea, poured it into a porcelain mug, and stepped onto his back deck. A full autumn moon lit up Fox Forest on the horizon. Creamy shafts of light illuminated the tops of the century-old trees and cast dark shadows on the walking path entrance. Old Man felt gut-deep pain. Somewhere in the shadows, his buddy was wounded.

"Hang on, little buddy. I will never ignore or leave you again," he whispered to the moon. Under the moon's hypnotic irradiation, he made the promise to find and walk his road to health, awareness, and redemption. Such journeys begin not with promises to others but with a closer, more examining accountability—a life-changing promise to yourself.

FOX WORLD BUDDY SYSTEM

The next morning, Old Man was out the door at daylight. Promises have alarm clocks, and he was up before his rang and he hiked swiftly to the forest where the autumn morning was warm. Old Man whistled and called out, but there were no signs of the wounded canine. Old Man walked on, mile after mile, as he explored the forest, including portions he had never seen up close. The briars cut into his sockless ankles. He paused to take a long pull of ice-cold Liquid IV from his aluminum water jug and attach a Band-Aid or two. Hearing N. Oldman's whistles, Mr. Fox emerged from the thicket along Fox River and, exhausted and hungry, he limped towards his friend. Head held high, Mr. Fox smiled and nodded, *we won*.

Old Man disagreed, "More like an insurmountable loss was wrestled by destiny into a painful tie." Mr. Fox was alive—barely. He was a survivor, a death dodger.

Over a stone bowl full of bison gumbo, Mr. Fox and Old Man forged an alliance. Operation Watch Over Me would entail one buddy from one world riding shotgun for a buddy from another world. Might seem dumb or farfetched to onlookers, but if a near-death did one thing, it clarified your mission and it united assets. They sat side by side, on stump and log, and discussed it if reflecting on it and hoping for it, qualifies as a discussion. Together, a fox and a human decided to explore and pursue fox-human bonds by softening the boundaries of dual worlds and building a rock wall of trust. Wait a minute, Old Man interjected in his head. That last sentence sounded too formal—like a Corporate World mission statement. Old Man laughed. No need for formal credos; just distill it down to fox terms. *Keep it fox simple,* Mr. Fox posited. *Little foxes only know simple ways.*

So, they did. They kept it fox simple. Fox World was a place of blissful escape; Old Man would partake of it. Fox World was a place of learning, and these animals had lessons to deal; Old Man would immerse himself in it. How? The answer to that question spanned the large chasm between knowing something in your head and committing to it with your heart. *Be here now,* Mr. Fox would say. Old Man heard the sages' lesson but was helpless in his understanding of how to achieve centered mindfulness. Fortunately for him, N. Oldman had chosen the right walking partner.

After silent reflection and more bone-broth infused with aspirin and antibiotics, Mr. Fox packed it in and limped up the trail to hill country. He looked over his shoulder with a final fox message: *Big Red will not be coming around anymore.* Old Man digested the message. His back against the wall, Mr. Fox had scored a way to advance. Infirmity and old age spark courage and ingenuity. Big Red had learned that lesson the hard way.

ONE EYE ALWAYS ON
THE HORIZON

October aged and brought more sun-drenched, toasty days and jacket nights. Summer's dash-here-and-there hurriedness was now stemmed. Parents, their vacation banks empty, were back at work. Children were settled back in the classroom and on sports fields. The net-net, as the Corporate World execs would say, is that the forest was quieter—fewer casual trekkers checking their smartphones and not as many kids throwing stones in the stream with shrill screams of delight.

Mr. Fox needed heal-up time in a calm environment. Big Red had hurt him substantially. It was a dual hurt—the physical rips and tears ached to the bone, and the crushing pain of exhaustion racked his old body. The hurt did not end there; he imagined the other animals' whispers: *We love our ole fox buddy, but he's getting old. He wouldn't have made it if the human had not intervened.* Mr. Fox was embarrassed. His crown had been toppled. In the animal kingdom, other challengers were sure to emerge. Ebbing confidence was a low fuel tank that both Mr. Fox and Old Man shared at this point in life.

Mr. Fox's eye injury from the Big Red fight looked better, but it was still crusty dry and painful. He sat on the spongy green moss mounds across Fox River. The moss cushioned his sore flank. Ignoring his injuries, he squared up to the west at sundown and watched the pale orange orb sink into the gray horizon. His one good eye true to the task, and the other squinted shut, he observed his daily ritual of paying due respect to the sun. Thankful for its warmth and grateful for one more day in Fox World, he studied the descending sun with the concentration of a scientist, the wonderment of a mystic, and the

product speech, a closing banquet, and a return flight. Repeat the following Monday.

Old Man digested these thoughts as he packed his roller suitcase: navy blazer (the armor of Corporate World); three dress shirt/silk tie/trouser combos; his lucky silk pocket square with foxes on it (for two press interviews and business TV show taping); khaki shorts/ golf shirt/golf shoes for the convention's kegger golf tournament; cordovan leather loafers; and a shaving kit filled with miniature-sized bottles, tubes, and samples. He added a handful of his favorite treats, Fox's Mints, in the corner zip pocket of the suitcase. He liked to pop one or two of the organic peppermints in his mouth while reading. This thought prompted him to toss in a couple of novels, Tom Coyne's and David Baldacci's latest. In the other corner pocket, he stuffed his compact birding binoculars (lots of new birds to chart in Arizona) and a pocket-size Nikon camera for morning desert walks.

As part of his foolhardy "run faster, try harder, do more" career comeback strategy devised on a plane flight weeks ago, Old Man had doubled down on stupidity with an idea to attain a prestigious career-capping industry designation at the sales conference. The fact that the sentence alone was more than a mouthful should have been a fire engine red warning flag. The professional designation required twelve lengthy exams, for which he should have studied for ten to twelve months. Old Man did the opposite and crammed daily for three weeks, and then took the twelve exams in two days. N. Oldman should have been happy with the passing grade, but, in fact, he was just exhausted. The exams had surprised Old Man; they were ridiculously hard. Old Man wondered what Mr. Fox would think about this; he would likely offer a succinct mental gem like *what you need to know to win or survive in life is not what you memorize; it is what you live.*

He rolled his suitcase to the front door and sat his messenger bag beside it. With an hour to spare before his plane ride to Arizona, he slipped on his tennis shoes, leashed his Jack Russell terriers, Beacon and Bounce, and headed out the back door to Fox World. The pups were joyed. They liked taking their human for a drag.

Mr. Fox was prone on a log, three feet off the ground. His posture looked relaxed; his gaze was one of worry. His eyes darted from the friendly dogs, which made his fox tail wave, to his human friend, where concern welled up inside. Mr. Fox did not like the exhaustion that he saw in his human's wry smile. Old Man looked more tired than ever.

As Mr. Fox ate his blueberry snacks, he watched Old Man and the two cute pups walk out of the forest and up the road to Human World. He mouthed goodbye. When finished, he hopped back atop the log, lay down, crossed his front paws, and rested his chin on his black leggings. He made a mental note to watch for the giant silver dragonfly to fly over in a couple of hours.

APOGEE'S APOLOGY

The exhilaration of reaching the mountain peak is often counter-balanced by a misstep and a fall down the back side of the mountain. Success and failure are separated by the micro edge of a straight razor, and it is not an edge for the tired or the clumsy.

Old Man returned from the industry symposium on the giant silver dragonfly five days later. Tan, smiling, and fresh from a four-hour plane nap, he walked through Dulles Airport confidently. After three business conferences in five weeks, including his industry's signature event, he wanted to kiss the home soil of Virginia. Sales conferences in resort locales are often defined by those who did not attend them as "paid corporate vacations". More like a "busman's holiday", Old Man concluded, as he rubbed his aching feet.

Old Man's gas tank was depleted. For seventy-two hours, it had been nonstop. Fifty new prospect coffee meetings. Press briefs on new products. Participation in an expert panel discussion. A podcast release. Taping of a business TV broadcast. On the last day, the Old Man had earned a coveted industry technical certification with other colleagues, noting the five talented individuals on the ceremonial stage were half his age. Maybe that is why they were fresh-faced and cheery, and he smiled through exhausted eyes. Regardless, this had been a high-water mark in his career, Old Man reflected humbly. He was grateful—deeply so.

As busy as his conference schedule had been, on each of the conference's three nights, Old Man had wandered into the calming desert after a foodie delight dinner and brought an African estate coffee to sip. The coffee and the stroll eased the digestion of the Wagyu beef from Snake River, Idaho, and the Arctic char from Bristol Bay. The banana tarte tatin had been a palate pleaser and Old Man admitted ashamedly that he had wanted seconds. He had relented to a second glass of Sanford pinot noir but declined the generously offered treat of a forty-year-old Taylor Fladgate port. He was not feeling well, and alcohol would add to that malaise.

Each evening in Arizona, he had tilted his head skyward and wished upon the brightest star. The stars in the indigo sky were the same ones hanging over Smiling Wife, the terriers and Mr. Fox two thousand miles away. Old Man smiled. There was a coyote howling among the saguaro cactus in the Sonoran Desert and another answered. A chain reaction of howls filled the desert night of "Fox World West." Old Man laughed at the joke and a bit at himself. Old Man's ego drive had dampened as his desire for a career comeback had been replaced by a desire to move on; there was a call of the wild in his heart. He looked at the brightest star in the desert sky and said, "Be home tomorrow, Mr. Fox. Hang in there. I will check on you Friday."

Old Man and Smiling Wife made frozen blender cocktails and grilled steaks when he returned from Scottsdale. Beacon and Bounce circled the ever-giving Weber grill on patrol for steak scrap droppings. Old Man's wife doted excessively over his framed certificate and gold pin. She was the most genuinely nice person that he had known in his life, he smiled. Her family were precious, warm, and principled people. When people used the term "married up" humorously, Old Man just nodded and agreed. He had.

Old Man capped off the "welcome home" party with a family tradition. He always purchased gifts when he went away on a long business trip. He gave his wife an assortment of French-milled lilac and vanilla scented soaps and hand creams. Beacon and Bounce jumped vertically into the air to retrieve their turkey jerky chew sticks and stuffed squeaker toys. Lastly, Old Man reached into the family gift bag and pulled out the last prize—a My Father cigar selected from the sizeable humidor at the Fox Cigar Bar in Scottsdale. He admired it, put it to his lips, and smelled the fragrant tobacco. He read the cigar band again. My Father. His father had loved an outdoor barbeque on a starlit evening, Old Man mused. With that thought, the Old Man lit the cigar and used the same wooden match to ignite the fire pit. Husband, wife, and the two furry kids snuggled into the loveseat cushions and fleece blankets.

"Victory cigar?" his wife asked with a celebratory smile.

Blue smoke from the cigar curled up to the stars. "No, this is an I've-never-been-happier-to-be-alive cigar. I want this moment to last to eternity."

Old Man's wife smiled deeper and rested her head on his shoulder. The terriers curled tighter into their blankets; their bellies delighted with filet mignon scraps. From the edge of the forest, Mr. Fox looked on at his human and canine friends. They looked happy and this made Mr. Fox smile. But the canine was also deeply worried. The day was here. Old Man would soon fall down the mountain.

THE LAND OF IN-BETWEEN

It was Friday, Old Man's favorite day. Somewhere in the universe it was written that Friday is designed as a half-day workday when the weather is good, Old Man laughed. A couple of decades ago in Corporate World, an energetic, focused salesperson could achieve their weekly sales quota in four days. Old Man remembered the process like it was stenciled on his wrist. Back then, Friday afternoon was for golf. Arrive at work at 6:30 on Friday morning. Do customer-call reports, log into customer relationship management software, do updates on key accounts, construct next week's sales funnel, complete expense accounts to replenish out-of-pocket money and submit all paperwork by mid-morning. Friday work calendars went dark after 11:15 a.m. Old Man laughed a second time as he recalled the creative calendaring for the Friday afternoon time block. The best entries were vague ones— "Prospecting," "Company Car Maintenance," "Mentoring Sessions," etc. These were secret code words for "Golf" and "Extended Happy Hour at a Chesapeake Bay deck bar", all of which was tolerated during the Fridays of summer—if, and only if, a salesperson met their sales quota. The mantra was "produce and no one asks questions of the golden goose." Where had the days of a results-oriented culture in Corporate World gone, Old Man lamented. Gone with the dinosaurs like him, he surmised. On this Friday, there were no such reindeer games to be played; Old Man had gone legit; today was logged as a one hundred percent legitimate write-it-down-official-as-hell vacation day. Old Man needed a mental health day.

He slept in until 7:00 a.m. Downstairs, he brewed coffee from exquisite beans that he had found in a shop in Old Scottsdale. He sniffed the aroma and sipped the licorice-black coffee. Whoa, strong. He punched the weather app on his iPhone. It read: "seventy-three degrees and sunny with a cold front and rain approaching midday", a forecast that would normally signal a golf day. His stiff, plane-weary muscles registered a complaint, nothing that a couple of Tylenols could not fix, but it did not matter. Old Man knew his plan. He was longing to spend six to eight hours in Fox World—walking, exploring, photographing birds, feeding apples to the deer, thinking quietly, thinking out loud if needed, catching up on phone calls with dear friends, walking some more, sitting by Fox River, and listening to podcasts or sports talk radio … and maybe … just maybe … seeing Mr. Fox. That would be a bonus because Mr. Fox was a dawn and dusk guy, not a middle of the day type of guy.

Old Man showered and donned khaki shorts and a navy golf shirt warm from the dryer. His feet were sore from standing all week at the conference, so he inserted Protalus orthotic inserts into his Brooks running shoes and slipped on no-show Bombas golf sock buffers. Ready. His dash bag, aka the fashionable green Tumi backpack, was fully stocked for a day hike. He put it over his shoulder and set his mental compass heading for Fox World. A happy-to-be-alive feeling rose in his chest. An ideal vacation day has a plan, and simultaneously, it does not. It should have an aspirational goal (e.g., hike a new trail) woven with a loose timeframe (e.g., hike until it is time for an impromptu nap).

Old Man decided to walk Fox World from end to end and make a day camp at the base of a massive oak high above Fox River for a picnic. The rest he would just figure out ad hoc and after kissing his wife, he began walking to the forested canopy on the horizon. He felt free, untethered, light in his shoes like a young lad on the first day of summer vacation. Time was timeless; possibilities and adventure were boundless. He sucked in two lungs' full of autumn morning air. He exhaled, took a taste of coffee from his thermos, and scanned Fox World. God, what beauty you crafted here, he reflected. Into the Fox World portal he walked, and behind him, the veil to Human World and Corporate World fell. He was immersed—how deep, he did not know yet. By day's end, he would have fate's answer.

By the banks of Beaver Lake, he photographed an eastern phoebe but then changed his mind and thought it might be a wood pewee. Consternation set in. Luckily, the laminated Virginia Birds chart in his dash bag was the official arbiter and ruled in favor of the former. Deja Blue the heron stood stick still on the edge of the pond fishing for breakfast and did not break character to say hello. She was stiff straight—not a blink or a twitch. There are no drive-thru lanes in Fox World or canned goods from the market. The food comes to you—if you are lucky and patient. Like a lightning bolt, her head snapped forward to spear a five-inch bluegill. Breakfast—fresh, free range, no additives.

Old Man retrieved the sketchbook from his backpack. *Look around you. See our animal landmarks. You do not need the smartphone's compass. Use the sun, the moon, and the forest as your data points.* He wrote the words "Fox World" at the top of the page and began to sketch a map with a charcoal pencil. He drew Beaver Lake and its beaver dam mound—regrettably, no longer inhabited by beavers. The top of the mound housed the fox burrow where Mr. Fox had been born and Old Man placed an "X" on the sketchbook's page. He added other landmarks including an "X" where Bucky the deer had been born near Snapping Turtle Pond. His artistry was sub-remedial level, which made Old Man laugh out loud. He looked at the page, and although he was not proud of the drawing talent, he was glad that he was recording these wildlife landmarks. One never knew when the animals might perish or leave. Old Man never pondered that he might be the one to expire first. Like every human, Old Man thought he was immortal.

Up ahead in the forest, Mr. Fox was making his morning rounds as the forest greeter. He looked up into the tall oaks and said good morning to Professor Owl and Colonel Hawk and their families. He stopped by a giant log and waited for Russell Raccoon to peek out in his bandit mask. They discussed the weather and the frogging forecast for Fox River. October was the tail end of frogging season. Their hope for a mild winter went unsaid, as food was always in short supply in their shrinking woodscape.

Mr. Fox did not know it was Friday. After all, how would he know what day of the week it was—he was a fox. There was no Outlook software in Fox World. But he knew something better; it was High Energy Day. It came every seven sunsets. The humans, who parked their cars in the asphalt parking lots that ringed the forest, were always more cheerful on High Energy Day. They laughed, and Mr. Fox heard them making plans "for the weekend" when they walked near the woods on their coffee breaks. Mr. Fox was not sure what the "weekend" was, but he figured it was that period—two sunsets out of seven—when there were no cars in the parking lots and no cigarette smokers on the edge of Fox Forest.

Mr. Fox liked to climb trees. He could not do it vertically—Red Foxes do not have curved claws like Gray Foxes—but he could leap five feet in the air to reach a sturdy lower branch and he did, and he looked all around Fox World. It was a palette of colors—canary yellow, tangerine, beet, harvest gold, and a smattering of holdover kelly-green here and there. There was an in-face breeze. He sniffed. The earth was damp after a stout overnight rain. The cool soil mixed with the warming autumn air to titillate the fox's olfactory sense. *What a day to be a canine,* Mr. Fox smiled.

From his roost centrally located in the forest, Mr. Fox could see more than halfway to Beaver Lake. He recalled fondly going there several weeks ago to visit his birthplace. Something was afoot on the western horizon. *Was there movement in the woods down by Beaver Lake? Did he hear a human laugh?*

The shape came into focus. It was N. Oldman, his friend. Delight filled the fox's heart. And the man had his backpack, which was welcomed news, because he always stayed longer when he brought his backpack. Mr. Fox hoped for a long walk and a handful of the most delicious substance on earth—cherry candies. He loved dried cherries. No one recalls how the moniker, cherry candies, was born. They were not actually candy and did not contain candy or added sugar per se. They were small, dried organic cherries—pinot noir-reddish in color.

Mr. Fox remained in the tree, five feet up. He watched his human friend walk and explore. Maybe he would surprise him and yip when he was close. He noted that his human friend did not have the fun little terriers with him. This both disappointed and delighted Mr. Fox. He liked the feisty Jack Russell terriers, but he knew that if they were not with him, it was likely that Old Man (or N. Oldman, as Mr. Fox had labeled him) would hike all day. Mr. Fox liked long hikes—almost as much as cherry candies.

Old Man paused; he felt "that thing." It was what he called his "eleventh sense" when he worked in New York City. There, if you walked in shady spots late at night, you'd best have all five senses working at 2x capacity along with your "head on a swivel" eleventh sense. He needed his eleventh sense but once in nine years in New York, but it had saved his wallet or his life. One night, departing Live Bait, a dive bar on 23rd, he had turned the wrong way. His eleventh sense was muted a bit by an oversized southern cuisine meal and a few too many beers served up by the establishment's flirtatious Ford Agency models/bartenders. He was a half block from trouble when he paused. A streetlight was out in mid-block - danger, danger.

Old Man heard a familiar sound, a high-pitched yip. It was not loud, and it sounded like it came from up in the air. His eleventh sense kicked in; he was being watched. Just as suddenly, his senses de-activated and he laughed heartily. Up ahead, about twenty degrees to the right and a few feet up on a V-shaped tree trunk, was Mr. Fox. And if a fox could smile, he was smiling.

"Come on down here, little buddy, and let's talk awhile," Old Man invited. He pulled a zippered plastic baggy from the olive-green backpack and poured out a, palmful of cherry candies. He placed them on a chair-sized stone embedded in the ground near the stream and then backed away to respect the wild animal's space. Mr. Fox was not a pet, and Old Man always respected that.

Mr. Fox nibbled the cherries slowly, savoring their exquisite taste. He listened as N. Oldman described his silver giant dragonfly ride to someplace called Arizona. He had seen a coyote as big as a German Shepherd in the desert. Mr. Fox shivered with fear, but N. Oldman explained that it was far away—a walk of a thousand moons. He told Mr. Fox that his career was winding down and he would be free in two to three years. Mr. Fox disagreed with that timeline, but he kept his fox opinion to himself.

"I am walking to the top of Fox Mountain today. I'd love to have you as my trail buddy. You up to it? You want to walk with an old man?" Old Man inquired hopefully. The human had no idea that when he spoke the words "old man", the fox heard "N. Oldman" and that had become the human's nickname in Fox World.

Mr. Fox pondered the invitation. He was worried about his human buddy, who looked very tired as of late. A tingly odd feeling told Mr. Fox that he should stay close to his human buddy today. He replied with a nod, *"of course, N. Oldman, that sounds like a fun day."*

They headed east. The grade of the climb was not steep, but neither was it shallow. If walked briskly, it caused a hitch or two in the diaphragm. The tandem ascended, climbing the route directly, and deciding that they would descend later via the alternate path to the left. Mr. Fox stopped every hundred paces or so and pricked his ears to engage his supersonic hearing sense and scan for threats. Old Man looked on curiously; the fox was diligent at his craft. Only once did he freeze on the trail as the hair rose on his burnt-orange neck and silky black ears as the static energy of a threat pulsed through him. A two-foot garter snake crossed the trail perpendicularly. It was more of a meal than a threat, and Mr. Fox let it pass. It slithered on and the old lions crested the apex of Fox Mountains two hundred paces later.

The peak of Fox Mountain is the highest accessible lookout to the bordering town. The nearby water tower is slightly higher but fenced off to animals and non-municipal workers. The horn beeps from the six-lane highway and the subway train's squeaky brakes were more pronounced on the peak as was the chilling sight of urban sprawl below them.

Mr. Fox admired the "mountaintop" view. Distant to the west was the mighty Shenandoah Valley. To the east, not quite as far, was the majestic Washington Monument. In the center was his hill, Fox Mountain. Mr. Fox felt taller here, his eyes were level with the top floors of the shiny glass buildings; these were the awful office towers that blocked his morning sun. Below, he could see acres of asphalt parking lots which flashfloods ran swiftly across, overfilled Fox River, and chased the forest animals to high ground. Progress, by human standards, has a definition indifferent to animals and further, Human World progress comes with a steep price. All too often, the invoice is handed to the animals. Mr. Fox accepted this burden, but he knew that his fox checkbook was growing thin.

Pride rose in Mr. Fox; his entire fiefdom was on splendid display from here, including his birthplace, Beaver Lake. His mom, Buttercup would be so proud that he'd made it to the top of Fox Mountain— physically and spiritually. He had forged partnerships and alliances with a community of many genetics—Bucky, the deer; Deja Blue, the heron; Professor Owl; Colonel Hawk; and Russell Raccoon. Mr. Fox looked to the stump where Old Man sat. Buttercup would be proud that her son had befriended the human who helped her during the "snowstorm of the century" many years ago. Old Man did not know it, but Mr. Fox would risk his life for him; the sentiment would be battle tested later in the valley.

The duo descended on the trailhead to the right, which made a wide circle down Fox Mountain through the oldest part of the deciduous forest. The tree canopy, tall and thick, cast a shadowy blanket on the trail even in midday on a bright-blue, sunny day. Old Man likened this part of the trail (and its tall, thick ancient trees) to Sequoia National Park. Here, the sounds of the highway traffic were muted by the massive tree trunks; the city's commotion was gone, deleted.

The stream to their right babbled gently over stones covered in a thin coating of moss. The brook's relaxing melody reminded Old Man of a desk-sized water fountain that he had selected in a Secret Santa drawing at work years ago. What a truly cool gift that had been. For years, the tiny fountain had brought the outdoors inside his 120 Wall Street office and was the theme music for power naps. Maybe a nap would be in order today, Old Man smiled, and Mr. Fox signaled agreement wholeheartedly with a smile.

Old Man checked his phone for messages. Hourly was the check-in limit and he had adhered to his self-imposed limit—so far. The AccuWeather app bolded a message: Rainstorm blowing in. This presented two choices: run miles to home or set up a buddy day camp. The old lions chose "B."

The camp was established along Fox River—on the high side of the riverbank where the pitch rose ten feet above the creek's surface. The high bank was lined across the top with thick green moss. This luxury upgrade made the campsite cushiony and inviting. Old Man had brought along a golf umbrella as a walking stick. Golf umbrellas have an oversized canopy; he opened his and inserted the handle into the back of a lightweight, low-slung, aluminum folding beach chair. He now had a sixty-eight-inch canopy overhead and his butt was off the ground in the seat of the small sand chair. The chair had two pocket sleeves on the arms. Phone and earbuds went into one, a cigar and lighter into the other. His coffee cup slid into the chair's cup receptacle. He pulled his Columbia fleece out of the backpack and draped it over the back of the camp chair. With the "man camp" set up, he scouted the area for a base camp for Mr. Fox. Although it was likely that Mr. Fox would run off when the rainstorm ensued, Old Man wanted a contingency plan for his canine buddy. Down the trail thirty paces was a perfect fox camp spot. Mr. Fox liked holly trees, and Fox World had a plethora of them. Old Man selected two small American holly trees and stretched a heavy-gauge plastic tarp from his backpack across the top of the two trees, creating a V-shaped tent. He left both ends open, as foxes like multiple egresses for escapes. Underneath the rain tent was Mr. Fox's favorite bed—spongy, emerald-green moss.

No man cave (or fox den) was truly operational without provisions. In this regard, Old Man had planned well. He surveyed the pantry in his green backpack. Nothing but good and better news in there. Two small plastic bowls, eating utensils, napkins in a waterproof zip bag, a Shenandoah Red Delicious apple, a cup of peanut butter topped in foil, bison jerky, dehydrated blueberries, instant coffee, a pouch of bone broth, a Snickers bar, peanut butter and cheese crackers (aka "nabs"), two bottles of water, and a diet Mountain Dew. In other words, a banquet.

Mr. Fox's nostrils flared. Old Man sensed it too. They both looked west in unison. Rain coming. They smelled the approaching moisture and the temperature dropped eight or ten degrees in the snap of his fingers as the breeze picked up. Just like that, the rain hit hard, and Old Man was trapped at the base of Fox Mountain with his wild canine adventurer, Mr. Fox.

Time to dig in, Old Man lit the coffee-cup-sized camp burner. Mr. Fox was jittery, as he looked way down the trail to his den. *It would be a long run; he would never make it before the storm bore down.* Time to up the offer, Old Man thought. He poured the pouch of bone broth into a small, stainless-steel bowl. He shredded small pieces of meat from a stick of organic-grade bison jerky and plunked the succulent protein into the small pot. The piece de resistance was the last ingredient, dehydrated blueberries. The berries plumped up in the bubbling water, and he added a couple of dollops of manuka honey. The aroma spoke delicious—by human or canine palette. Mr. Fox's nostrils flared again, but he was not playing weatherman this time. He was a sous chef smelling the aroma of a maestro's creation.

The breeze stiffened another notch, and the temperature sunk a couple more clicks. Old Man reached to the back of his pack chair for his steel-gray fleece jacket. Much needed with the rain-chilled breeze, he rolled his arms into it. With a fleece, a hot coffee, and the wide protection of the golf umbrella, he would do okay in the rainstorm.

Old Man carried the bowl of fox broth thirty paces down the trail and put it under the makeshift, plastic-tarp-covered fox den. It would never work, he thought. Mr. Fox was either laughing at him or scared out of his fox wits by the storm at this point. But hey, it was a vacation day, and that meant magic was always possible. That, too, was a rule written down somewhere in the universe, Old Man was convinced.

The beefy broth's aroma was a homing signal. Better stated, it worked like a Star Trek tractor beam—especially when the sheets of rain began to fall onto Fox World. Mr. Fox circled the fox tent three times—always three circles. He always circled three times before reclining for a nap. Is three a mystic number in fox land? Mr. Fox crawled under the clear plastic tarp draped over the two small holly trees and assessed its suitability. It had good head room in the ceiling, and the floor was carpeted in the finest grade of bryophyte. The tarp's sides were weighted down with mediumweight stones, blocking the wind-driven rain. Warm, dry, soft bedding whispered "nap." Broth, chunky with bison and blueberries, screamed "yum." A trusted friend just down the trail to look over him and protect him from predators spoke "trust."

Mr. Fox felt blessed and so did Old Man. He settled into the comfy chair under the canopy of the large Callaway umbrella, dry as stored flour. The thick fleece fended off the rain-induced chill as did the metallic space blanket across his knees. Coffee warmed his innards, and he relaxed knowing that he was well stocked with coffee supplies for a second and third cup. His stomach growled loudly. Mr. Fox's ears pricked thirty yards away. Foxes can hear mice crawling under six feet of dirt. The Old Man's stomach agitations must have been deafening to the fox. About then, the rain pace stoked higher. Time to break the emergency glass on the Snickers bar and the My Father cigar. *No need to suffer*, Mr. Fox concurred ever slyly.

Old Man lit the cigar, tuned his radio to sports talk, and bit a chunk out of the heavenly candy bar. What a luxury a candy bar was these days. He had cut his weight twenty-nine pounds over the past year. He was at his lowest body weight and best pulse rate in two decades, his family doctor had said. He felt good about that. Good achievements, he thought proudly. Yet, he thought, as he did on the plane a few weeks ago, why was he so blasted tired at times? Was the tingly feeling in the back of his neck just a minor ailment stemming from dehydration? The thought creased his brain. He was sick or tired or both, but that worry was not for a vacation day. He dabbed his cigar on a wet leaf and put it down. He adjusted the backpack chair's settings, pulled up the fleece under his chin, and eased back. Within seconds, the euphonic rhythms of falling rain and the now fast-moving brook hypnotized Old Man into a paralyzing doze. Thirty feet away, Mr. Fox synchronized his snores with the human as both slept in the hidden inner sanctum of Fox World.

The rain eased eventually, leaving the forest squishy and jungle fragrant. Old Man hardly saw anyone in the forest at any time, but for sure, not now. It was a workday which meant few casual walkers and the mud puddles and drippy leaves were effective barriers to entry.

He stood to stretch his locked knees. A half-dozen bone pops and cracks later, he walked down the trail—away from Mr. Fox. No need to spoil his slumber. Old Man was on the north side of Fox River. This was the high side of the riverbank; the creek had cut a deep channel over the decades. Old Man was ten feet above the water's surface, and the path was slick-wet with fallen autumn leaves. As a precaution, he steered a couple feet away from the creek bank's edge. He noted that the creek's water level—driven by parking-lot runoff from nearby Corporate World—had risen from the normal level of twelve to fifteen inches to twice that. He noticed one more thing on the bank below him—a thick as his forearm, four and one-half foot northern water snake. It was irritated too, flushed out of its hole by the rising rains. Old Man cringed. There were two things that shook his core—snakes and clear-air turbulence on cross-continental flights. He had handled and fought to a draw most of life's maladies. Snakes and turbulence, though, had his number. He shuddered as he looked at the northern water snake, known for its long, sharp teeth. It looked as nasty as Big Red, the fox that had attacked Mr. Fox a month ago.

Filled with snake fear, Old Man turned and headed back towards the "man cave" camp. The woods became still. Oddly quiet. His neck tingled. He had a flash of a what-is-going-on premonition as he reached into his back pocket for his cellular phone. Even though it was a vacation day, Old Man wanted to check his business email account. *Work hard, run fast, do more.* It was the last time that he would ever mumble that mantra.

Sudden cardiac arrest was true to its name; it struck lightning quick. The electrical-charge sensation hit the base of his skull and the top of his spine felt like a Fourth of July sparkler—bright, tingly, sparkly, with a scratchy static sound. At ear level, the iPhone floated out of his limp hand and off into space. There was a second flash that pulsed his electrical system—head to toe. Muscles loosened their tension and his began to fold downward. In a desperate, futile attempt to stave

hand in the backpack for Mr. Fox's arthritis. The baby aspirin might save his life today.

He crawled. His body, lethargic from lack of oxygen, strained and achingly complied. His head fog cleared a smidge. He looked down at his hands and chest. His skin was violet, which startled him. Had he died and gone to Pandora? Was he an Avatar now? Even in death, there was humor. Aided by the leftover blueberry taste on his teeth and gums, he realized that he must have vomited the dried blueberries he'd been chewing before he blacked out. He was not an Avatar; he was covered with blueberry stains.

Knee shuffle by knee shuffle, he crawled to the backpack. Scared, he was never happier than to see the olive-green ballistic nylon pack. He sipped from the water bottle and thumbed two eighty-one milligram aspirin under his tongue. He was weak; he needed help. He patted the pockets of his stone khaki shorts. No phone. What? It was gone. It was somewhere back down the trail. Mr. Fox was a few feet away. His head swiveled left, then right, scanning for danger. Back in full wild fox mode, he had activated his protective predator radar.

Old Man did the math. He was two miles from home. Half of that was a wooded walk with no access to people. Even if he made it to the parking lot area, it was Friday afternoon. No one from Corporate World would be walking the wood's edge for a cigarette now.

There was one shortcut. If he crossed Fox River, he could reach a safe area sooner and try to get medical attention. This would necessitate a slide down Fox River's steep bank and ford the two-foot-deep stream. Yes, the creek was flowing fast after the rain, and he was shaky and weak. And there was the snake he had seen earlier. Yeah, there was that. Time to roll the dice. Like most things in life, the options were Mr. Bad and his brother, Worse Than.

Afraid of a fall if he walked down the stream bank, he locked in on options two—slide down the orange clay mud that caked the sides of the stream. Old man slid amazingly fast in the rain-slickened clay and stopped with an abrupt jolt and a loud splash as his feet hit the stream's bottom. It startled him and a wave of dizziness hit him again.

Old Man had to get up and get moving. If he blacked out again, he would drown in the stream.

He looked right, upstream, hoping to put a GPS fix on the snake before he forded the current. He scanned and located the snake again—the thick coiled serpent was thirty feet upstream. It was irritated both by the stronger current from the storm and the human intruder in its little hideaway. The good news was that Fox River was narrow here. With luck, Old Man would make it across the mossy-slick stones in the stream even if the snake swam towards him. The math worked. The man had fifteen feet to go to cross the stream. The snake had twice that mileage to reach him. Old Man was safe.

Frighteningly, he was not. Old Man looked back up the steep muddy bank that he had scooted down. Mr. Fox was perched high above on the green moss and the old fox was on high alert. His steely-eyed stare was fixated on a spot in the stream—fifteen feet downstream and to Old Man's left. What was the fox staring at, Old Man thought? Old Man had forgotten a hiking rule that his grandfather had taught him fifty years ago. Where there is one snake, there are usually two. Coiled feet from his left calf muscle was a second five-foot northern water snake. It had recovered from the big ripples generated by Old Man's splash. Now it was fighting mad. If Old Man moved—even an inch—there were going to be fireworks. Old Man's body was in no shape to handle more danger. He turned to look back at Mr. Fox above him.

Mr. Fox saw the danger; his friend was in trouble. Mr. Fox would normally make lunch out of a snake, but not one this big. The snake in the stream was a monster, the largest that the little fox had ever seen. Mr. Fox gulped hard. Weeks ago, he had almost been killed by Big Red and N. Oldman had charged into the middle of the fight to save him. Mr. Fox was alive today because of it and he was tired of nasty snakes beating good people. He echoed Old Man's earlier thoughts—sometimes bravery is being foolish enough to believe astronomical odds are beatable. It is best to act before you have time to think about it, and Mr. Fox did.

As Old Man turned to see the fox, the unbelievable and unforgettable unfolded in slow motion. A twelve-pound ball of piercing orange fur, fangs bared, and employing his tail as an aileron, launched from the green moss patch ten feet above. If the two old lions were not bonded before, the act forthcoming would bond them forever.

Splash!

Foamy white-water droplets shot up into the air as a loud kerplunk echoed up and down the stream bed. Mr. Fox landed heavily on top of the coiled snake. The snake, not expecting an aerial attack, never saw the king of the forest coming. The fight had the span of a peak era Mike Tyson knockout. Mr. Fox delivered a snap of his jaws behind the head of the thick snake and shook it vigorously with 180-degree jerks of his canine head.

Old Man, frozen by this incredulous sight and weakened again by a second round of heaviness at the base of his skull, acted. He angled right and away from the snake and in five lunging steps leapt out of the stream. He then scaled the shallower bank on the stream's other side and made it to a large, ottoman-sized stone. He sat, breathing hard, and scanned desperately for his fox buddy. The snake was floating limp down the stream. Dazed or dead, Old Man did not know. He felt sorrow. Old Man was not a snake fan, but he did not like to see any human or animal harmed.

Mr. Fox had moved downstream twenty-five paces, shaking off water like a dog emerging from a flea bath. His eyes were bulging with adrenaline rush, he had crossed the boundaries of human-fox interaction. There was no going back. He accepted that. In fact, he liked that.

Greek historian Herodotus said that "death is a delightful hiding spot for weary men." Old Man and Mr. Fox, exhausted by worry and a fear-fueled fight, chose to be weary—and alive.

Mr. Fox tailed his friend back to the safety of Human World. Mr. Fox had never seen his friend move so slowly. What was wrong with the human he did not know, but he knew the look of ache and fatigue. Big Red memories flooded his fox thoughts. He had crawled into the shrubs after his fight with Big Red and N. Oldman had stayed with him and left water and berries. Mr. Fox tracked N. Oldman now with the same devotion. Old Man stumbled on the root-infested asphalt path. He tripped and his knee crunched on the asphalt. Blood oozed down his calf. Mr. Fox winced. His human stood up, centered his wobbly ankles under him, and hobbled forward. Mr. Fox watched in amazement. N. Oldman was hurt but he moved determinedly like Mr. Fox's big strong friend, Bucky the deer. On cue, Bucky appeared a hundred yards away in a clearing and alertly ambled toward them. Colonel Hawk strafed the crow clan to activate their alarm calls high in the oaks—*Help, help, our beloved Peanut Man is hurt.* The brigade moved forward. Old Man's head hurt, and he was racked with dizziness, but the sounds and sights of his animal friends buoyed his injured heart. Ahead, he saw a guy on a skateboard riding circles in a parking lot behind an office building. Old Man began to shake in violent uncontrollable waves like he did twenty years ago when he had almost drowned in a Cancun riptide. Afterwards, he shook uncontrollably on the Mexico sand due to shock. It was happening again; he was going into shock. He needed help fast. Old Man waved both arms desperately as if he were on the shores of Cancun again. "Hey, buddy, I need help. May I make a call on your mobile phone?"

Old Man collapsed as fear, exhaustion, and confusion filled his being. What had happened? Where did he go when the butterflies came? How did he come back? Who gave him the three feathery kisses on the neck? Were they real? Had he died? Had he died and this was all a dream?

"My man, you ok? You look tired. Your face and leg are bleeding."

"I'm not sure. I think that I may just have had some type of heart failure. I need help."

Skateboarder Guy moved back a step as Old Man relayed the story in a tired whisper—startled, reflecting on, and digesting what he had just heard. He listened to the man repeat the story to his wife on the phone. Skateboarder Guy was in awe that this gentleman had made it almost two miles after what was apparently a heart attack. Further, he was astonished at the scene near the corporate parking lot. At the edge of the forest was a fox. Why had the fox been following the man, and why was the fox watching injured man now? It would not be the last time Skateboarder Guy would see the fox and ask himself questions.

Mr. Fox watched from atop the Cherry Candies Stone. It provided sufficient height for Mr. Fox to see N. Oldman, and it was surrounded by blackberry vines to hide him from others. The woman with the sweet voice and beautiful smile came quickly, and she and others helped Old Man into the car's reclined front seat.

Mr. Fox felt a pang in his heart. N. Oldman was ill and injured. *What had happened in the forest?* Mr. Fox pondered. *For several minutes, N. Oldman had looked as though he was dead on the forest floor. Was Old Man ever coming back?* For now, he watched the sun sink in the westward trees of Fox World. Night came and the moon rose, and the fox curled into a furry ball in a pile of pine needles and waited for N. Oldman.

For twenty-two sunsets.

THE COMPASS POINTS
TO GOOGLE NORTH

Old Man's mind drifted aimlessly. He was not afraid. Alternatively, he did not feel safe or know what to expect next. There had been a shocking, numbing pain in his neck, followed by gold butterflies and then the most serene feeling ever. Now he was in the hospital. Where was Mr. Fox? What had happened to their Friday afternoon picnic? How did he get here?

The phrase "road to redemption" is often a lyric in a song describing a spiritual quest. The road to redemption is a journey to explore one's conflicting thoughts, enhance one's life, or right one's mistakes. It is not a single, start-stop trip to a map-drawn destination. The road to redemption does not have a smoothly paved, gently sloping entrance ramp. More likely, a person must jump over a barbed-wire fence by the road to escape something bad, and then and there, she or he are on the road. Redemption road is well disguised at first—pleasant, alluring, and intriguing. It is a road, but it is not driven. It is walked up calf-burning, steep hills and around twisting, nausea-inducing curves through arid, sand-blown desert trails. It soon morphs into what it is meant to be—a vision quest where you walk, and you walk, and you walk until the facades of an inauthentic existence are peeled back and the seeker finds their core truths. Excruciating is the alternative—continuing to live unaligned with a life purpose.

In Old Man's case, his road to redemption began gazing at ceiling tiles in hospital examination rooms and recovery-room beds in the Mayo Clinic and Cleveland Clinic-branded centers in Arlington,

Virginia and Washington, DC. For days he looked up and dim yellow lights and water-stained tiles stared back.

Four times the cardiac surgeon and electrophysiologist operated on his heart. Four times it had stopped with arrhythmia surges, they said. Twelve seconds. Fifteen seconds. Twenty seconds. Thirty seconds. Pacemaker inserted, and within days, it failed. Emergency surgery to replace it a week later. Stent bridges inserted. Atrial fibrillation ablation zaps to the heart. The eleven hours of surgeries caused collateral damage. Deep vein thrombosis blood clots, a half-dozen of them, brought paralyzing pain to Old Man's left arm, shoulder, chest wall, thigh. In and out of hospitals, in and out of consciousness, he held serve as best as he could.

In the ether of the alpha state, he wondered about Mr. Fox. How was his dear friend? Was he cold as winter started? Had his injuries from the fight with Big Red healed? When he was not counting ceiling tiles, N. Oldman watched autumn age outside the hospital window. The disabled business executive missed the forest, the pine scents, and the bird calls. He was resigned to a single certainty; he was no longer in control. Whether that was good or bad did not matter. Fact is—it just was.

The cupped rubber edge of the hissing oxygen mask came down towards his face. Adjusted in place by the blonde anesthesiologist, who whispered with mock flirtation, "I'm beginning to think you like me, because you seem to be doing anything you can to come back and see me again." He smiled. Three breaths in and the anesthesia curtain fell.

He drifted to a place of peace—Utah a thousand days ago. He was in red rock canyon country in the high desert, twenty miles north of the Arizona border. If one were to name the area "Secluded," one would be overstating the population considerably. Old Man was alone in the desert. Well, not exactly. He was on a red rock sand trail, dotted with buckhorn cholla, with an eight-year-old McNab Shepherd shelter dog named Google.

Google was a dual color dog—milk chocolate and cream. The former color covered his head, ears, torso, and a dessert-plate sized circle on his neck. The latter covered his nose, a twelve-inch ring around his neck, and his front legs and back feet, like ankle-cut athletic socks. His coat was coarse on top to handle rough weather days yet slightly fluffy underneath on a tummy that invited belly rubs. His oversized amber eyes were soulful and bespoke one who is searching, one who cleverly hides his mental pain, and one who has a spiritual message for quiet listeners. Google was not a barker. He was an eye talker and a willing walker. Old Man's trail mate was of kind heart, pleasant in demeanor, but appropriately prickly when not allowed to chase tiger whiptail lizards. Google was an incredible dog by all measures. He had one not-his-fault flaw: he had no home. He had lived in a rescue shelter most of his life. Six of his eight years. Before that, he had been an energetic puppy bound to a tree with a heavy iron chain. A chain dog. That explained the sad eyes. The lonely dog ... always waiting ... and no one comes to play.

Google and Old Lion (Google attached this moniker after hearing Old Man talk to the animal shelter volunteers and telling them that he was a stressed-out business executive looking for a speck of solitude and peace) walked miles on this brisk, high-desert morning. Stress went poof, muscle tensions dissipated, worries lifted. The shelter dog lead Old Lion blissfully down the trail. Were they walking his Road to Redemption or Google's magic path? Before the sun set that evening, Old Lion would have his answer.

Authentic German doughnuts and strong black coffee in the red buttes of Utah are a king's brunch. Google and Old Lion paused and sat on a pink-red, automobile-sized boulder. The temperature crossed fifty-five degrees as the emerging sunlight warmed their faces. He opened the bag from the German bakery, a star-crossed lucky find in rural Utah. There were dog biscuits and succulent doughnuts inside the brown paper bag dotted with hot oil circles. Compared to the sweet treat doughnuts, the organic dog biscuits were spartan. The scents of sweet baked and fried doughy treats filled the crisp air. Google's head snapped around and his nose tipped upward as he ran canine diagnostics on the doughnut vapor trail. He wanted one, and he did not mean a crunchy biscuit.

Google wanted many things; most never came. He had lived a life of silver medals, no gold. Thus, if proffered, he would gladly accept a biscuit. But for now, he focused elsewhere to the vista of Zion National Park on the western horizon with the occasional side glance at the doughnut bag.

Old Lion (aka Old Man aka N. Oldman) stretched his legs fully on the boulder and leaned back on another stone—not before checking for Mojave rattlesnakes. His fear of snakes was irrational but deep seated. All safe, he relaxed and poured a bowl of mineral water for Google and doled out a generous handful of organic meat treats. Google gave him a *where-did-those-come-from* look. The shelter dog moved closer, nibbled on the succulent treats, and dropped his guard a bit. As much as he wanted a forever dad or mom, he feared the thought. Visitors like Old Lion came, and they went. *Temporary friends*, he categorized them. Maybe a gift package addressed to "Google" would arrive later. But no one came back to take him home—ever.

A shelter dog, a stressed business guy, unlimited beautiful solitude to reflect in, and a mutual sugar addiction were a chef's pot in which to cook up a batch of trust. *These were the building blocks of a friendship*, both reflected in the silence of the morning desert. Old Lion decided to up the ante and inserted his hand into the pastry shop bag, rattled the tissues inside, and palmed two bakery doughnuts of two different flavors: Apple Berliner, a tasty pastry made with fine butter-dough sweetened with apple filling and coated in cinnamon sugar, and Carnival Berliner, a doughnut batter filled with sweet curd and finished with a final roll in raw sugar. He placed the baker's creations equidistant between the two hikers on the wind-polished, rose-pink flat stone.

Google's amber eyes darted between the two tempting pastries. His large nostrils sucked in their steaminess. Like any canine, he liked meat. But Google's lifelong secret was that he had a sweet tooth. Old Lion would readily confess that he too needed a Twelve-Step Sugar Anonymous intervention most days in his life. Fate had married two sugar addicts on this hike. Bonds often have unusual origins.

Google, normally painfully shy, locked eyes with the old guy for the first time that morning. Well mannered, he was too timid to plead for a doughnut. It was human food, and he was not allowed to have that. But if a tree falls deep in the forest, does anyone hear it? Same for a doughnut. If a couple of doughnuts disappear in the vast expanse of southern Utah, does anyone really know? Google's eyes, filled with wisdom and the heaviness of the world, softened and twinkled. With a nod of his head to the left, he chose the Apple Berliner.

Good strategy, Old Lion thought as he tore the apple doughnut into two pieces. Start with a simple entrée and then on to the gluttonous, crème-filled offering. With his left hand he pinched the doughnut piece between thumb and index finger and offered it to Google's lips. With his right hand, he fed himself. Jaw smacking ensued, and it was the most heavenly sound ever created in the morning still. Two boys bonding by indulging in a deeply coveted secret—sugar.

Old Lion told Google his story. It was a tale of thankful blessings and a deep regret or two. Reaching his mid-fifties, he knew inside his heart that he had not done what he loved in life, but he had managed to love what he had done. The chasm grew as Earth years went by. He told Google about oceans crossed and big cities far away. He explained to Google that there are kind people and evil people, but that animals are all good. His ears pricked as he listened attentively. Old Lion hugged Google deeply and told him that he was valued and valuable.

Old Lion had come here seeking an epiphany in the cool, dry October air and the starry skies of Utah's high desert. Both he and Google laughed at that hope. Changes and solutions are not light-switch events. Google had seen many come for that—some catching a moment of clarity in a bottle, others leaving more confused and disoriented than before. Maybe the best that you can hope for is to feel settled and centered for a bit, and Old Lion was. He hugged his trail buddy again affectionately. Google sheepishly consented and leaned into him.

The best tales on the trail are not the ones you tell; they are the ones that you hear, and Old Man wanted to hear Google share his story so he parted the second doughnut into trail buddy breakfast portions. Google gratefully accepted the Carnival Berliner, and an *oh-my* look broke across his canine face. He chomped down on the doughnut, and the cream inside squirted out onto the milk chocolate fur of his nose. He retrieved the errant glob with his big pink tongue and with a twinkly smile in his eyes. Bingo! Those eyes were less heavy now. Google was having fun.

Old Lion dipped a napkin in the water bowl, cleaned Google's snout, and wiped the trail dust from his eyes. Refreshed and sugar satiated, Google twirled into a ball and put his head in the man's lap. "Tell me your story, Google," the man requested. Google began …

> I am a desert dog. I have lived life long in the red rock sand. I think and dream of the faraway ocean. Not of the waters, but of the waves. I imagine the rhythmic waves of the ocean bringing my hopes closer. I wait for one big, huge Google wave to roll in and bring all the things a desert dog dreams of.
>
> Someday, my wave will bring the comforting shade of an evergreen pine and lots of cool, cool green grass on my belly as I nap beneath a perfect aqua sky. And a warm breeze from the desert blows across my face as someone twirls my ears.
>
> My wave will bring a picnic. A picnic with plenty of treats. A long day nap with all-around quiet. The chance to see the sun set while my dimming eyes are still adequate. A sun that is yellow, then orange, then rose-pink, and then fading. Followed by a long talk at night—for it is then that I am most lonely. I cannot see the stars well now, but I imagine someone describing their twinkly brightness to me as I rest my head in their lap. And maybe later, we sneak into the park in town, and I dip my paws into the fountain waters as I imagine the waves of the ocean. The Atlantic. The Pacific.
>
> My wave will bring a long, carefree run through the streets of my hometown, Kanab. A run so fast that I feel as light and bouncy as a puppy again. No aching

bones—just running like the wind. Smiling and yelping,
I will run.

My wave will bring a circle of love on my birthday as I
hear stories of my life from many fathers, many mothers.
And I can walk around to each caregiver, one by one,
greet them, and give them lots of Google kisses.

My wave will bring from everyone who knows me an
understanding of why I am so shy. So many eyes have
looked at me, but no one took me home. So now I just
look away or I look down. If my eyes do not meet yours, I
hurt less.

My wave will bring acceptance. I'm old now. It
feels good to be lifted and carried when I am tired or
uncertain in my gait. I love being held tight when I am
scared, or to get a shoulder rub when arthritis' advance
makes me twitch.

My wave will bring an opportunity to share with all
in my life how much I love them; how much I find my
forever home in their hearts.

Old Lion looked down at the aging shelter dog asleep in his lap and twirled his ears. He rubbed his strong, stout shoulders and held him tight until the long shadows of autumn began to cast. He thanked Google for the gift of this day, for the generosity of opening his calm spirit, for being vulnerable and teaching him to be the same.

It is those that have the least to give, who give the most, Old Man had observed often. This phrase defined Google from tip to tail. He was selfless, put others first and suffered silently. Giving willingly from the depths of a broken soul is the north-star compass point on the road to redemption. Be humble, be self-aware be vulnerable—only then are you open and free. This was the Google credo, and going forward, it was the compass heading that Old Lion would always call "Google North."

The dream of the Utah hike with Google scrunched down to a nickel-sized blip like an old TV when the picture tube clicks off. Google faded. The calm desert evaporated. Red rock dust swirled upward with the hint of a light zephyr. The ceiling tiles reappeared blink by blink and framed the face of a beautiful dark-haired lady. Old Man, no longer the desert-traversing Old Lion, awoke slowly. After five hours of surgery, every muscle felt paralyzed, except his eyelids. He half-opened his eyes and above him was his wife's tear-streaked face.

"You're back," she said softly.

"That is all I got; I am so very, very tired," he whispered.

"Far from it, Old Man. In a few days, you will be walking the forest trail with your fox buddy—just as you did with Google years ago." She smiled and lit his heart. Old Man's wife had many qualities, one of many was prescience. She knew that the road to redemption, started by Google the dog in the Utah desert, would ensue again and veer into Fox World.

TWENTY-TWO SUNSETS

For twenty-two sunsets, Mr. Fox paced the boundaries of Fox World. When he wasn't walking, he found a good hiding spot and watched Old Man's house. Animals are blessed with many endearing attributes—unlimited patience being near the top of the list. Still, it was downright devotion that spurred the old fox through the last few sunsets.

Mr. Fox saw Donnie, the driver of the brown express package delivery truck. He wanted to jump out of the forest and ask about Old Man. He nodded to Donnie instead. Little did Mr. Fox know that Donnie would report the Mr. Fox sighting to Smiling Wife, and the fox buddy sighting would brace N. Oldman's recovery stamina.

Mr. Fox went on a "walk and talk" around the forest. He spoke to Russell Raccoon, Deja Blue the heron, Bucky the deer, Professor Owl, and Colonel Hawk. No one had seen Old Man in the woods. Bucky reported that he had seen the white Range Rover drive by, and it looked like Old Man was riding, not driving. *He always drives,* Mr. Fox pondered. *Must not have been Old Man.* Bucky, the twelve-pointer, went on to add that the man in the passenger window looked tired, and he was not smiling.

The sweet lady brought blueberries and snacks. She walked alone though. She looked exhausted, and it was always dark when she came. Mr. Fox never let her walk home unescorted. Finally, one day she spotted his stealthy chivalry. She turned and said, "Hello, brave little Mr. Fox. It is particularly good to see you. Are you ok? Are you finding your nutritious treats? My husband is ill. They cut on his chest and made him better. He is getting stronger, and he misses walking with you. He needs your help when he returns. He needs to relax."

Mr. Fox snapped to attention immediately. *Yes. How? What? Anything. Just tell me.* His fox brain was filled with ideas. His heart was happy that his buddy was alive. He whispered their mantra under his breath—*if you're alive, you've won*—and with that, Mr. Fox hatched a plan.

HOSPITAL FOOD IS
ACTUALLY TASTY

Thanksgiving eve came. Old Man and his wife watched the November sun set in the battleship-gray sky outside the hospital window. It was his last day in the medical center—all hoped. This piece of news sparked an idea for a party. The customary hospital food tray offering was eschewed in favor of delectable dining of a higher calling. Old Man and Smiling Wife laughed out loud—to speak the truth, there was but one alternative to a hospital tray dinner. It was a Subway franchise in the hospital canteen. "Everything you need on one sandwich," Old Man's father had said once when they visited him in Tennessee years ago. The sandwiches had "everything": proteins (turkey and cheese), vegetables (lettuce, tomato, green peppers, black olives), and carbohydrates (six-inch whole wheat submarine bread). Further, Jack Silvin would add (and Old Man and his wife mouthed the words in unison), "They have big-as-wagon-wheel chocolate chip cookies for dessert—just in case you need some sugar." Who didn't like sugar? Old Man liked a Snickers bar on occasion. Smiling Wife was a petite Snickerdoodle cookie fiend. Google liked German doughnuts. Mr. Fox liked cherry pie. And Jack Silvin loved chocolate chip cookies.

Old Man's wife kissed him on the cheek and told him to read his book or listen to a podcast while she went on a Subway food run. The gray skies parted, and Old Man watched the last drips of the pale, pink-orange sunset from his window-side bed. Mr. Fox, his buddy, was a dedicated sunset watcher, part of his fox code, and Old Man wished he was back in Fox World with Mr. Fox.

The fox had no wristwatch or alarm clock in his den. He was a "sundial" kind of fox. Sunsets, sunrises, and shadows were his time-pieces. Old Man loved the old fox's rituals and principles. As he pulled the flannel blanket up and over his chest, he watched the stiff wind shake the bare branches outside. It looked bitter cold. He telegraphed a message westward to Fox Forest—*I hope that you are not cold, Mr. Fox. I hope that you are not hungry. I hope that your old bones do not hurt too much in the night's chill. I am ok. I am coming home tomorrow.*

Seventeen miles away, Mr. Fox's heart sank with the sun. Another earth day punched out, and his human buddy was not back. *Was he ok?* His fox intuition told him yes, and he trusted it. Suddenly, the orange downy hair on the back of his neck bristled and his canine ESP antenna spooled up. Incoming Morse code message. He listened and translated. *Tomorrow is what humans call Thanksgiving—Thanksgiving Day—and it will be a day when everyone in Fox World gives thanks, for N. Oldman is coming home.*

Old Man and his wife dined at a makeshift table on the side of the hospital bed. There was a rosebud vase in the middle between two place settings of the finest paper china (Royal Doulton porcelain in one's imagination). The banquet was three courses—paper-wrapped turkey sandwiches (loaded with everything you need), side dishes of Doritos and low-salt "crisps" (as his golfing mates in St. Andrews would call them), and make-believe champagne (aka Sprite soda). The piece de resistance of this champions dinner were the cookies, the big-as-a-wagon-wheel cookies. Ooh's and ah's greeted the milk chocolate chip and white chocolate macadamia nut cookies as they took their honorary place on the celebration party table. "Le Subway" catering, a VIP table, and a beautiful dinner date. It was the best dinner of their marriage.

"Tell me a story about why you love our life together," she asked.

He grinned, his first pain-absent smile in days. His dream of walking with Google in the desert flashed in his mind again, and he told Smiling Wife about his dream during surgery. She smiled; she loved the McNab Shepherd named Google. Old Man's thoughts turned to another rescue dog adventure years ago—an odyssey that he had shared with his wife. It was a "roll down your truck windows and smell the summer air and mowed grass on the back roads of America" type of road trip. It was replete with Americana trimmings—an oversized wire-bound road atlas, a Sharpie pen to circle good backroad routes, quick-grab road burgers, XM/Sirius tunes blaring, sneakers unlaced, and a new pair of sunglasses (a summer rite of passage and approved splurge from the annual mad-money budget). At the end of the road, the most moving of motivations waited: five shelter dogs. All five had execution dates hanging around their necks in kill shelters in faraway central Kentucky and southwest Virginia.

Old Man and his darling wife topped up their plastic cups, borrowed from the nurse's station, with the bubbly, ice cold Sprite. They toasted, and Old Man began the story, an ode to his wife and her wisdom, her toughness, and her endless grace.

> Years ago, there were five dogs in trouble. They ranged from age two to twelve. Their health status ranked from young and randy to old and why bother. They had one thing in common—a ticking clock in a kill shelter.
>
> To save them on short notice, the list of needs was daunting. Kind souls to "pull" them from the kill shelters. Health exams and medical certificates for across state border travel. Living supplies. Toys for fun socialization. A Jack Russell terrier sanctuary to go to, live for a while, and stabilize physically. Long-term medical treatment.
>
> Angels appeared. Two ladies in Kentucky saved the dogs from the gallows and arranged for their medical exams and their travel papers. A single-breed sanctuary for JRTs in South Carolina stepped into the leader's role and promised the five dislocated dogs a home and big hope. The sanctuary's czar coordinated the entire set of rescue logistics.
>
> The beleaguered kill-shelter dogs needed supplies, and they needed transportation for a 1,900-mile

freedom ride. This is where two other Jack Russell terriers came into the picture. Beacon and Bounce broke into their piggy bank, took an Uber to their favorite big-box, Petco, and shopped supplies for their Jack Russell cousins in Kentucky.

Five crates. Five blankets. Five harnesses and leashes. Five collars stenciled with their names. A personalized name tag connotes VIP, and these five souls deserved VIP status after their trials and tribulations. Five food packs (food, bowls, water dishes). Five gift boxes of toys and stuffed-animal mates. Beacon and Bounce did not miss a thing. They delivered a bounty.

The freedom ride was mapped into a 1,965-mile loop through Virginia, Maryland, West Virginia, Pennsylvania, Kentucky, Tennessee, the Carolinas and back home to the Old Dominion. With the SUV packed, Beacon jumped in the shotgun seat and fastened his doggy sunglasses in place. Your husband and trusty terrier were ready to launch. On the horizon were five amazing dogs and seven incredible people that would change the arc of our lives. And along the way, there was an overdue reunion with a cherished, long-not-seen relative. It was a trip that would forever ground us with what is enormously important in life— family and making new friends.

As you know, I knew nothing about dog rescue. I was as naïve about the hidden pitfalls of shelter dog transportation as any one person could be. Operating only with faith, good intentions, a full tank of gas, and a twelve-year old canine co-pilot, the chances for peril and disconnects were set high by the oddsmakers.

It was ninety degrees in northern Virginia at the 7:30 a.m. wheels-up departure. That is hot for 7:30 a.m. Thankful for the long sunlight hours of an early July, the trip to Lexington, Kentucky would consume most of the day. Beacon liked the windows down, so we were wind-blown and gritty by the time we crossed the Kentucky state line. We drove on, westward into the setting sun. We pulled into Lexington at 8:00 p.m. I was dog tired, and Beacon was human tired. He and I enjoyed room service hamburgers at the JW Marriott and ingested them al fresco on the balcony as the sun set over the golf course below. We fell asleep on top of the comforter, lamp on, Beacon curled to my chest. We missed you, my dear wife.

Next morning, Beacon and I awoke to a blinding sun poking through the sheer drapes and a double Tylenol ache in our bones. Beacon had a full canine breakfast. I washed down meds with a minibar orange juice and a pack of peanuts. Sleep tank full, breakfast in our bellies, and old lion aches warded off by pharmaceuticals, we walked the kelly-green edge of the golf course to loosen our muscles. It was hot. Desert hot. Africa hot. The forecast heat and the reality of an amateur rescuing five stressed canines gave me pause. I realized that navigating the mountains and back roads of Kentucky and western Virginia to South Carolina solo with five rescue dogs in sweltering weather was not safe for the dogs or me.

So, I did what I have always done over the years when I have overcommitted or made a dumb mistake: I called home. You answered on the first ring, almost as if you expected my call, and listened patiently. You made a note or two and told me to stay by the telephone. A few minutes later, you called back with a flight number for the next morning.

Next morning, the calvary arrived—you walked down the escalator at Lexington's Blue Grass Airport. Your smile spoke both happiness to see me and a pinch of *what ridiculous thing did you do now?* Guilty as charged. You needed a mood booster after your air travel, and I did my best to script a full fun day for you. Bourbon Trail distillery tours. A first-ever tiny glass of Pappy Van Winkle 23. A two-hour ride through Kentucky's blue grass thoroughbred farms. A visit to Secretariat's grave and a picnic at the Kentucky Horse Park. Late afternoon, we took a swim at the JW Marriott spa pool to cool ourselves, followed by a steakhouse dinner. After coffee, we strolled through the hotel's beautiful gardens for one of Beacon's favorite activities—barking at bunny rabbits. Glorious Kentucky had soothed us.

We departed the hotel at o-dark-my-gosh hour the next morning. Little did we know that a ten-hour trip to Cassatt, South Carolina was destined to take twice that amount of time. Coffee cups on the dash, we drove south fast. First stop: 6:15 a.m., and we were late. Around daylight, we pulled into in Somerset, Kentucky—a town of eleven or twelve thousand. In Kentucky's lake country, the main drag is Route 27, which was dotted with tourist type businesses—food, beer, ice cream, boat parts, etc.

There, in a fast-food chain parking lot, we met two of the kindest, most heroic people who have ever graced our lives. We learned that they devote most of their non-working hours to rescuing dogs in Kentucky's kill shelters. It is a daily devotion. It never stops. In most worlds, helping at the shelter on a Saturday morning is a good way to feel charitable. In this town, miss one day and a dog dies. You and I were in awe of them. They were warriors. Four Jack Russell terriers peeked from their crates: Cleo, Cora Bell, Brady, and Jenna. The four sleepy darlings were quiet, tentative, and a bit scared. Yet hope's sparkle was in their eyes. They sensed adventure and they smelled hope.

Brady was the most enthusiastic among them. He called shotgun and took the front window seat. We discovered two things about Brady. He was a dedicated hang-his-head-out-the-window dog. It was also his first car ride. He painted a yellow stripe along the side of our white SUV with his queasy stomach contents. To be exact, four yellow stripes.

We drove east on the Daniel Boone Trail, so twisty and curvy that you and I almost joined Brady with our heads out the window. We drove through mountainous areas where iPhones, GPS, and satellite radio did not work. In fact, we had to do two things on a car trip that I have not done in forty years—stop at a filling station and buy a detailed state road map and play the harmonica to entertain ourselves. The dogs joined in on the singing, especially Jenna and Cora.

It was a return to the simplest of times, to innocent days gone by. Magically, time stood still. How often have we all secretly wished for that to happen? We got lost. Twice. The dogs got car sick. Four times. We had a dog escape. Once. We were run off the road by a tractor trailer, and five dog crates went askew. But on this road trip, at wits' end with the switch-back curves and the soaking humidity, an angel and an oasis appeared.

The angel was a nine-year old boy who walked up to us at a highway rest stop and said, "I'm Kaiser, and you look like you need some help." Oh, did we. He played with and held all five dogs. He helped us hydrate them and wash their faces with ice water. He petted each of them and told them to enjoy the trip. A calm set in with the dogs as he touched them. I will never forget it. As quickly as he appeared, angelic Kaiser answered the call of his mom and vanished.

Two hundred and fifty-five miles later, we entered Wise, Virginia. The name was ironic. Nothing wise about being in this despondent, run-out-of-luck town, which while green and lush in July, was most certainly monotone gray and brown with coal dust come January snow season. Sprinkle in the meth-state hopelessness and the attitude of a life milestone is a new tattoo, and you have a rundown coal town.

The crown jewel in this town was the saint of a woman credited with saving over two thousand kill-shelter dogs in coal-country Virginia. She was tireless and unrelenting in her desire to help needy dogs. She was a mixture of your lovable, caring aunt and a demanding, successful Olympic athlete. We loaded up a beautiful, smooth-coated terrier named Dody. She jumped in excitedly and joined Jenna, Brady, Cora Bell, and Cleo. She smiled from her crate after finding out that she had her own fluffy blanket and assortment of toys.

We sat under a wide shade tree to cool and water the dogs and hear the woman's many stories of animal mistreatment in southwest Virginia. Breath-stopping tales, sobering and sad. In this anthracite-hard town, we found a soft-hearted angel amidst the crusty shell of despair and poverty.

Next stop was Abingdon, Virginia. The truck had become stuffy, closed in. Two humans, one co-pilot, five crates, and two duffle bags packed the Evoque. We needed cooler temps, stretched legs, and open space. We parked on a shady street beside a hilltop park. Temps dropped a smidge. What we saw below was an oasis, a promise of a chilled thermometer. It took the form of a tall water fountain and a two-foot-deep wading pool. In the center of the bubbling pool was a sculpture titled *Midsummer Night's Dream*. The fountain was ringed with bronze carvings of animals, including wolf pups. We smiled as I told you the story of Abingdon's previous name, Wolf Hills. A go-west explorer had found a cave with wolf pups in it, and the moniker had stuck.

How do you get five shelter dogs unfamiliar with each other to walk anywhere as a team on a sweltering hot day? Promise them a swim. We did, and they honed it on the spray of water from the fountain and its core-temperature-replenishing waters. After a dip, a brisk shake, and a handful of organic beef treats, the fabulous five huddled and settled. These mistreated shelter dogs with nicks and scars on their bodies and in their souls rallied around the hope of a better life that every mile brought. The fab five were all in with the mission and its challenges. Their eyes registered unconditional gratefulness.

We had a picnic spread of sparkling waters, iced tea, dog biscuits, country ham biscuits, deviled eggs, and banana pudding. It was a queen's banquet. We unlaced our boat shoes and dipped our toes. Whoa, it was cold. This was Virginia spring water, icy from the depths. We soaked in the cool Zen of Abingdon. All too soon, we had to leave the quaint township, but not before pausing to place yellow roses on long-passed parent's graves and introduce them to the Fab Five.

On we went—several more hours to Statesville, North Carolina. There we had a far-too-short visit with my father's sister and her beloved beagle, Rosie. Her home was beautiful and welcoming. The fenced yard was spacious and lush green—a dog's paradise. Rosie and the Fab Five chased playfully after each other in the Ireland-green grass. The spirit of the five shelter dogs rose visibly. Tail wags increased exponentially and tapped out a message in canine Morse code: *We are free ... really free.*

Driving on into the dark, we were met by one last challenge in our odyssey. It was a DUI roadblock in rural South Carolina. The law enforcement officer laughed when he shined his flashlight into our SUV. When he read my driver's license, he said, "So what are a guy and a lady from Virginia doing in the middle of South Carolina at midnight with a Range Rover full of Jack Russell's?"

You replied, "Saving them, sir, by delivering them to Raintree Jacks."

At this point, he hollered at another police officer in front of us, "Clear the road; rescue vehicle coming through!" He turned to us and grinned. "Get those babies to Raintree Jacks."

We arrived in Cassatt, South Carolina at 12:30 a.m., nineteen hours after leaving Lexington, Kentucky. Raintree Jacks Sanctuary is on a large horse farm. It is a special place for an extraordinary canine breed. The magnificent woman who put this place together assists over one hundred terriers annually. She is otherworldly in her grace, energy level, and capacity for kindness.

In the midnight hour, Raintree Jacks is a stone-deaf quiet place. Noise and light pollution do not exist there. Every star is a brightly lit diamond on a cloud-less summer night. The only sounds one hears are the low soothing hum of nocturnal insects. Fireflies twinkle in the inky darkness. To say it is magical is to undershoot its majestic resonance.

We hugged goodbyes to our faithful five. Thirteen-year-old Cora Bell, thought to be too fragile for rescue and for the nineteen-hour freedom trip, emerged first. Fresh as a daisy after riding on our laps for the last six hours, she displayed her alpha female spirit on her new frontier called Raintree Jacks. She sniffed the breeze and she smelled safety, loving kindness, good friends. The others disembarked and explored the still darkness and the scents of the South Carolina pines. This was home. This was Heaven. We bear-hugged the matriarch of Raintree Jacks. We wanted to stay and talk over coffee and get to know this wonderful lady. But this is a working farm and the roosters crow early. We left with promises to return, which we did fifty-three days later with a marvelous rescue dog named Memphis.

Arriving at our hotel at 3:30 a.m., we were fatigued but could not sleep. Thoughts of the five shelter dogs and the miracle humans who helped them circled through our heads. We talked about them in our hotel bed, lit dimly by the Waffle House sign across the parking lot. We re-traced our miles. We'd embarked on a miraculous adventure in Kentucky, got wiser in Wise, discovered a water oasis in Abingdon, found long-lost family in Statesville, passed a DUI check in Camden, met the Mother Theresa of canine rescue in Cassatt, and fell in love with five unique canine souls.

Road trip complete, the adrenaline drained. There were no more mountains to climb—literally or figuratively. Reality set in. We missed them. The Fab Five had touched every point in our emotional register. They made us laugh (Brady with his head out the truck window); they made us worried (Cora was so weak that we didn't know if she would survive); they made us marvel at miracles (when nine-year old Kaiser walked up unexpectedly at a rest stop). We missed, admired, and respected their indomitable spirit.

Old Man's voice trailed off. He looked at the remnants on the plate of their hospital room feast. Only bread and cookie crumbs remained, a successful end to a meal in his wife's view. Old Man touched his wife's hand and squeezed it softly and gave her a smile that foreshadowed the healing days ahead. She slid Keurig-made coffees onto the hospital tray and upped the offering with another wheel-sized chocolate chip cookie. She broke off a small piece of cookie and fed him. He reciprocated with a bigger chunk for her that made her laugh. Old Man went on. She smiled warmly through her fatigue. "That was the greatest story ever. Some would say we made a difference. Instead, it was the shelter dogs and the people on the trip that made the difference. They changed us."

The nursing assistant came with pain medication, a cup of water, and a pillow and blanket for his wife. She dropped into sleep rapidly. Old Man leaned as far right as the IV line and EKG patches would permit. His left chest wound throbbed. He kept reaching and wincing. He pulled the blanket up around his wife. He could not hug her, but he squeezed her left hand. Goodnight, angel.

Outside the third-floor hospital window, the full moon perched atop a single tall green pine like a golf ball on a tee. Old Man enjoyed the moon rise, a simple pleasure that no longer escaped him and he had Mr. Fox to thank for that. "If you're alive, you've won," he whispered to himself. He longed to see the old fox again. As for walking with him soon, the immediate future was uncertain. He had a lot of chest trauma and blood clots, the doctors said.

Seventeen miles west, Mr. Fox tilted his head upward to Professor Owl's tree, the full moon was lingering low in the sky, gaining altitude inch by inch. Mr. Fox had not seen his human friend since the last full moon. He missed N. Oldman and his stories of faraway places. He crawled into the hollow log under Professor Owl's tree and lowered his chin on his crossed-over velvety black paws. He exhaled a breath of worry and said goodnight to Professor Owl, Bucky, Colonel Hawk, Deja Blue, and Russell Raccoon. Their good nights echoed back one by one. Restlessly, the Fox World animal team tossed and turned during the night. Waiting is hard, they agreed.

Tomorrow was Thanksgiving—a happy thought for the forest animals. On Thanksgiving Day, the Corporate World parking lots were desolate and posed no threat to the animals. Annually, it was the day for a community meal in Fox World. N. Oldman, Smiling Wife, and Beacon and Bounce always pulled a blue wagon to the forest, and it was filled to the upper edges with special treats—cherries, blueberries, eggs, sardines, small cubes of cheese, sliced apples, pumpkin pie, shelled corn, timothy hay, and more. But it was not about the food and treats this year. As delicious as this feast sounded, they just wanted to see N. Oldman again.

Mr. Fox knew one thing dead darn certain. If N. Oldman could just make it back to Fox World, he would fix him. And he would fix the things that broke his heart.

GRATEFUL FOR
A PLATEFUL

Troubles, like scrambled ideas on a chalkboard, sometimes need to sort themselves out. Accept the mess, Old Man decided, and find a new plan. Optimism rose, and he did his best to temper it, but he was ready to find his hiking boots and cushy wool socks, take his waxed waterproof jacket and knit cap off the wall peg, tuck his sunglasses in his shirt pocket, and start walking. Old Man was hospital-free, on his way home, and he longed to see the old fox.

The doctors were united in their opinions—find a way to relax or he would die. His heart had stopped four times, four strikes and Old Man was still standing at the plate, but he could not risk taking another high inside pitch. It was time to find a different way, a new path. He was weakened by the setback, possibly beyond repair and his compass was spinning, but he felt the energy of a new life ahead. Mr. Fox would say, *there are no setbacks in life. There are just sit-backs. Yes, sit back and let it all go. All of it.*

Thanksgiving Day dawned sunny and bright with a faint chill. It was an "I'm grateful for a plateful" day, as Old Man's mother had always called Thanksgiving. Old Man and Smiling Wife drove seventeen miles on the empty holiday beltway to home. Old Man joked that he now knew what a rescue dog on a freedom ride felt like. His wife gave his knee a reassuring pat and said, "We'll be home in a few minutes. I have a special day planned."

Home, Old Man sat by the brownstone's window in a chair that he had owned for twenty years. It fit like old khakis. The ottoman elevated his aching legs. An ice pack and sling comforted the residual pain in his left chest. The morning sun streaking in, a decaf coffee, and terriers on his lap warmed him. On the side table was a yellow hundred-page legal pad, college-ruled, with the words "Relax or Die" in black rollerball ink at the top. His wife would go berserk if she saw the inscription, so he covered the legal pad with newspapers, The Washington Post and The Washington Times. Cryptic numbers were jotted in the margin of the legal pad: 52 times 4 equals 208. Fifty-two weeks in a year with an average of four walks a week with Mr. Fox. A total of 208 walks in a year. Fox World's forest easy path is 1.6 miles long. Out and back is 3.2 miles. Walk it 208 times and the total mileage walked it in one year would be 665.6 miles. Reduce that number by twenty-five percent to account for the tough early days of heart surgery/blood clot recovery. Old Man circled the answer, 499.2, three times on the pad.

Four hundred ninety-nine point two miles in one year. The math work continued. Old Man liked big, challenging, are-you-crazy goals. Five hundred miles was exactly that—nuts. He had barely been able to walk to the car from the hospital door that morning. How was he going to walk five hundred miles? He did what Corporate World had taught him to do regarding goals: break it down, chunk it up. Take 499.2 miles times 1,760 yards (number of yards in a mile) and it equals 878,592 yards, or approximately one million steps. One million steps in one year. Or, by separate measure, two million steps for a four-legged fox or four-pawed Jack Russell terrier. Could Old Man and Mr. Fox walk 500 miles together in one year? And a better question was, why would a fox join him? A business executive would be stumped by this question and have no answer. A reformed, on his deathbed, business executive would just smile and trust the universe. Necessity births ideas. Ideas, married up with a plan, become a mission. A mission generates focus and intent, the baker's best ingredients in a successful cake.

The scent of roasted turkey and oyster dressing wafted from the kitchen's oven. Real bone china and gleaming Irish crystal, not the paper plate and plastic cup loaners from the hospital, were arranged on the cherrywood table. The family hand-me-down silver sat in a mahogany box on the buffet cabinet. This would be the first year that they had dined alone on Thanksgiving—a bit sad, but it was good to be home in Casa de Oldman.

Old Man left the yellow legal pad and the penned micro goals on the chair. He was locked in, he said to himself. He walked twenty paces to the beautifully set Thanksgiving dinner table, a sight that would have Norman Rockwell priming his paintbrushes. Old Man had never been more grateful for a plateful. He prayed thanks to God in the meal's blessing and a profound gratitude for God's gift of healing. He further thanked God for his wife across the table and the two terriers at his feet—stationed there somewhat out of adoration, but primarily positioned for crumb catching.

A feast followed. Old Man's eyes were bigger than his stomach. It was the first time in decades that he did not go back for seconds (or thirds). With nutmeg-spiced pumpkin pie, they sat by the orangey heat of the gas fireplace, the Green Bay Packers game turned down low in the background. They enjoyed the richness of Irish-Crème coffee (decaf and with no Bailey's this year). Next to the front door was a wood crate. With all her worries and endless list of tasks to ready the house for his homecoming, Old Man's wife, bless her heart, had not forgotten the animals. The rough-hewn wood box was brim-filled with bags topped by orange tied bows. Inside the pouches were beef treats for the Jack Russell terriers; peanuts in a shell for Russell Raccoon and Julius Caesar the chipmunk; cubes of Swiss cheese for Professor Owl and Colonel Hawk; fresh sardines for Deja Blue the heron; whole corn and sliced Shenandoah red apples for Bucky the deer; blueberries and cherries dipped in honey for Mr. Fox and Buttons.

Old Man looked at the wooden crate. His wife did too. She shook her head defiantly as in—"Heck no, you cannot go with me." Old Man's eyes pleaded yes. She softened, "Well, ok, but you are staying in the car. She loaded the treat crate in the trunk of the SUV and pulled it to the curb, where Old Man had shuffled to the sidewalk. "You are not getting out of the car," she repeated.

"Ok," he replied with a lie.

Leaving their gated community and following the labyrinth of Corporate World office park streets, they drove the 270-degree semi-circle route (three rights and no lefts) to the forest. It was a two-mile drive, far less as the crow flies. With the sun's shallow angle this time of year, it would be dark in fifteen minutes.

Mr. Fox was angled southwest. He rested on his haunches; his long tail brush swept around his lower body as a windscreen. The last of the day's sunbeams warmed his puffed-out chest and blazed his focused eyes a fiery amber. Sunrise and sunset were his two minutes of earth devotion daily; he cherished the amps and the solar-energy recharge.

Mr. Fox heard the truck door shut. He snapped his head right. *No cars came to the Corporate World parking lot on Thanksgiving Day. Who then?* It was his walking buddy's wife, and she had a big box in her arms. Mr. Fox was happy to see her, but she was alone again. His heart panged with disappointment. She spread treats around the woods on logs, tree-limb perches, and flat stones. Fox World's citizens gathered and sang, *it is Thanksgiving, and we give thanks for these wonderful treats on a cold winter afternoon.* She smiled and teared with happiness.

A second car door shut.

The animals were digging into their holiday treats and did not notice the car door opening. Everyone except for one. Mr. Fox ran—half hopeful and half afraid to hope—to the edge of the woods. Leaning against the white sports utility vehicle was Old Man. His arm was bent and tied to his chest; he looked pale and tired. With his other hand, he waved. He smiled and called out, "Hey there, Mr. Fox! How are you, dear friend? Would you like to walk with an old man in a few days?"

You better believe I would, N. Oldman!

There was a slight but noticeable twitch in the white tip of Mr. Fox's tail. The motion built to a fervent tail wag. Mr. Fox walked closer, twirled around three times, and descended into prone resting position. In wild fox language, this translated to comfort and trust. Old Man sat on a stump and relayed the million-step walking plan to

Mr. Fox. Mr. Fox listened intently and nodded. *Sign me up. I am rock solid all in with that plan,* he telegraphed.

Buttons walked up to join her mate, Mr. Fox and they nuzzled. Their thoughts buzzed through the frosty November air into a message: *Welcome home, N. Oldman. Thank you for coming to see us. Heal your chest and your mind. We will be right here waiting for you in Fox World. Thank you and your beautiful wife—we're grateful for a plateful (of cherries).*

BEACON IS THE
PRAETORIAN GUARD

Old Man eased into bed on Thanksgiving night at six o'clock, a timeframe that he had not observed since he was five years old. Getting old often means discovering the best aspects of childhood again, he laughed. Tummy full of holiday sustenance and exhausted from a short walk to the edge of Fox World, it was time to be horizontal. His wife had made a "recovery suite" in the master bedroom. Old Man stated repeatedly that it was not necessary, was overkill, was tantamount to excessive doting, and so on. A wave of her hand dismissed his grumblings.

The Keurig machine was on a nearby table for quick prep of coffee and hot peppermint tea. The latest books by Sanford, Child, Baldacci, Coyne, Moon, and DeMille were on the nightstand, along with a Waterford crystal bowl of blue-wrapped Fox's Mints from the UK. He smiled; the clear hard candy mints were his favorite accompaniment when reading a novel. He had discovered Fox's Mints walking through Heathrow Airport ten years ago and had initiated a life-long, sugar-loving bond with them after purchasing the first blue bag. On the bed were two homemade, patch-woven "homecoming blankets" sent by friends in the Carolinas. They were warmly thick and decorated with fox and hiking patches. His wife placed one over his legs and made a small puffy dog bed with the other.

Beacon, the fourteen-year-old, short-legged, tri-color Jack Russell jumped from the floor to the dressing bench to the high antique bed. He reversed his position to face the foot of the bed, reclined with a deep dog sigh, and leaned against the hip of his dad. He stayed in that position for days. His mom carried him out for brief bathroom breaks and brought his food bowl twice a day. If loyalty was brought in buckets, Beacon delivered a steam-shovel bucketful to those he loved. This was the little dog's style—everything he did, he did all in. As a puppy, he traveled to a casual Jack Russell terrier race meet ostensibly to make new friends, but he did not engage in casual frolic and puppy play with the others. He was fixated on the older Jacks running trial heats on the fifty-yard racetrack. His begging glances cajoled his mom into paying the twenty-dollar entrance fee. He ran, and won several races. Over the next ten years, he captured twenty-nine races and eight championships. At the age of twelve, three months after having a cancer operation and spending a week at the University of Pennsylvania Animal Hospital in Philadelphia, Beacon raced one more time at Montpelier, the estate of James Madison. It was a sunny autumn day at the steeplechase. Beacon's race was supposed to be ceremonial due to his age. One lap—just one lap by himself. During the practice runs, he watched the competitors warm up with adrenaline-fueled wide eyes. Suddenly, he backed out of his chest harness, jumped the snow fence, and ran down all the competitors on the track. "Let the little dog run a real race", the crowd cheered, so Old Man entered him in the next heat. The little guy won it and later won the bronze medal in the finals.

Mega heart, Old Man thought as he scratched the fur on his buddy's neck.

Old Man stared out the window to Fox World. His mind and memory rolled back. Thirteen years earlier, Beacon and Old Man had been walking on a cold December morning—just after daylight. A rail-thin red fox crossed the walking bridge ahead of them. Its head swiveled to present a bright, white, toothy smile. It was a yearling fox. Far too thin. It stopped—not from fear, but to flash a "help me" look. To the young fox, the man looked gentle, and the seven-month-old puppy looked bubbly and energetic and not a threat.

Time froze. The man, the terrier, and the fox were motionless except for their darting, connecting eyes. It was the first fox that Old Man had ever seen closely. Old Man took in all her features:

burnt-orange coat, velvet black leggings, white underbelly, eyes bright with intellect. Old Man reached in his down coat packet and retrieved a packet of bison jerky strips. He tossed a jerky stick to the young female fox. She sniffed it, took it, walked away a few steps, and ate it hungrily. Old Man and Beacon expected her to dash off. She returned and sat on her back legs. Her pink tongue traced the fur around her lips. She wanted another portion of jerky. Old Man had an idea. He broke the twelve-inch strip into three pieces, one large and two bite-size. He and Beacon kept one each and gave the large portion to their new friend. He toasted their new friendship, and everyone said cheers and ate their bounty. The ceremony initiated a series of Saturday morning bridge brunches. Old Man believed in separation of church and state when it came to feeding a wild animal. A human had to carefully weigh the danger of creating a dependency. But he could not let an animal starve, especially when mankind had stressed its natural resources.

Old Man eventually named the female fox Buttercup, because in the summer she would nap in a thick patch of bay-green grass and cheese-gold buttercup flowers. Old Man and his wife called the field Green Bay Land, because of the green and yellow tint to the field. At age four, Buttercup gave birth to two male fox kits. One was Mr. Fox; the other was his brother, Favre.

One animal had spanned the long arc of Buttercup and Mr. Fox. It was Beacon—the race champion, the snuggle boy, the canine-to-wild animal diplomat, and the immensely loyal friend. Old Man rubbed his buddy's shoulders again. The faithful terrier had been a fixture in one-quarter of Old Man's lifespan. He hugged Beacon closer and told him about his five-hundred-mile walk plan. Beacon exhaled a long breath calmly, wiggled closer, and winked. *You had me at I gotta plan.* Step one in the plan was to heal. They closed their eyes and slept for days.

# WONDER WALL

In most respects, Old Man never woke up; a new man did, it could be said. And by new, the word was in no way a descriptor to connote fresh and energetic. The illness had not broken him physically, but it had smashed his life-long mental paradigms. The outdated, overused dogma of "work hard, run fast, do more" had been pulverized into dust. N. Oldman was now in a new state of mind, or at least, on the front edge of it.

In his current circumstance, he was now a man <u>of</u> the moment who just needed to learn how to live <u>in</u> the moment. His life going forward would be bereft of options except for two: relax or die. These choice points were harsh in their dichotomy for a reason: wrong choice equated to a permanent penalty. Life is not without luck, and at this juncture, life had decided to show Old Man a lucky hole card. Life was forcing a rebuild. Half the rebuild was already done—the walls of disillusionment were down. Now, Old Man needed tools and a teacher, and he knew exactly where to find both. Fox World, frighteningly harmed and abandoned by humans, was beckoning. He was entering the animals' world as a beggar and he was not too proud to accept their mentoring.

With human hubris traded in for bottom-of-the-food chain humility, N. Oldman began his journey, a never to be forgotten stroll with a fox.

"Even that which they build, if a fox go up,
he shall break down their stone wall."

Nehemiah 4:3

MILE MARKER 0.1
STUMBLING BLOCKS

A man chooses his trail; he cannot choose his journey. Partners along the trail determine that.

The physical trauma of the past weeks had an unexpected side effect. Old Man was having fuzzy mental periods, so he had installed two ad hoc memory patches—a journal, an orange one, and a roller-ball pen, a black ink one. His million-step walking plan was tucked inside the orange journal.

He wrote "Mile One" in the journal. Walking one million steps with ix blood clots and a fresh chest wound was more a fool's errand than an achievable goal, drawing the comparison of balancing an appropriate level of confidence and unchecked ego. He shrugged, laughed (at himself), and hobbled to the sock drawer. Old Man selected asparagus-green, knee-length wool socks from Ireland, which hugged his calves with comfortable thickness, not too bulky to overfill the boot, not too thin for the crispy cold bite of a December morning. Three decades old, the socks were aging better with each passing year. They were top shelf in quality—as was the lady from Baltimore who had put them in his Christmas morning stocking thirty years ago. Quality ages beautifully, and he was sure that her character, grace, principles, and kindness had afforded her the many splendors of beauty. He silently thanked her for the lessons and the socks that she had shared.

Boots came next after the socks. Old Man had purchased the beaver-brown, ankle-high hiking boots on Christmas Eve seventeen years ago while walking along the main avenue of historic Frederick, Maryland. The boots were a self-gift on the first "alone holiday" after his divorce. Red and green holiday lights blinked hope through the plate glass windows. Old Man was planning an Appalachian Trail "clear the head" hike on New Year's Eve and the boots were a practical purchase. Two blocks later, he made a heart-pulsed purchase, a trail buddy. Benji was a ten-week-old eastern cottontail rabbit in a large glass store window, playing in pine shavings under a hand drawn "ADOPT ME" sign. Old Man paid the seventeen-dollar adoption fee, added a bag of bunny food and an adorable rabbit sweater with a snowman embroidered on it. On New Year's Eve, a man and a sweatered rabbit hiked for miles on the Appalachian Trail, stopping along the mountain path for a hot chocolate break for Old Man and banana chips for Benji. Fueled and happy, they walked and walked to the horizon's hope of a new year.

His mind ricocheted back to the present. Warm socks, quality boots, and a trail buddy—the requisite ingredients of a hike and a spiritual reckoning. He had two of three in his home; the third was in Fox World.

A mile away, Mr. Fox woke up. Sunrise was brightening the forest. It was not touching the furnace thermostat, though. It was a bone-chiller morning as Mr. Fox rose from his bed of crunchy brown leaves. He looked around Fox World. He liked cold, dry, sunny weather in the forest. It heightened the olfactory senses, and he detected the best of scents. Mr. Fox smelled hope. He walked stiff legged through the massive oaks. He was not hungry, but a few blue-berries would be nice, he reflected. His destination was the paved cart path where it turned into a S-curve on the woods' edge. From there, he had a 270-degree view of Human World. He curled on the path, chin on front paws, and waited on his hope's manifestation.

The throaty rumble of the Range Rover's engine crested the hill. It came to rest in the empty corporate parking lot next to Fox World. Three passengers jumped out—two energetic terriers and the wife with the warmest smile ever. Slowly and in pain, a fourth disem-barked, shuffled his feet stiffly, taking a measurably long time to cover the fifty feet to the asphalt path that trifurcated Fox World, Corporate World, and Human World. Smiling Wife assisted with a hand under his armpit. Mr. Fox saw the grimace, but he knew that a grimace is just a smile waiting on hope and healing. He wagged his tail to Old Man—signaling that hope had arrived in bunches.

Mr. Fox heard the Smiling Wife say, "I understand that you want to start walking in the forest again, but it is too much too soon."

Old Man replied confidently in a raspy voice, "I am going to walk five hundred miles in a year. And I'm going to do the first mile today."

Mr. Fox watched and listened as he sat casually on his fluffy tail, sensing that today was a big day, a gamechanger, and he was excited. In the back of his fox mind, the switch clicked from "Patient to Impatient" and he did a very un-foxlike thing. He barked; he barked three times. One-two-three!!! It was their secret guy code: "One-two-three-for-you-and-me."

Old Man turned stiffly, and as he did, the painful grimace trans-formed into a smile. It was Mr. Fox! Mr. Fox had come to see him and to co-walk the first steps of his cardiac rehabilitation walk. Old Man cupped his hands and queried Mr. Fox, "Do you want to take a walk with an old man? Let's walk a mile together today." Mr. Fox heard this and angled his long canine nose skyward and yipped, *Of course I want to walk with you, N. Oldman!*

Prior to a couple of weeks ago, Old Man never knew that when he said, "Do you want to walk with an old man?" the foxes heard "N. Oldman." To them, he was N. Oldman. If Old Man had known that his formal name in Fox World was N. Oldman, he would have laughed endlessly. The epiphany hung in the morning air—people do not always hear what you thought you said. Communication has many tones, inflections, and interpretations, Old Man made a note.

Without ceremony or speeches, which differentiated this day from any Corporate World launch event that Old Man had ever attended, the odd couple, N. Oldman and Mr. Fox, embarked on their five-hundred-mile journey. Old Man's rigidly set goal was one mile on day one. The day ahead had but one success: he learned a lesson about rigid goals as the tandem suffered a pain-ridden start.

Fifty-five stiff-legged steps were the recorded achievement on the pedometer. On step fifty-six, Old Man's leg buckled inward awkwardly. There was a pop and an audible groan as he stumbled to the macadam. With his left arm in a navy-blue medical sling, he had little to soften the drop and he hit the paved path hard, knee first and then shoulder. There were two crunches and two flashes of white-hot pain. Under a heavy dose of blood thinner for the DVT blood clots, the result was immediate and certain. Seconds later, the knees of his khakis were red blotched with a volume of blood that resembled a gunshot wound. Old Man felt weak and embarrassed. He had failed and was now a bloody mess. Up the trail, Mr. Fox was the ultimate optimist. *You didn't fail. You took fifty-six more steps than you did yesterday. I'm proud of you. Patch yourself up and I'll see you tomorrow.*

N. Oldman had found a coach. Game on.

Smiling Wife ended their journey then and there. Buttons, Mr. Fox's wife, watching from afar, agreed. Buttons scolded Mr. Fox for encouraging his buddy to walk so soon after surgery. It was obvious that the man was still ill. Buttons would have a longer talk with her husband later. N. Oldman and Mr. Fox locked eyes. They were in trouble with their spouses, so their smiles of collusion were masked cleverly. Both nodded and winked a cryptic Morse code message to each other: *s-e-e -y-o-u -h-e-r-e- t-o-m-o-r-r-o-w*.

Their journey was underway.

MILE MARKER 1.2
THE EASY DAY WAS
YESTERDAY

An axiom of the Navy SEALS, generally described, is "the only easy day was yesterday." Mr. Fox, although not a SEAL, thought the same as the frosty morning broke. His bones responded slowly to the brain's call to get up. He took stock of his life. He was nearly a decade old, was healing from a horrible fight with Big Red, and a wind-blown gritty debris in his swollen eye, and that was the good news. The bad news was that Old Man was in worse shape—pale, weak, hobbled. Mr. Fox laughed, not at Old Man, but at their collective plight. *Between them, they did not have a full body of working parts. Enough inventory taking and excuse making*, Mr. Fox groused. He was one-half of an expedition team of two old fools planning a multi-hundred-mile walk. Provisions had to be gathered.

It was either a fool's errand—or a noble calling, Mr. Fox surmised. The latter was more motivational, so he puffed out his snow-white, sprinkled with charcoal flecks, chest and did his morning fox stretches. He kissed Buttons on the forehead and whispered, *"I'm going hunting. Be back soon."* She nodded assent and then curled her fluffy tail over her head and went back to sleep in their pine needle nest. Mr. Fox ambled down to Fox River, stuck his orange snout through a crack in the ice, and had a refreshing drink of water. His puffy eye stared back at him in the swollen eye reflection. *One eye short on the second day of a mission? Make do*, he thought.

Mr. Fox knew what they needed: help, just a little help—that was all. He set his canine GPS and headed to the center of the forest, where a once towering beechwood tree had grown. The windstorm, which had messed up his eye, had cracked the towering beechwood. Many of the tree's once sky-reaching branches were now scattered on the ground near the base. Mr. Fox nosed through the branches, sorting the timber. The choosing, selecting, and discarding continued until he found the one, the ace. Some would call it a cane. Old Man would not like that word and thus, Mr. Fox renamed it a walking staff—a five-hundred-mile walking staff. Old Man needed a smidge of help and the beechwood support would steady him. No more bloody knees.

The fox snatched the slim, strong stick in his mouth and began walking. It was one mile, five thousand fox steps, back to the edge of the forest. He welcomed the warmth the walk generated. Condensation flared from his nostrils into downward cone-shaped clouds. This was hard work, but he was dedicated to it gladly. *The only easy day was yesterday*, he mused.

Human World would never accept (or believe) that a fox selected and gave a walking staff to a man. Moreover, the outside world would laugh if told that Russell Raccoon meticulously gnawed both ends of the walking staff into smooth crowns. *Truly animal-crafted? Depends on whether one believes in animal magic*, the elderly fox posited. When

Old Man arrived an hour later, the carved beechwood walking staff was right there—on the ground—exactly where he had stumbled and fallen the day before. Old Man stopped, stared at, and admired the gift. Fox World had accepted the challenge and sent the calvary. The sight of the walking staff on the asphalt path was an omen. The first mile of five hundred was going down today, and his confidence crested as he picked up the fox-crafted stick and steadied his stance with it. The cane/staff fit Old Man's hand as if custom-made by a world-famous cane craftsman.

Old Man looked downrange to the horizon where he saw confidence booster number two. Fifty meters up the path, Mr. Fox sat with a look of steeled confidence on his face. *Let's do this*, his face read. They started deliberately, chipping away at the one-mile goal. It was painful, as one buddy had a swollen eye and arthritic shoulders, and the other buddy was the remnants of a six-digit Blue Cross hospital bill. When they grew tired, they sat on Helping Hands Bridge, the span over Fox River, and on a patch of green moss Old Man called Ireland. Each break, they enjoyed a sip of black coffee, or a bit of bone broth tea infused with blueberries. They walked and walked until N. Oldman's fitness watch clicked: one mile.

Smiling Wife trailed them. What was Mr. Fox doing? Where did the walking cane come from? It was right on the path where her husband had fallen the day before. How far would the two old lions walk? Was her husband well enough to do this? What was happening? Where the heck were the two old lions going?

On the other side of Fox River, Buttons pondered the same questions. Both wives realized two things: day two was in the books and the boys had done better than day one. Buttons and Smiling Wife also knew that they were witnessing a strong, uncommon bond between animal and human. The bond would be tested again and again in coming months. At Mr. Fox and Old Man's advanced ages and with the infirmities that had (and would have), the oddsmakers were silent on Mr. Fox and Old Man's chances for success.

MILE MARKER 10.8
WALKING, TALKING
AND NO BALKING

Winter hit and stayed on like an unemployed, broke house guest. Mr. Fox and Old Man met daily and walked baby fox steps. Sometimes they walked in the morning, other times in the afternoon—depending on Old Man's work-at-home schedule. Timely as a Swiss-made pocket watch, Mr. Fox was always there on the path, waiting. But on this morning, Mr. Fox was not. It was daybreak and nineteen degrees. Old Man scanned the forest and saw no sign of the fiery orange canine. Mr. Fox had a well-hidden shelter deep in a briar thicket above the stream and ideally located with eastern exposure to gather the morning sun's warmth. The den's architecture flared away from the prevailing winds. Old Man, beechwood cane providing traction, scaled the embankment. His pacemaker throttled up, his tender chest muscles tightened, but he kept climbing.

Old Man whistled twice, expecting nothing. After all, Mr. Fox was not a stray dog; he was a fox. Old Man felt embarrassed at his Human World hubris. Who was he to expect the fox to be here or to come immediately when beckoned?

Mr. Fox emerged, shook off den dust, breathed in frigid air, and exhaled vapor more voluminous than a double-barreled Marlboro smoker. He yipped. Old Man was startled. Did Mr. Fox just answer back? Yes, no doubt. Mr. Fox was barely able to walk due to his wobbly morning legs and shoulders bound by aging canine stiffness. The eye abrasion from the recent windstorm was still noticeable from a distance. The abrasion and the resulting infection, no longer raging, were still in need of attention.

His appearance warmed Old Man's hopes. Mr. Fox was ready for another walk. Old Man, mindful of wild animal boundaries, coaxed him slowly to an open spot in the forest and gave him two meat-balls with a dusting of antibiotic and a speck of crushed baby aspirin powder inside. From a blue thermos, he poured a piping hot bone broth drink into Mr. Fox's stone bowl. The broth was made chunky with bison bits and halved blueberries. Old Man added a teaspoon of Manuka honey; its antibiotic properties were needed dearly. Like Old Man, Mr. Fox liked a sugar fix, so Old Man sweetened the broth with dried cherries (aka "cherry candies"). The phrase made both laugh— and made Mr. Fox salivate.

Old Man backed off and walked a hundred yards down the trail to fluff Mr. Fox's daybed with a thick layer of grass. Snuggle pockets were made on all four compass points of a large oak tree. Any time of day, Mr. Fox could maximize the sun's warming rays and block the wind by choosing a compass point in the bed. Medicine, nutrition, naps, and vitamin D from sunlight were the doctor's script for Mr. Fox's damaged eye. Only so much that one human could do to help an old arthritis-bound fox, Old Man regretted. Probably the same limited amount that an aging fox could do for a human with a hunk of titanium in his chest.

Old Man returned in late afternoon after work with more broth. Mr. Fox was atop the green moss mounds across Fox River. Mr. Fox's stare was a mix of mustered-up courage and sheepish glad-to-see-you gratitude. Darn, it was icicle-forming cold in Fox World. How could Mr. Fox not be shivering, Old Man worried.

Mr. Fox telegraphed stoically, *go home, N. Oldman—get out of this cold wind, buddy. You should not be here in this ice storm. This is my fight, mine alone.*

Not a chance, Mr. Fox. Old Man pulled his wool cap over his ears and snapped the buttons on his Fjallraven parka around his neck. The air-activated chemical pouches in his boots warmed his toes. Staring down the harshness of a brutally cold day was exhilarating, Old Man regaled. It was a seldom seen victory in a losing season, and he cherished it. Mr. Fox curled in a tight ball and wrapped his fluffy tail to trap a toasty pocket of body-warmed air. Both trail buddies napped briefly in the peace of windswept Fox World.

From the car, where the heater and electric seats were working overtime, Smiling Wife watched her husband on the frozen tundra. Her instinct was to go get him and warm him. She did not. He needed his small victories after what he had survived, and there was a miracle unfolding out there on the ice. "Let it be," she whispered as she reclined the car seat and rested her tired eyes.

MILE MARKER 17.9
THE BEAUTY OF ONE
HUNDRED DAY PLANS

Winter was here in force, rapping on the forest's door with icy knuckles. Old Man watched Mr. Fox sleep on the frozen ground. With the wind whipping across the green moss mounds, it was a bone-chilling place to grab a nap.

Old Man set up his portable camp chair, poured a smoking hot coffee, and dug into his front coat flap pocket for his emergency cigar. He had not smoked a cigar for months—the last one being the day he collapsed or "died medically." Cigars were a treat now. Even though his heart issue had been electrical in nature and not a plumbing blockage, the cigar was probably not the best idea. He lit it anyway. He puffed the corona-sized mellow Connecticut shade tobacco. Old Man felt the relaxation that only a guilty pleasure brings. His mind drifted to an old article that he had read about action planning. The gist of the article described how any circumstance in life can be substantially altered for the better in one hundred days. Draw a red circle on the calendar one hundred days out, make micro-sized tactical goals and use short bursts of energy to accomplish a few steps every day. Follow the recipe. Bake the cake. Eat the cake. Celebrate.

In short, one hundred days are long enough to be strategic without all the blue sky, wishy-washiness that comes with "annual planning," the article had said, and a hundred-day horizon is concise enough to prompt action and see success validated each day. The hundred-day approach blends both thinking and doing. What an elusive elixir, Old Man laughed.

Does the formula work? Old Man raised his hand yes. He had "one-hundred day'd" his way out of divorce, job loss, nine corporate transfers, lonely times in new cities, and more. His current endeavor was different though, one hundred days seemed like an eternity with the physical challenges that Mr. Fox and he had. Maybe the five-hundred-mile walk idea was a deck stacked the wrong way by a card shark. But Old Man had a wild card in the deck, emphasis on wild. Old Man grinned. He had a simple, highly motivational reason to rise on cold mornings and keep walking—he was worried about the old fox. Going out and finding Mr. Fox every day made Old Man want to walk—even if his weak heart and stiff limbs protested. What rational, properly thinking, successful business executive would find motivation in helping a little fox?

Uh, a changed one.

MILE MARKER 24.1
CORPORATE WORLD CALLS

Old Man, having lived in two worlds for a half century, was now beckoned by a third. He finished the Windsor knot in his silk tie as he looked out the loft's window to the forest. He lived in Human World; he made a living in Corporate World, but it was Fox World that made him feel alive. Old Man felt genuine and accepted in Fox World. There was no need for "an act" in its serenity. And even if Old Man fabricated a facade, Mr. Fox would see through it like cellophane. Fox World had a strict no bovine merde policy. Be real or be gone and alone. Being a lone wolf most of his life, Old Man liked the escapism aspect of Fox World a bit more than he should. For now, though, there was a mortgage to pay and a 401k to fund. He cinched the necktie's knot tighter.

After a month in and out of the hospital for heart surgeries in November and a few miles of comeback walks in December, Old Man returned to his downtown Washington, DC office in January. As coincidence would have it, it was "executive headshot" day—photographs used for press releases, industry speaking engagements, magazine articles, etc. Over coffee and hazelnut pastry, he would laugh with colleagues and call it in jest a comeback day photo. Technically and physically, it was. Mentally, he was not so sure.

The executive headshot photo came in an email from the photographer a day later. Old Man opened the file. There was one aspect the photograph did not show—a huge blood stain. Driving south on the George Washington Parkway on the morning of the photo shoot, Old Man had reached under his shirt and scratched his itchy chest scar lightly, very lightly. Unbeknownst to him, his super-strength blood thinner decided to assert its efficacy. A tiny, undetectable, slow leak opened. Arriving at his office in downtown Washington, DC, Old Man went to the washroom to freshen up for the photographer's visit. In the mirror and to his horror, he saw a baseball-sized blood spot on his white shirt. Life was laughing at Old Man, as if to say, *I (not you) will decide when you are ready for a comeback.*

No time to make repairs, he buttoned his suit jacket to hide the bloody spot, brushed his teeth, and combed his hair. Three minutes later, a wry was mustered, the camera clicked, and comeback day was recorded—officially. Old Man later walked three blocks south towards the White House, stopping at Brooks Brothers to purchase a new shirt. Afterwards, he crossed the street to CVS to buy Band-Aids, the first of ten or eleven boxes purchased over the next year. When the summer months came later, he would learn that every mosquito bite incurred on a Fox World hike would spawn a mini geyser.

Back at his desk, he locked in his focus on business, made a few calls, and jotted down sales goals, and doodled on the legal pad. His sense of humor peaked at the irony—one day back in Corporate World and he was already bleeding.

MILE MARKER 30.1
SUNRISES AND
RECKONINGS

Old Man and Mr. Fox built miles slowly.

With a severe winter storm approaching Virginia, Old Man rose early to check on Mr. Fox before driving to work. He sipped a healthy vitamin-infused coffee as he hiked to the entrance of Fox World. His mind scrolled through the bright spots and the scary spots in his life. He was healing and he felt optimistic, even though more heart procedures were possible on the horizon. Old Man feared, however, that each day might be the last for the old fox. Old age, severe injury, brutal cold, and the unknown of the wild made the fear more than a grain of a thought.

He had not seen Mr. Fox in two days. He whistled through frozen lips, which resulted in an erratic half-whistle. Silence hung in the air like an un-rung bell. There was a stirring in the brush. Mr. Fox emerged onto the moss across Fox Creek and barked back a raspy hello from a throat constricted by the nine-degree air. He stretched deeply and stiffly as if to say, *all is good, buddy. The dirt floor in my den is a bit hard on my old bones, but I'm ok.*

Mr. Fox turned east to observe a ritual. Whether encoded or born of his devotion to Mother Earth, he watched the sun rise every day with singular focus. He ignored the camera, the coffee thermos, and Old Man. Mr. Fox had a subtle lesson to share: *enjoy every day, every minute of it, including the first minute.* Old Man felt small in Mr. Fox's world at that moment. N. Oldman had seen the sun rise many times, not once had he experienced it like this little fox. The fox was immersed in the yellow orange orb ascending to warm his world. The commuting executive would be in his climate-controlled car in an hour. Mr. Fox had no central heat in his den; he needed the rising orb's few extra degrees to survive. Mr. Fox had only the sun, the moon, and the forest—he was dirt poor by Corporate World standards. In Old Man's eyes, though, Mr. Fox had immense riches.

Mr. Fox meditated as the sun rose—*it is possible to have nothing and have everything.*

MILE MARKER 35.9
BLUE SUEDE SHOE DAY

It's one for the money,
two for the show,
three to get ready,
now go fox go ...

Old Man sat on his packable seat cushion, a hiking gift from his wife, and leaned back on the trunk of The Great Oak. Elvis, alive or dead, would be eighty-three today. The verb tense depended on whether one thought Elvis was still with us. Old Man's mother had loved Elvis, and thus it was imperative that she visit Graceland. After Elvis passed (or disappeared, as his mother would have claimed), she made the pilgrimage. As Old Man sat on a log in Fox Forest (wearing blue suede shoes in her and Elvis' honor), Old Man regretted that he had not gone with his mother to Memphis decades ago. As far as following silly little dreams in life, it was her apex. Good for her, it is important to chase silly dreams, Old Man thought, and he regretted that he seldom did.

As he was humming Elvis tunes, Buttons appeared. Mr. Fox's wife sat far away—across Fox River near Foxville. Old Man pulled his binoculars from his pack and dialed the lens on her. She peered down to the valley where Old Man and Mr. Fox were singing Elvis songs and telling stories. Midway, Mr. Fox had dozed off and begun snoring on a log twenty feet away from Old Man. Buttons smiled. *Tsk, tsk, what are those old lions doing?* She had warm thoughts about the human. Old Man was brave. He had chased armed poachers out of Fox World and things were safe for a while. Buttons' thoughts were of a maternal nature. It was mating season. Her "to do" list for sprucing up her fox den was longer than her luxuriant fox tail, but it was done. The cycle renewed; it was time; she needed Mr. Fox.

The fox mating ritual has a small twist. It is the female fox who is the pursuer. When she is ready, she calls to her chosen mate. It is a loud squall—plaintive in sound but beckoning in its nature. Buttons squalled; Mr. Fox awoke, stretched, and nodded farewell. He trotted off to Foxville, his old arthritic bones cracking. He ambled up Fox Hill dutifully. The best genes in the forest were needed to perpetuate Fox World. Old Man smiled—he was excited in his heart to know that the fox clan would live on and on, thanks to Mr. Fox and Buttons. Old Man lit his My Father cigar and watched the cold front push the gray-blue smoke through the air. He stood, watched the sun set over the winter-quiet forest, and smiled with an idea. Old Man did a happy-in-the-heart dance in his blue suede lace-ups; slow at first, but then a full burst twist to the Elvis music. He looked up to the treetops in Fox World and called to his mother's spirit, "Come dance with me, Mom, on the portico of Graceland. Elvis is playing." With a final pirouette on the frozen green moss mounds, Old Man cocked his ear. Was that a whispering Elvis ghost in the wind saying "Thank ya, thank ya very much".

Nah, it couldn't be. Everyone knows Elvis is still alive.

MILE MARKER 41.3
BLUEBIRDS AND NAPS

Late January brought a thaw—the infamous Virginia "false spring." Humans are always fooled; animals just enjoy it for what it is—a needed reprieve for a week.

The mating season on, Mr. Fox had been gone for five days. Old Man hoped that Mr. Fox was relaxing, exploring, sniffing, running, and strengthening his legs in the late January thaw that now blessed Fox World. Old Man missed him, though, and he worried a bit. The trail buddies had logged many miles towards their goal and their health was mending a bit. Old Man was finding the cadence of Corporate

World again. Things were good—was the trend smooth? Or was it a "false spring"?

Old Man recalled "the agreement" that he and Mr. Fox had made on their New Year's Eve walk. Old Man had asked his canine buddy what gift he wanted for the new year. The fox locked eyes, studied Old Man's face intently, and then stepped onto the green moss, flopped down on his side, and dropped into paralyzing sleep. At his advanced age, he wanted sunny day naps. Safe, undisturbed naps. Old Man's role was to watch over him while he napped, i.e., be a sentry to stymy big dogs off-leash or stop marauding, territory-hungry younger foxes. Thankfully, Old Man had a lot of practice with that in Corporate World.

Old Man made good on the bargain. For weeks he watched the tired, stressed fox sleep on the moss on sunny afternoons—both warm ones and cold ones. Mr. Fox slept contently, his stomach rising and falling with restful breaths, bearing proof of his trust. Mr. Fox opened one eye and winked a message: *And you, N. Oldman, what is your wish?*

"Bluebirds. I want the bluebirds to come back, Mr. Fox. They have been gone from the forest for three years. I want them to come back for a visit. Their blue flashes lift my soul, and it is my hope to see them in Fox World again."

That conversation was weeks ago. Old Man tugged the green backpack higher on his shoulder and continued to walk the edges of Fox World looking for Mr. Fox. The walking cane helped him manage his energy diligently and the sunny January day added welcomed encouragement. It was a delightful day—the type when winter yawns, and spring jumps in. Suddenly, streaks of blue flashed through the air. One here, another there, one over yonder. The air was ubiquitous blue with over a dozen bluebirds buzzing his head. Bluebirds in late January? How could that be? After three years, they were now appearing in the dead of winter, albeit a "thaw day. Old Man reveled in the rare sight. He strained to hear their muted tweets. Bluebirds are always closer than they sound, he remembered. Bluebird song-call geometry suggests that bluebirds are fifty percent closer and one-third lower in the tree than a birder might estimate. He applied the geometry and found their roosting spots and they posed for crystal-clear photographs. They left no doubt—they were back! Old Man was ecstatic.

Lost in the wandering of his walk, Old Man realized that he had forgotten to check the green moss mounds of Ireland. This was one of Mr. Fox's favorite sunny day pads. He turned right. The bluebirds followed in a tight flight pattern. He expected to see the luxuriant green moss mounds empty. Mr. Fox was curled there with a sunbeam warming his face. He was asleep—both ears down, eyes shut. He felt cradle safe. Old Man did not wake him, but instead mouthed the words, "Thank you for the bluebirds, Mr. Fox. You are a good friend. I will always watch over you if my old bones will carry me here."

Old Man watched over Mr. Fox until dark. Before leaving, he left bison soup in his rock bowl with blueberries sprinkled on the stone rim. He thumbed a "be home soon" text to his wife, who was probably worried with dark falling. He slipped away quietly, avoiding the crunchy leaves. He reached in his down vest and clicked the on switch to the 1100 lumen flashlight. The cone of light pushed back the night. Even at thirty degrees, it was not a cold walk home. Old Man was warm inside. Bluebirds and a little fox had lit his heart.

MILE MARKER 44.9
JANUARY 23RD IS
1-2-3-GO DAY!!!

Psychologists assert this day on the annual calendar is potentially the blue-est day of the year. It is the third Monday (or thereabouts) in a gray, cold, and dreary month when December holiday cheer has faded. The "we overdid it a little" credit card bills arrive and resolutions, steadfastly made on New Year's morning, either followed the twenty-one-day habit-forming formula or they didn't. Most hopes and changes are quietly abandoned and un-done by the arrival of Blue Monday. Spring and its warmth and long sunshine-filled days are miles and miles away. Blue Monday is truly blue.

Fortunately, hope appears where we invent it. Decades ago, Old Man decided 1-23 or 1/23 or January 23rd would be a fun creation in his January calendar, and he gave the blue day the cheerful moniker of 1-2-3-Go Day or New Beginning Day. It was a mind trick, aka a re-boot tool, to kickstart a fresh perspective .

"One ... Two ... Three ... Go!" was reminiscent of a simpler, more joyful era in life, Old Man had decided. The words initiated every playground race or impromptu competition in younger years. In a fifty-yard dash, you could try your hardest, do your best, scream with joy, experience victory. If you lost, you could simply say, "One-Two-Three-Go" and do it again.

Over a cup of Irish Crème coffee, Old Man pondered how to celebrate New Beginning Day. He smiled dismissively at his dumb idea. Maybe America did not need another made-up reason to purchase a greeting card. But maybe in his life, he did. This was the first year of a life that should have ended three months ago, and he was excited to celebrate a freshly granted life. He began to list things to do: A frosty morning hike along the edge of Fox Forest? Mr. Fox would like that. Call two or three old friends and check in on their lives? Yes, an excellent way to commemorate 1-2-3 Day. Write a letter to someone who is not expecting one? Check. Go to the market and buy flowers for a certain special lady? Double check. Visit the butcher and select ingredients for a cook-it-all-day Bolognese gravy (not ever called sauce if you ever lived in New Jersey)? Absolutely, yes. Hug two lovable Jack Russell terriers? Check and check.

As the 1-2-3-Go Day list grew with ways to bless others' lives, Blue Monday and its ills faded permanently. Old Man stirred the Bolognese sauce and smiled. Hope is the magic ingredient in every secret sauce, especially the bison Bolognese sauce, which Old Man delivered to Mr. Fox on an icy evening. Old Man watched Mr. Fox nibble his Italian supper and afterwards, his beloved cherry candies. With a plump tummy, the old fox yawned and reclined for a nap. Through tired eyes, he looked at Old Man, and blinked a message: *Hope is where you get up and invent it.*

Easy as one-two-three, Mr. Fox.

MILE MARKER 49.5
COFFEE BEANS AND
THE SNOWPLOW GUY

The snowplow's hard scrape, accompanied by sparks from the iron blade, filled his ears and eyes at 3:05 a.m. Old Man opened the plantation shutters on the bedroom window to see a few flakes of snow and he uttered an inaudible unmentionable. Getting an early jump on the half-inch snowstorm, are you, snowplow guy? What does a man in his fifties do when awake at 3:05 a.m.? What he does not do is go back to sleep. Thank you very much, overeager snowplow guy. Grind the beans. Add filtered water. Flip the switch to BREW. Minutes later, inhale. The smell of caffeine filled Old Man's nostrils for the approximate 10,000th go-to-work morning of his career. Routine? Rote? Not a chance. A shaky heart and an aging fox had awakened his head with a piquancy that dispelled any expectations of daily sameness. The game was in overtime now. Roll in all the marbles, Old Man had decided. The stillness of the night passed, and the work hour approached. He pondered: "another brutally cold night ... did Mr. Fox make it?" Best to go see, Old Man decided. He made manuka honey meatballs and heated bone broth. Would Mr. Fox be there waiting at daylight Old Man wondered. No chance, it was too early, it was too cold. Mr. Fox's bones were too old and achy to be up and about at dawn.

Mr. Fox sat looking east. No sunrise was visible in the gray, snowy, eastern sky, yet his compass took dead aim. He waited unexpectantly with no high hopes. He did not understand Human World, but he knew enough to realize that human have things that come up. Mr. Fox waited for the sunset and his friend. He turned and the expression on his face was painted admiration. *I don't expect you to come, but I'm grateful when you do. That's why I wait.* Silence dropped like a curtain as the fox lesson was transferred. Are there others in our lives who wait and are grateful when we come? Mr. Fox sipped his piping hot bone broth and broke the serious mood with a sly fox grin— *did you hear that darn snowplow guy last night? He woke me up.*

"Me too, Mr. Fox, and I'm glad because now I am here in the forest with you," Old Man said. They both smiled you-are-my-buddy smiles. "Thank you, snowplow guy," Old Man added under his breath. He also etched a permanent note in his mind—do not wait to go and see those who wait for you.

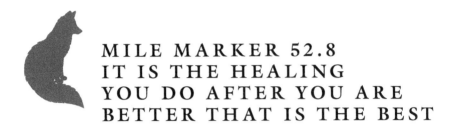

MILE MARKER 52.8
IT IS THE HEALING
YOU DO AFTER YOU ARE
BETTER THAT IS THE BEST

Is the healing that comes after you think you are better the best kind? Old Man rolled this perplexing thought in his mind as he inched achingly slow in morning traffic on the George Washington Parkway.

Mr. Fox had recovered, Old Man observed. His left eye injury from the Christmas windstorm had healed and the eye had re-opened. The hip injury from the marauding fox attack was healed as well as an aging fox could expect. There was a noticeable limp on cold mornings, just another war injury and injustice from a hardscrabble life. With old fox wisdom and a gut instinct for survival, Mr. Fox was atop his perch again. For now, at least—Nature has no guaranteed contracts.

Healed, Mr. Fox was moving on and Old Man sensed it. Mr. Fox was acting differently. Thankful for Old Man's help, he wanted to be a wild fox again. Or at least that was Old Man's conclusion. Nimbly, with the fox in the lead, Old Man and Mr. Fox navigated the roughest trail in the woods. Across the stream, over the Lincoln Logs, through the briar bushes to the center of the forest, far deep into the woods, to a spot called Foxville. It was the last inner sanctum in the animals' Fox World domain. Humans did not go there, because of the rough terrain. Foxville differed from the remainder of Fox World in distinct ways. It was high ground, like Fox Mountain, which guaranteed dryness even in the spring rain season. Further, the forest floor was covered with eighteen inch tall, strawy, yellow-burnt-orange grass, providing camouflage for its fox residents. Lastly, hollow logs, big enough to drive a tricycle into, lined the edges of the forest. And all of this was ringed by thorny blackberry bushes which foxes walked under but upon which humans were snagged. Foxville, capitol of Fox World, wore the state crown with pride and caution.

Mr. Fox stopped, looked at Old Man, and then peered all around Foxville. A soft bark followed. Winter's dried leaves crackled behind the dense brush. Slowly, timidly, reluctantly—for she had experienced little human contact—Buttons appeared. Her coat had a deep red-orange sheen which framed a fluffy white chest that bespoke freshly spun cotton. Mr. Fox gave her a doting look. This was his treasured mate, the love of his life. Mr. Fox had doubled down on his trust in Old Man by bringing him to he and Buttons' private sanctuary. Buttons greeted Old Man graciously with a kind smile that only those of the softest hearts possess. She was not afraid of Old Man; she had seen him in the forest and her mate vouched with high praise. Mr. Fox had spoken of only two humans in that reserved regard—Old Man and his wife with the sweet, soft voice.

This was their Secret Garden, and it was spectacularly beautiful—even in the dormancy of the winter season. There were hollow logs, tree stumps for perches, and copious amounts of eastern wild rye, American holly, and Virginia juniper for cover. A small feeder tributary to Fox River provided fresh water. The ground was set high above the watershed, safe from the flood zone.

Mr. Fox sat next to Buttons, nuzzled her ear, and puffed his gray-white chest. She was his wife, and he was proud of her and their home. Old Man understood now; Mr. Fox was not moving on or leaving him; it was an affair of the heart. Fox life called now. His world and Old Man's, united for mutual survival, would be divided for a while, as it should be. Knowing looks, eye to soul, were exchanged between the man and the fox. Old Man felt a strong love for the old fox. Harsh life challenges and hard-won trust had bonded them together on this journey. Today was a win for the old lions. *"We're ok now, buddy,"* both said silently and simultaneously.

As he walked home, his heart glowed like a fireplace ember in his chest. He rubbed the scar below his collarbone through an opening in his buttoned shirt. The wound had healed, and the stitches had dissolved, but there was more going on. The emotional void in his heart was filling in. These walks with the fox were suspending reality (i.e., no one would believe what he and the old fox were doing) and that is exactly what Old Man needed—a new reality. He and the old fox were building it. With Fox World's gentle post-op care, Old Man was excited about life again.

MILE MARKER 55.7
THE QUEST FOR
SIMPLICITY

Disruptive technology. Transformative innovation. Artificial intelligence. Bots. Robots. Fascinating and game changing or simply exhausting? Old Man pondered this as he looked out onto Connecticut Avenue from his ninth-floor office in Washington, DC. Do we really desire more speed-of-light change to digest (despite the indigestion that accompanies such a rapidly devoured meal)? Or is it still-quiet simplicity that we crave? Oh boy, the ramblings of an out-of-touch old lion, Old Man sighed, told himself to get to work. He drew up a sales funnel for the day and began making sales calls. High tech be damned, someone still had to ask for the sale. Even dinosaurs knew that.

He drove the rote path home from Corporate World in the darkening winter sky. Exit the parking garage, left turn on M Street, pass the steakhouse and the Camelot cabaret club on the right, travel farther west to the hotels and health clubs in Washington's West End, enter the eastern end of Georgetown dotted with bars, bistros, ice cream shops, lofts, and pretty winter-wrapped university ladies. Window down, the chilled air of the incoming cold front calmed Old Man's buzzing mind. The chatter of sales quotas and unfinished marketing strategy white papers prattled in his head. His place in Corporate World was slipping, he knew. The things—the sales problems, the marketing quandaries, the new ventures—that once excited him were now annoying and trifling. His once sharp mind was letting go of Corporate World.

The car crossed the Key Bridge and began the twelve-mile run northwest on the George Washington Parkway, the Potomac River starboard. Even on a slate gray day in February, it was spectacular scenery. In October, in a convertible, it was a movie set. He exited the Beltway at Fox World. Right signal light on, he turned into pet supermarket and inside, he walked the aisles until he found two trail trays of high nutrient cat food. His spirits rose. He needed a dose of Fox World, clarity and simplicity abounded there.

N. Oldman walked along the edge of the woods and examined the western sky. Across the stream, over the log, and through the briary brush was Fox World. The stakes there were simple and high. Find food, duck out of the cold front, and advance another day. No PowerPoints. No international airports. Just gut it out and survive in a forest threatened by urban sprawl.

Peeling back the aluminum foil on the cat food tray, he scanned the forest and squinted into the dim light. Is that a fox in the distance? Nah, can't be. Fox World and its curative calm were not same without Mr. Fox and Old Man was quietly sad that Mr. Fox was not waiting. The impromptu trip with a tin of cat food at dark was not what he thought it would be—it was unsuccessful. He pulled his coat collar higher and turned for the car. Behind him, he heard a crunchy rustling in the leaves. *Where are you headed, buddy? Back to Human World?* asked Mr. Fox with a curious stare. He nibbled the proffered nourishment, not waiting for an answer. Old Man's heart glowed as he watched the old fox lick his food-caked whiskers. To see the old fox for just a moment soothed a frustrating day like a happy hour ice-cold vodka martini. Old Man took a mental sip and inhaled the essence of the calming fox.

Cold front coming, N. Oldman. I feel it in my right hip. That darn arthritis is always hurting and double the pain on bad days. Kind of like those cryptic sales reports that you write, huh? Simplicity is not knowing why your hip hurts; it is knowing that you can outrun your enemy with a hurt hip. That's the pass-fail clarity of Fox World. Old Man swallowed the nugget of wisdom. He needed to "slim-plify" his problems, i.e., reduce them quantitatively and re-order them in perceived rancor. Life wasn't as hard as he was making it.

Darkness' veil fell and Mr. Fox vanished. There was a whisper in the wind. *Next time, buddy, bring some of those cherry candies.*

MILE MARKER 60.8
BRUISED STERNUM

The backstory, destined to be a hilarious campfire story someday, unfolded on an icy morning hike. Old Man saw Mr. Fox crossing Fox Bridge II (aka a narrow log) on the forest's horizon, and he followed—a questionable action weeks after heart surgery, but Mr. Fox was in the lead, so Old Man fell into formation with the operative word being "fell."

Fox Bridge II is the second of two log bridges that span Fox Creek. The log was dusted with snow, which covered the clear ice patches underneath. The tread of Old Man's hiking boots gripped the snow powder firmly, and he began the crossing, his boot marks erasing the small paw prints of Mr. Fox's earlier transit. All was well in the man-fox train until N. Oldman's boots hit black ice. The first stage of the fall was a step upward as his feet went skyward. AOld Man rolled his body in a last ditch attempt to miss the log on the way down and protect his spine. It worked—partially. He hit the log butt-first. This was good fortune, as he was well cushioned in the flank. The butt-hit flipped him face down to the iced-covered creek five feet below. There, two catastrophes occurred—one minor, one major. Of lesser concern was the extended zoom lens on the camera around his neck. The lens struck the ice first and shattered. Old Man landed with a thud on top of the shattered Nikon. There was an audible crack and the breath shot out of his lungs.

Mr. Fox snapped around. *Where did Old Man go? What was that loud sound? You know, the one of a heavy man falling flat on his face on brick hard ice.* He heard Old Man laughing. "All I've been through and I'm going to buy the farm on an icy log?" Even though each laugh made his chest ache, he had to smile—he had fallen off a log while walking with a fox in the dead of winter, and he was ok with that. Oh my, his world perspective had certainly changed. ll

He rose with an exaggerated slowness to let his body and mind run a diagnostic check. Had the loud crack been an injury to his sternum or ribs? His puffy Mountain Hardwear parka had thankfully absorbed some of the strike, but his chest was aching. On the plus side, a life-long tightness in his neck was gone. What did that mean? Was his neck numb or was it miraculously healed? Old Man dusted off his fleece-lined khakis, adjusted his wool cap, picked up the busted lens, skated across the ice, and climbed the steep embankment on the stream's edge. He was lucky to be in one piece; unfortunately, his Nikon camera did not win the great log fall lottery and he poured the busted camera pieces into the avocado green backpack. After a brief rest and regroup, he began the walk home. The pain in his chest was noticeable and pain in his chest had been the bane of his existence for three months now. He was too scared to be scared; he could not let his wife know about this act of folly. He stopped and shouted to Mr. Fox across Fox Creek, "Hey, buddy, let's keep this a secret and not tell our wives."

Good idea, N. Oldman. My fox lips are sealed.

Smiling Wife was standing at the front door, car keys in hand and a worry crease lined her forehead. The pacemaker monitoring system had issued an alert when the jolt of the Fox Bridge accident had interrupted his pacemaker rhythm.

"In the car. Your doctor called from the hospital. You have a code yellow on your pacemaker. We are headed to the hospital," she said. There was silence in the car during the twenty-minute drive. Old Man was embarrassed at his foolishness and disheartened that he had brought more stress into her life. Smiling Wife was upset, and she was worried, but she admired the man in the seat next to her. Physically, he was a shadow of the man he had been three months ago, but he was not giving in. There was fight left in him, and the old fox sparked his survival instinct.

X-rays showed a badly bruised sternum, but no bone cracks. A pacemaker interrogation was completed, the device was recalibrated, and normalcy was restored. Adding to the good news, Old Man learned that the "ice log incident," as his wife would refer to it forevermore, had delivered an unexpected gift. The ice log tumble had jarred misaligned vertebra in his neck, triggering a spinal re-set. His decade-long neck pain diminished markedly. Old Man rubbed the thick chest scar through his oxford cloth button down and touched the tender purple and yellow bruise. A few miles into their journey, the old lions were already in a box canyon.

MILE MARKER 63.3
THE MAP OF FOX WORLD

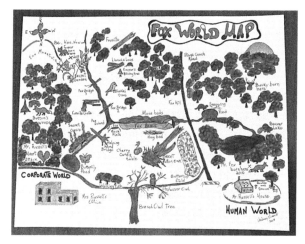

Old Man rested for a couple of days with the faithful terrier, Beacon, snuggled into his armpit. With an ice pack on his chest and, under a wife-imposed moratorium on forest walks, Old Man took it easy. He caught up on work assignments, connected with customers by telephone, organized his remaining camera equipment, and worked on a Fox World map. He repeated: "a successful mission requires a vision, milestones, focus, and a map." He had obviously forgotten a map in his battle plan to walk hundreds of miles with an old fox. Time to do it—or finish it. Truth was there would be no more walks until he drew a map of Fox World and agreed to file a flight plan with Smiling Wife before each fox walk.

Old Man had drawn a pencil draft of a Fox World map three months ago while walking with Mr. Fox. The fox engineer had marked all the key locations. Old Man, the land surveyor, had recorded them.

During this wife-imposed and dog-accompanied rest period, he needed to finish the map. It would be a fanciful distraction during the mending process.

The hand-sketched map was crude at best; Old Man was not an artist, but all the requisite locations were recorded, e.g., Beaver Lake, Snapping Turtle Pond, Fox River, Foxville, Cherry Candies Table, Old Man's Heart Attack Tree, etc. The purpose of the map was to allow Smiling Wife to locate him if he was injured or sick. Map 1.0 was accurate, but it looked like a kindergarten student had drawn it. It needed color, pizzaz, and a true artist's touch. Fortunately, he knew a talented wildlife artist in Canada, and he sent his Fox World scribblings to her. A few days later, a bright, colorful map of Fox World arrived.

Old Man's wife set forth firm orders—trips into Fox World alone were banned for the time being, and there was to be no tree climbing, log crossing, or stream fording. She threatened an ankle surveillance bracelet (and she was likely not jesting), but she made time to stroll with Old Man and their Jack Russell terriers in Fox World. Mr. Fox was always waiting on the Human World side of Fox River—a noted concession to the wife-issued executive order of no more river crossings on the log bridge. Mr. Fox did not look well, he scratched incessantly, his fox coat was blotchy, and his eyes were half slits. Was he just up from a nap in scratchy leaves or was there another problem?

Mr. Fox read his thoughts and gave him a mocking sideways look that said, *speak for yourself, old lion; you're the one setting off heart alarms.* Mr. Fox continued his sunset gazing until the midwinter sun dropped below the treetops. The orb gone, he curled into a ball on the forest floor. Old Man and Smiling Wife exchanged knowing glances; they never wanted to leave Mr. Fox after their walks with him. How great it would be to spread a wool blanket over his arthritic hip and shoulder as he napped. Mr. Fox picked up on their empathy, *your love warms my fox heart, and that is all I need through the cold night.*

MILE MARKER 68.1
BE A FOX WARRIOR

The miles increased. The odd couple met daily and chipped away at the five-hundred-mile journey. The miles were hardly important; the walks and talks were all that mattered. Old Man was learning to speak fox and he was happy.

On this day, Mr. Fox and Old Man walked west to Beaver Lake. It was a dry, cold, late-winter day. Low humidity in the air masked how cold the day really was. Light snow dust kicked up in white puffs as the fox leader took point. They made it to Beaver Lake two hours before sunset. Old Man pitched camp and began heating coffee and the bone broth and slicing bison jerky with his utility knife. It was an old lion's banquet—assured by a top-shelf dessert of cherry candies for Mr. Fox and a Snickers bar for Old Man. All the camp-out needed was a fireside story and Mr. Fox had one to tell. He tongue-lapped the bowl of broth, sat back, and began:

> I was born right over there—about twenty paces from us. It was the greatest snowfall in the history of Virginia. Mom Fox kept my brother and I warm in our den on the hill overlooking Beaver Lake. Even though I was only a few days old, I realized how special this time was. I was safe, warm, fed, and most of all, loved. Mom licked our fur and snuggled us close. Three heartbeats, three breaths—harmonized.
>
> My brother and I drank a lot of milk, sapping Mom's energy. Our dad died before we were born. Mom could

not leave us alone, so the math was simple—no hunting meant no food. She held strong, balancing her fear of starvation with the euphoria of a mother's love.

On the fourth day, we heard crunching in the deep snow above our den. We were little tikes, fearful of this noise, but Mom gave us a "don't worry" nod. Then, I remember it like it was yesterday, a wonderful aroma filled our den, one redolent of a just-in-time holiday care package. Mom climbed up and out of the den and poked her head to the top of the snow. Boot tracks came to our den's door and then turned back to the brush, across the log, and over the stream. By our den door was a steaming-hot roasted chicken. Yes, a full chicken! Mom gave a long knowing look east. She returned inside happy—and relieved. She placed the chicken near us. The steam warmed our cave, and the flavorful chicken aroma filled our baby fox nostrils. Mom feasted and replenished her energy. Brother and I had our morning milk and we drifted into a blissful nap.

Mom whispered, "Don't worry, young ones. We are foxes. We are warriors."

Later that year, tragedy would befall Mom. And soon thereafter, my brother left, and he did not return. I moved forward as best as a juvenile fox could. Mom had taught us how to hunt, but I went hungry many days. I wandered into neighborhoods looking for outside dog bowls and I looked near commercial dumpsters behind restaurants for scraps—a French fry or two, a packet of ketchup, scraps of old bread. By winter, I was in rough shape. I was not finding enough calories to warm my thin body. Hunting, especially fruitlessly, was depleting my energy. Mom's words sustained me: "Don't worry. We are foxes. We are warriors."

Only one of ten abandoned or orphaned foxes make it in the wild. I decided to be one of them. I chose to survive.

On Christmas Eve, it snowed a couple of inches. It was beautiful in Fox World, but it was frightfully cold and hunger pangs racked by body. I saw you and your dog walking on a path. You stopped and petted the dog and fed him juicy treats. Oh, how I wanted some. They smelled delicious. I remembered Mom's words—be a warrior. I left my hiding spot and walked to within a few feet of you. I was shaking. In my weakened state, the terrier could have easily caught me. I just stood there. Pleading. You emptied the bag of liver treats on the paved path, gathered Beacon in your arms, and walked away slowly. I ate them one by one—savoring each. The protein-rich morsels filled my stomach, and hope began to fill my soul. Most of all, I was topped with confidence. I had taken a chance and trusted.

On Christmas morning, a crunching noise in the snow roused me. I was in my leaf bed under the holly tree. I peered stealthily through the low hanging holly branches. Something was on the ground near me. The aroma rushed into my nostrils; it was a steaming-hot roasted chicken and those long-ago feelings twinkled in my heart. I felt safe, warm, loved.

With your help, N. Oldman, I made it. I am alive and I am a fox warrior.

MILE MARKER 71.2
HAPPY NINTH
BIRTHDAY, MR. FOX

The best gifts received are the ones you do not expect.

Mr. Fox had known tough times mostly in his life—orphaned, habitat cut in half, territorial fights, loneliness, bitter cold winters, hunger. Today he felt joy, and he was not sure why. He talked to himself: *yesterday, N. Oldman said that he will come tomorrow for my birthday. What is a birthday? Why was it a special day? Why would anyone know that it was my birthday? Why would anyone care*, he sadly reflected? He felt the lump in his throat with the next thought—*will I live to see another?*

Mr. Fox waited for N. Oldman. It was cold—more so than most late February days. Old Man came in early afternoon, and Mr. Fox spotted him quickly and closed the gap. N. Oldman had a big plastic bag and a covered tray in his hands. He placed a four-foot by four-foot square of plastic tarp over the frozen ground. "This will be a dampness protection layer," he heard Old Man say. He then dumped two bags of timothy hay—purchased in the rabbit section at PetSmart—on top of the tarp. He shaped the hay into a deep-sided bowl, making wind-blocking high walls. Inside, it was warm, fluffy, and cushiony. With roof cover from the holly tree, a moisture barrier underneath, and the wind blocked below by the timothy hay, the new and improved fox fort would be an excellent day den. Old Man added a bonus—he stuffed dried cherries, peanut butter biscuits, and bison jerky in the nooks and crannies of the hay. Mr. Fox would sniff them out later in the evening when he went in the bed. Unexpected late-night snacks on a cold night would be a birthday delight.

Old Man looked up from his construction project. Mr. Fox was observing with wrinkled brow and cocked head. *What was N. Oldman up to?* Next, N. Oldman opened the snap-top lid of the plastic container. It held a treasure inside. The "bison, blueberry birthday cake" had been made by Chef Oldman. Ground bison meat formed in a circle, decorated with fresh, honey-dripped blackberries. In the middle of the "cake" was the numeral "9," fashioned with cherry candies. The chef had made enough cake for two, so Mr. Fox would be able to invite Buttons to his birthday party. "Happy birthday, buddy. I am filled with joy to celebrate with you on your special day. Enjoy your birthday surprises and know that you are loved. You are a brave little fox. Happy birthday, old warrior."

Mr. Fox felt joy inside. He had a brand-new fluffy bed, a bison cake with real blueberries, and time with his friend. He climbed in his new bed. It molded around his arthritic hip and cushioned his sore shoulders. He peeked over the rim and smiled at N. Oldman, who signed their one-two-three-for-you-and-me greeting and said, "I will watch over you. Take a nice birthday afternoon nap." Soon, Mr. Fox was sleeping soundly, as he always did with his human guard on post. Old age was tiring at times, and uninterrupted naps were a delightful tonic. Old Man stood guard, the coyotes did not come, winter's nip did not bite, and hunger's ache was allayed.

It was his special day; it was his birthday, and Old Man had remembered.

Even the mighty, thick oaks on dry, high ground had snapped like stale bread sticks. The fracture points were eight or ten feet up their fifty-foot height. Old Man tried to imagine the wind force required to break healthy trees with thirty-six-inch diameters into splinters. As a child, Old Man had called these mighty oaks "no hugs" because two kids could hug the tree and not touch fingers. The oaks, fractured and splintered, held on with all their strength and Old Man respected their resiliency amidst the flotsam of broken branches and debris. The century-old oaks had fallen near Mr. Fox's den. Was the old fox ok? Was he safe? Worried, Old Man climbed onto the broken trunk of the largest felled oak. From six feet off the ground, he had a vantage point to look west to the setting sun.

Mr. Fox climbed atop a log a hundred yards away and looked east across the forest. He spotted N. Oldman atop a log. Mr. Fox wagged his tail like an orange signal flag—*I'm over here! I'm ok!* N. Oldman waved back and made their signature one-two-three-for-you-and-me chest pound. Old Man was overjoyed; Mr. Fox was alive. The duo began walking towards each other, both relieved.

Oaks, like foxes, might bend. Their branches, like bones, might break. But their roots, like hearts, stay strong and reach for the sky again. Old Man hope to be like foxes and oaks someday.

MILE MARKER 88.1
AND THEN THEY CAME

The Super Moon hung in the dawn sky as Old Man drove the 5:00 a.m. traffic-free roads to the hospital. He was alone except for a stuffed fox toy placed on the car dash by his wife. She named the five-inch-tall stuffed fox, "Med Fox". He parked the car in a moonlit parking lot at the hospital and walked in. Today was heart checkpoint day. Get a green flag or get ready for more surgery, the surgeon summarized on the front end of a full day of diagnostic tests. Old Man missed his rock, his wife. Other than today, she had walked every step with him, handholding, offering a Diet Pepsi on ice, and telling a story to make him laugh. Today, she left Med Fox on the car dash and a love note in his backpack. He laughed—a corporate exec with stuffed animals and love notes—the stuff of nonsense. Bah humbug, he would have said a few months ago.

141

Red is the international sign of danger. In the blood screening lab, Old Man's hands were shaking, and his mind was racing, prompted by the talk of getting a green flag or bust. Stakes elevated, the repeated needle sticks to find a vein made him twist and turn in anguish. Finally, the IV needle pierced the vein and he twitched. The needle went clean through, and the vein popped. With a high level of blood thinner in his system, things escalated. Blood gushed, painting his hand and arm into a red glove. He bled for minutes before the medical experts could stem the flow. With an embarrassing apology and a time out to bandage up Old Man, things began again, and the blood samples were taken.

Red is an omen; Old Man knew it. This would not be the last time Old Man would see red this day, his gut signaled, it would be shed elsewhere. Hours later, the nuclear medicine stress test done, the echocardiogram completed, and other test names that he could not pronounce in the finished column, Old Man visited the hospital cafeteria for a coffee and white chocolate macadamia nut cookies from Subway. He passed time listening to podcasts while he waited on the medical test results. He nibbled a cookie and paged mentally through the past hundred days. He should have died, they said. The cycle had repeated three times—each loop plagued with different complications and near-death paths. He had rested for weeks and had begun slowly to walk again. An old red fox had joined him, and they had walked almost one hundred miles. He had returned to work in his downtown office and had seen signs of sustained recovery, yet here he was eating a cookie in a hospital and waiting on the verdict of a green or red flag.

Then, in his mind's eye, he saw the flashing red sign of danger. There was trouble, his radar screamed it. He gathered his backpack and car keys quickly. Fast, no time to spare. The test results could be discussed tomorrow or Monday. He put his foot into the SUV's accelerator and raced the seventeen miles to Fox World. The entire way there he chided himself for leaving the hospital. Was he losing his mind or was he finally after fifty plus years, beginning to listen to his gut?

Old Man found Mr. Fox on the sandy beach of Fox River—in the middle of the stream bed that divides the two spheres of Fox World and Human World. Mr. Fox would argue there is only one world, and it is called, "Be Here Now." *Be in it,* he would say. Now, he did not look like he was well enough to say anything. His face and fur were red. Puncture marks in the side of his left jaw oozed. He tried to stand but his front legs buckled. Another sign. Foxes fight with their front legs. His front limbs were exhausted; his front paws also had defensive scrapes.

His position on the stream's rocks was strategically defensive. Surrounded by the wide sandy beach area, his head was on a swivel for future attacks and the open ground would discourage predators. He was in the demilitarized zone—Switzerland neutral, he hoped. Why had his enemies come for him again? What was it? Cave rights? Food supply? Jealousy of his ability to cross the stream and talk to humans? What? Why? Mr. Fox is a fairminded old fellow, and a threat to no one. He is a helper, a fox who shares everything and a beautiful old soul who watches the sun rise and the sun set. He gives gifts—bluebirds. He teaches lessons and he is a survivor.

There was the answer. Mr. Fox was a survivor. As much as the world loves the story of the survivor, there are those who find a sense of victory, albeit hollow, in hunting down the gentle survivor.

Old Man opened his Fox World dash bag, which he had thankfully left in the SUV. He placed a tray of protein laced with antibiotics and a bowl of filtered water before Mr. Fox and placed the fox medical kit back into his pack. He sat on the sand near the old canine. Mr. Fox's breathing was shallow and labored. He had fought to the point of collapsing exhaustion. Old Man did not need Cleveland or Mayo Clinic heart experts any longer. No weak or injured heart could feel like this much pain and not fail. Mr. Fox had bite marks on his face and paws. Coyote? Bobcat? At this point, it did not matter. The old fox was suffering. The wounds were superficial for the most part, his bloodied fur looked made it look worse than it was. The old fox was exhausted and weakened by the adrenaline surge.

Mr. Fox walked to the shallow edges of Fox River and washed the blood crust from his fur. He shook off the water droplets, fluffed his fur, and trotted to his birthday haybed. Old Man waited with him there in silence, both old lions trembling.

The mobile phone ring startled Old Man out of his tunnel of thoughts. The message was curt. More heart tests were needed, surgery likely. The road to redemption had just entered a treacherous mountain pass.

MILE MARKER 91.9
SKATEBOARDER GUY
AND THE COYOTE

A decade or so ago, *The Washington Post* wrote an article about the coyotes that roam the rim of the Washington Beltway. A burst of new home construction had broken their habitat into pieces and scattered them. Confused, some went east towards the city, not west and away to the mountains. The *Post* article expressed pity for their plight, warned of their aggressiveness, and spun romanticism about wild animals coexisting with civilization. Eventually, the coyotes (most of them) moved west to the Shenandoah Valley. But every two or three years, a stray coyote, looking for territory, walks east into the suburbs.

Old Man fast-walked to Fox World. Mr. Fox had been injured for the second time (third if he counted the eye irritation) in a handful of months, and he looked sickly, too. His fur was scruffy, and he scratched his chest and chewed his tail aggressively. Two thirds of the way to Fox World, Old Man took a short cut through the parking lot of a building where an internet industry corporate giant was once housed. It was there that Old Man encountered (i.e., nearly knocked over) Skateboarder Guy, the man who had summoned medical help for Old Man weeks ago. They had not seen each other since then. He liked Skateboarder Guy; he was highly mindful for one so young. Old Man and Skateboarder Guy were decades apart in age. One was a nine-to-five corporate executive office dweller; the other had the career freedom of a part-time coder contract. One was a walker and cigar smoker; the other was an expert boarder and bud toker.

Old Man apologized to the young man for not watching where he was walking. Both flipped up their Native sunglasses on their forehead and laughed. The coder had shoulder length brown hair and husky-dog blue eyes steeled with intellect and was youth thin. He wore expensive, distressed jeans, a Johnnie-O hoodie, stylish Vans board shoes, and a high-end Thousand "brain bucket." Old Man felt comfortable but ancient in the young man's presence.

"No problem, bruh," said the coder as he dismounted his Birdhouse Tony Hawk Falcon 3 board.

"No, I was clumsy and not watching what I was doing or where I was going. Again, I apologize," Old Man added.

Boarder Guy stepped back and examined Old Man admiringly. "Glad you are feeling better. You are that fox guy. The man who walks with the old fox. I often watch you guys. That old fox is so cool, bruh. And watching you and him walking together is a blast. My friends don't believe me when I tell them. You are streaming incredible fox Zen, my man. Big ups to you. I am happy that you are walking better. You were weak then. Are the fox walks making you stronger?"

Old Man extended his hand and offered, "Thank you. I am better and stronger. Your board skills are rad—as you would say." Both laughed and lit up their herb of choice.

Boarder Guy said straight up, "Your fox is a hero. Couple days ago, there was a young fox limping over there by those green moss mounds. A big gray coyote was stalking it and ready to pounce. Then, like … whoa … there was this orange flash and … bam … your old fox hit the gray coyote like a linebacker and rolled him. They fought for a bit. The fox was smaller, but he fought ferociously. The coyote ran as fast as a leopard out of the woods. He won't be back. No way."

Old Man was stunned. For many reasons. To hear about the incident from an eyewitness was helpful in assessing Mr. Fox's injury and the future threat of the coyote. To hear about it from a skateboarder made it even more special. He was mega-cool, and he loved Mr. Fox as much as Old Man did. Old Man and Mr. Fox now had a young friend. Old Man felt younger at heart with his new association. Skateboarder Guy felt wiser in years with his new buddy. Mr. Fox, watching from the tree line in the forest, felt lucky to know them both. "I never knew that you watched me and my walks with the fox. You are a quiet observer and, as I said, an expert boarder. You carve up the asphalt like Silver Surfer."

"Silver Surfer, huh? You read that comic book?"

Old Man replied, "I have dozens of them. Some are almost as old as me."

They laughed. Silver Surfer—another commonality across generations. They exchanged good-byes. The skateboarder rolled off in a pillow-sized cloud of blue smoke. Old Man puffed on his My Father cigar, turned, and headed into Fox World. He needed to help Mr. Fox with his injuries, and secretly, he hoped the coyote was ok too. He wished all animals good health and prosperity. He recalled the long-forgotten words from his comic book hero. The Silver Surfer had said often, "Responsibility is not the issue now. A solution is." With that sage wisdom from his comic book hero, Old Man stepped into Fox World to find Mr. Fox.

Mr. Fox, looking at N. Oldman and the skateboarder from behind a fat oak, thought the very same thought. A solution would soon be needed. Not for him, the old fox decided. While he had a few injuries from the brief scuffle with the coyote, he would heal.

Mr. Fox smelled more danger coming for N. Oldman.

MILE MARKER 103.6
TOUGH TIMES RETURN

Sarcoptic mange is insidious; it strikes hard and fast. Sarcoptic mange is like having an army of ants (miles) burrowing under the skin. An intense itch follows and within weeks, the fox is overwhelmed. With the incessant itching, the fox cannot focus on hunting or food gathering. Hunger and malnutrition come next. In cold weather, hypothermia may set in, as protective fur is lost due to scratching and self-biting. Sarcoptic mange is often fatal if contracted in the winter.

Icy windy mornings were now the norm as the hiking buddies approached the century mile mark in their hike. N. Oldman needed to talk with his canine friend. His heart was ailing again, and his cardiologist and electrophysiologist had recommended another heart procedure. Something called a heart ablation.

Pacemakers establish a steady minimum heart rate—usually around sixty beats per minute. For arrythmia sufferers, it is a crucial device to sustain life. Premature ventricular contractions are an extra heartbeat in-between two normal beats, an unchecked number of PVCs is potentially deadly. PVCs are galloping horses in the chest and Old Man felt the ponies, their rumbling hooves, and the loss of energy that the horses sapped out of him. Four months into the man-fox journey, diagnostic tests confirmed Old Man was headed back to the hospital.

Old Man stopped cold in his snow tracks when he saw Mr. Fox. His buddy's hair was falling out in chunks, his drooped eyes were fatigued, and his mood was agitated and anxious. The malady was obvious. Mr. Fox had contracted sarcoptic mange. Mr. Fox, sensing that N. Oldman needed help, puffed his chest bravely and smiled *I'm ok. Old age comes and the hair goes. Nothing wrong here, buddy. How are you doing? What is worrying you?* Old Man admired Mr. Fox's stoicism and selflessness, but he was not fooled. The old fox was in trouble. Old Man was heartbroken—physically with PVCs and emotionally with the sight of his sick pal. Life was throwing a prizefighter haymaker at Fox World again.

The old lions had overcome so much in their walkabout quest. Were they now to be undone by mites and horses? He looked at Mr. Fox's tattered coat. Old Man was heading to the hospital in one week and he had much work to do if Mr. Fox was going to survive. Old Man was worried, and the anxiety stirred the horses in his heart. He rubbed his chest, the horses galloped, and his energy waned.

MILE MARKER 105.9
LOOKING FOR A FIX AS
THE HORSES KICK

His own health status in critical stages, no one would have faulted Old Man for walking away from Mr. Fox. It was an easy choice. Walk away. Abandon this dumb five-hundred-mile walk idea. Forget the little fox. All things come to an end. Get his heart fixed, retire, and get some long-needed rest. Say goodbye to magical Fox World. Go to the beach and golf. It was the right choice for a good, safe life. Old Man recoiled from the thought, and he rejected the choice of abandonment categorically. The little fox had not abandoned him the day that Old Man had almost died; he had stood and fought. Mr. Fox and Old Man would keep walking—maladies be damned.

Old Man spent hours that evening doing internet scanning and talking on the telephone with a fox expert. He attempted to be calm, but he was frenetic. Mr. Fox was in immediate peril and Old Man had a date with his cardiologist and his heart electrophysiologist in seven days. Stress rose and the chest stallions began to gallop. Old Man drank two cups of calming herbal tea, did his box breathing exercises, and dug deeper into the web. He jotted down notes from his research and a wildlife rehabber's phone number. There was an antidote, he was told, and he could make the concoction if he had the requisite ingredients. The nearest source of the healing element was thirty-five miles away. Open at 8:00 a.m., Old Man would be on the store's doorstep then. He would assemble the medicine and administer a dose to Mr. Fox fast, followed by a booster in five days. The medication, if paired with organic supplements and manuka honey to build up his immune system, would take hold quickly.

Hopefully as fast as the galloping horses in Old Man's chest.

MILE MARKER 110.0
WHEN RIVERS RAGE,
CHAMPIONS SWIM THEM

The next day, Mr. Fox cooperated. *Veni, vidi, vici*, the Romans would say. Mr. Fox came, he saw, and he conquered (i.e., wolfed down) the healing cocktail and immune boosters. A game of duck and weave with the weather ensued. Days of rain set in, followed by ice and teeth-chattering drizzle. Fox needed a booster bundle of meds, and Old Man was due in the hospital in two days. This left one option—don the raingear and go find the ailing fox. The second dose would stop the sarcoptic mange in its tracks. One week of high nutrient food, uninterrupted sleep, and he would heal.

Old Man worried as he walked. He whistled and called out, "Mr. Fox! Hey buddy!" The creek was swelling, becoming a river. Old Man kept looking. Expectantly. Frustratingly. Old Man knew that Mr. Fox would not be out in this weather. And even if was, he could not cross the raging river.

Splash! Old Man wheeled. What was that?

Mr. Fox was swimming the fast-moving, white-capped river. Orange head bobbing, black socks pedaling, bushy tail acting as a rudder, he swam skillfully. *If his friend would come out in this storm to bring medicine, he would swim to get it*, Mr. Fox decided. He needed Old Man's help. Achy bones and swollen eyes were ailments he could overcome, but mange was killing him quickly. So, Mr. Fox swam. On and on, he swam for his life. The river was too deep for his paws to touch the rocks beneath the surface, so he pumped his fox paws like pistons through the stiff current.

In awe, Old Man watched this magnificent animal. Mr. Fox's eyes were focused on N. Oldman; their beam locked in with gritty determination, not an ounce of fear. Mr. Fox had the heart of a champion. Years of struggle had not discouraged him; they had instead honed his champion's spirit. He landed, emerged, and groomed his matted fur. His eyes sparkled and radiated, *I made it*. His eyes were moist from the river and no doubt a tear or two of pain dotted them. Old Man responded with a tear of admiration in his own eyes. He respected the old fox. When rivers rage, champions swim them.

Old Man poured the courageous old lion a hot broth—a compote of chunky protein, berries, healing manuka honey, antibiotics, and mange-fighting potion. Old Man sipped a coffee with a wee bit of Blanton's bourbon. "Sore shoulder medicine" he liked to call it. He checked a sports news app on his phone while Mr. Fox ate. He was tracking a good friend's progress in a professional golf tournament in South Florida. His friend, a canine-loving guy, had been injured and aching for two to three years. During an injury drought, victory becomes a back corner of the mind thought and is replaced with the nagging thought: *will the pain stop and will victory ever happen again?* In Human World, there are many measurements of "success," and the success ladder takes its toll.

Mr. Fox looked up from his bowl of healing broth and winked. *There is only determinant of success in Fox World. If you're alive, you've won.* Mr. Fox appreciated N. Oldman's persistent efforts to deliver a cure—especially in this icy rainstorm. *Thank you, N. Oldman. I will be here when you come home from the hospital. We have miles to go. Be a champion.* There was another splash and Mr. Fox was back in the river, navigating down current with ease this time.

Old Man watched his friend float down the raging, bloated stream. Mr. Fox dug at the swift, frothy current hard with his right paw to force his body left to the riverbank's edge. The alert bell on Old Man's smartphone chimed. It brought news from sun-filled Boca Raton to Fox World. The screen read: Results Final—PGA Champions Tour. Old Man's oft-injured friend had won the professional golf tournament, the e-article said. He was alive; he had won.

When rivers rage, champions swim them.

MILE MARKER 111.1
HOT CHOCOLATE HOPES

Old Man smiled grimly as he pulled into the hospital garage—
every challenge brings an opportunity to smile. When life hurls
a knock-out punch, smile back at life, and keep walking. Old Man
smiled again when he thought of his trail buddy. The old guy had
swum a river to get the meds he needed to survive.

It was Old Man's turn. First, a bevy of medical tests. He knew
the drill—pokes and prods all day. The results would determine the
extent of the surgical procedure on day two. At the end of the day,
there would be a consultation with the heart surgeon. Old Man's wife
had come along for moral support, and her wide, beautiful smile was
doing just that.

Between lab tests, they sat in the floor-to-ceiling glass lobby. It was
filled with natural light—like an airport hangar with a steel and glass
roof. They told jokes to break the tension and laughed hesitantly.
They mocked Old Man's bandaged wrists and called them "mummy
hands." They counted how many times (fifteen was their guesstimate)
they had sat in this lobby previously—each time she politely did not
drink her beloved coffee because his pre-test protocol prohibited a
taste of caffeine. Underneath her omnipresent smile, she was a tough
and steady woman, his rock and anchor.

Armed with optimism, they took on another hospital day in high
spirits. They shared Mr. Fox stories, drawing strength from his plight
and courage. They dined in the Mayo Clinic café. She ate a grilled
chicken salad; he sipped a water. He took pics of her to look at on his
phone while he sacrificed more blood that afternoon. She protested

and they giggled. He kissed her and headed to the nuclear medicine wing for the afternoon.

Two hours later, he walked the long corridor back to the airport-lookalike hospital lobby. Oh boy, hospitals and airports, how Old Man hated both. There along the bank of sun-filled windows was the lady dressed in red, bespectacled in tortoise-shell-rimmed glasses, reading a novel. Smiling Wife was the "librarian look" done perfectly. She handed him an espresso shot and an extra-large hot chocolate with a you-need-caffeine look. He winked thanks, downed the shot, and started on the hot chocolate. From there, the caffeine did the talking.

"Let's go see a surgeon!" he exclaimed—his caffeine high stoked by chocolate and sugar. In the cardiologist's office, they learned that day two at the hospital was going to be harder. Time to go home and pack a bag. On the way home, it snowed. Old Man turned left on the road to Fox World. He liked to watch it snow in the forest. Snow flurries calmed his mind, and a blanket of snow made a quiet place quieter.

Old Man and his wife walked to the head of the trail where they saw a canine butt print in the snow and little pawprints heading away to the east. Mr. Fox had come for their daily walk, Old Man had missed him, and Mr. Fox had walked home alone. Old Man thought silently—I will miss our walk tomorrow and the next and the next. The horses galloped in his heavy heart.

Smiling Wife hugged him and whispered, "We will leave at 6:30 a.m. tomorrow, fifteen minutes early. With all the snow coming tonight, Mr. Fox is going to need an early morning hot bone broth." For the second time in one day, she had come to the rescue of the guys in her life. She knew a trade secret—hot chocolate, bone broth, and a good night's sleep neutralized all ills.

MILE MARKER 115.4
TRACTION

"Traction" is a word used more often than the situation prob- ably merits. In Corporate World, the phrase "we're getting traction now" signals success, when in reality, the situation is not more that ot sliding backwards. Merriam-Webster defines traction as "the adhesive friction of a body on a surface on which it moves." Ouch, sounds painful.

Mr. Fox gladly accepted the lesser Merriam-Webster definition. He was not moving backwards. Mange's assault had been halted by the Dr. N. Oldman potion and Mr. Fox felt the change internally. He was calmer, the urge to scratch his tail and chest had dropped to zero. He was no longer restless or anxious and he took healing naps in the safety of his refurbished haybed. The bed's fluffiness soothed his

Would Mr. Fox get well? This was the only question that needed to be answered. What were the advance signs of recovery? Signs—that word made him think of another Corporate World process, KPIs. Key Performance Indicators are milestones in a project. Follow the rights KPI beacons and success is imminent, Corporate World believes.

Old Man stopped the pencil work and laughed out loud. He was acting like a corporate executive, not a freshly minted forest walker and fox watcher. Mr. Fox, true to his nature, was smiling at his buddy's foolishness. *I love my human buddy, but he sure takes the long way around to get to a solution in Human World. Maybe I can share a lesson with my buddy. In Fox World, life's tests are straight-lined*, Mr. Fox explained. *Did you wake up after a night of freezing temperatures? Can you find something to eat? Can you defend your territory? Fox World is a pass-failure test. There are no KPIs. Just survive and advance.*

Old Man pondered the data. Mr. Fox's appetite was strong. He was hunting game. His coat was thin, but the hair loss had diminished. The hair loss in his tail was at eighty percent, a concern because he could not use his tail as a warm blanket. Old Man continued his observation. Mr. Fox's energy level was noticeably higher. He walked briskly with his tail held high. He pushed proffered blueberries around and flipped them into the air and caught them. He posed for photographs. He jumped up on a log and surveyed the forest. When he saw his fun, pesky fox, friend Santa Claus (the moniker chosen because this fox's large white mane matched the fringe on Santa's coat), he barked a playful greeting and chased Santa Claus through the woods. As they sped by, Santa Claus always gave Old Man a sideways smiling glance as if to say: *Look, N. Oldman, I'm making the old fox get some exercise.*

Old Man took another sip of his coffee and crumpled the notebook paper with the list of Fox World KPIs. Corporate World analytics did not work here. In Fox World, KPIs, metrics and expensive consultant buzzwords were irrelevant. There is only one determinant of success in Fox World: If you're alive, you've won. Mr. Fox nodded agreement. *N. Oldman has miles more to go before he gets it, but he is walking in the right direction.*

On cue, N. Oldman grabbed his walking staff and avocado backpack and headed up the trail and Mr. Fox fell dutifully in behind him.

MILE MARKER 122.2
SECRET WEAPONS:
BOUNCE THE TERRIER
AND ARNOLD
PALMER'S PUTTING

Old Man and Mr. Fox had been walking for four months. Some days were hard; others were scary. The six DVT blood clots in his chest, arm, and leg were healing but at times they drained his energy. Tired bones made it difficult to muster the energy to change out of a suit and into a cold-weather parka for a walk into the woods. Every time he went into the forest on an ultra-chilly day, he held his breath. Mr. Fox's vitals were improving but he was vulnerable with his mange-driven hair loss. And, last evening had been very cold, in fact, the coldest night of the winter. Had Mr. Fox made it through the night?

Old Man wrapped himself in a puffy down parka and wool scarf. It was ten degrees, and the wind was gusting to 40 mph. It was going to be a brutal walk to Fox World and the long jaunt brought no guarantee of seeing Mr. Fox. Old Man needed two things to calm his frenetic state of mind. First, he needed a highly disciplined motivational thought to focus his mind on positive outcomes. Secondly, and more importantly, a walking partner for the trip would be a mental boost. Bounce, his ten-year-old Jack Russell terrier, was hovering. With Bounce being a dog that could not tolerate frigid cold temperatures, Old Man was reluctant to take her, but she persisted with unending circles around his feet and Old Man relented. Besides, Mr. Fox loved the tiny tike; it would make the old fox happy. Old Man dressed her in a clingy, form fitting fleece and topped that with a heavy wool dog sweater and he stuffed the sweater with heat packs. She wiggled into it, excited by the prospects of a brisk walk outside. Old Man laughed as he noted the orange fox embroidered on the back of her thick gray sweater. She was "fox ready" and "weather enabled."

As Old Man and Bounce made the weather-slowed trek to Fox World, Old Man scrolled his mind for an inspirational thought. Think positive and believe, he whispered as he bit into his frozen lower lip. Arnold Palmer was a great in-the-clutch putter. The reason for his putting prowess, golf writers and analysts said, was not his putting stroke. In fact, his putting stance was unorthodox, which is a cleaned-up way of saying ugly. It did not matter—Arnold Palmer made impossible putts to win championships because he willed the ball into the hole with sheer, steel-hard determination. Mr. Palmer envisioned no outcome but success. "He believed," Old Man whispered and locked onto the mantra. Bounce joined in. *Just believe, Dad. Believe the best will happen.*

Mr. Fox was deadly still in his hay bed. Old Man regretted his choice of words almost as soon as he formed them. Mr. Fox faced eastward away from Old Man and Bounce. The bottom half of his body was buried in the deep-bowled haybed. His head was cocked sideways and awkwardly, almost as if his neck was broken. The lack of any discernible movement was startling and immensely sad. Mr. Fox needed sleep, and he liked to sleep when he knew Old Man was on his flank, but he had never slept this soundly. Mr. Fox's vigilant state of alertness in the wild explained his long-life tenure. He was always on guard—until now.

Silence ruled the moment on the frozen landscape as barren as an iced-over North Dakota wheat field. Winter's winds swirled tiny snow spouts into the air and rippled the orange fur on the back of Mr. Fox's neck. His black ears flopped in the wind as if sewn onto a stuffed animal toy. Afraid, Old Man choked back a whistle. What if there was no response? For four months, he had whistled, Mr. Fox had come, and they had walked. This was their buddy pact. But now, Mr. Fox was not moving. Mr. Fox appeared to be dead; his body was eerily still. Maybe he should whistle one time—for old time's sake. Before he could draw in a breath to whistle, Bounce the white and caramel colored terrier took charge and pitched a high soprano note into the air. Old Man's ears almost did not register the ring-of-hope note, but a canine did as Bounce's high-pitched whine cut through the rustling wind. Old Man watched, frozen in expectation. A black silky ear tweaked sideways. Was that the wind? Was the frigid breeze simply rustling the fur of a deceased animal? Another Bounce whine followed. Mr. Fox's head rose and turned his ever so slightly—almost indistinguishably. Mr. Fox was alive! Was he too ill to move?

The answer came next. Drunken with post-nap sleep, there was a shake of the head, a focusing of his eyes, and a sly fox grin. He was alive! Mr. Fox was alive! Bounce barked softly, as if not to startle her fox friend, and her tail twitched like a windshield wiper on the intermittent setting. Puppy whines, fox yips, and copious tail wagging followed. After a cup of bone broth, thickened with high nutrient chicken livers, there was more courtship. With his signature arthritic limp, Mr. Fox walked back and forth near Old Man and his dog—checking out Bounce's fox sweater. Stomach fortified and spirits brightened, he climbed the highest log he could find and puffed his chest. And while he preened and danced with Bounce, Old Man slipped a flannel pillowcase with a dozen hand warmers inside under the straw of his hay bed. A little extra comfort tonight, ole buddy. The overnight forecast was zero degrees, but with a nutritious supper, a toasty bed, and a get-well visit by Bounce, Mr. Fox was primed for success.

Mr. Palmer willed a lot of putts into the hole at Augusta in his victorious 1958, 1960, 1962, and 1964 campaigns. With will as unbending as Pittsburgh steel, Mr. Palmer never considered outcome other than winning. Neither did Mr. Fox. He was a survivor and a winner, and he was tough as railroad spikes. There was a cheer of joy in Fox World on this day, reminiscent of a crowd's roar greeting a Palmer charge amongst the pines of Augusta. Mr. Fox had made it through another day.

MILE MARKER 125.0
TATTERED WARRIOR

Take the hard road. The jagged rocks on the difficult trail cut open the soul and let the light in. Redemption road batters the walker without mercy or repose. Every challenge can be bone-jarring hard. Victory is momentary, replaced by more hardship—the deeper, longer kind. The calculus of survival is straightforward. When limits and ceilings are maxed out and an insurmountable challenge is faced, the math becomes concrete—win one more than you lose. Face circumstances eyeball to eyeball and say with fire in the throat, "I'm all in—outcome be damned." Old Man and Mr. Fox had fixed that bayonet many times. *Just need to win one more than we lose*, they agreed.

Old Man sat with Mr. Fox for hours on the first day of spring. Sleep was Mr. Fox's ally at this point, so Old Man watched over him dutifully. Mr. Fox characterized the care as excessive doting. Old Man laughed—where had he heard that phrase before? He read the winter alert on his smartphone. One final winter onslaught was priming. Mr. Fox's battle with sarcoptic mange was half won at this point. The disease, cured by Old Man's potion, was no longer active in his body. This was the good news.

Stage two of the recovery was daunting (bad news) when the scenarios were war gamed. Mr. Fox had lost underbelly hair, which provided insulation from the frozen ground. Equally concerning was the denuding of his fluffy tail, his fox blanket on windy nights. Now it was tattered and threadbare. If this atrocity was not enough gristle to chew on, there was a cold front approaching that would last four days. Radar indicated that it would bring snow—up to six inches.

Old Man shook his head in disbelief. Mr. Fox had fought off the fatal disease, but now he was likely to succumb to hyperthermia. He needed the warmth that the First Day of Spring on the calendar had not delivered. Old Man sipped his coffee and formulated a plan in his mind. If Old Man needed motivation or urgency, what he saw next brought a tractor-trailer load of it. Mr. Fox rose from the forest leaves excruciatingly slowly. He quivered in pain and with the exasperation of "all this rescue effort might not succeed." He fought to lift his head. Every ache was apparent as he shook. He fell back a little to the ground. The forest sighed. All the animals were rooting for their king. "Don't give up, Mr. Fox," Old Man encouraged. Mr. Fox doubled down on fortitude and tried again, his energy tank empty. He looked to the sky defiantly and he spat on Ole Man Winter in disgust. In any language, the message rang: *I'm still standing.*

Old Man responded with glowing respect. "Immense love for you, old warrior. Winter and disease took your majestic orange coat. The winds chilled your bare legs. Competitors came when you were down. Luck left town. But no one could take your warrior heart." With that spoken word, Old Man began a rescue plan.

MILE MARKER 128.0
A FOX BLANKET AND
A CAT CHALET

With the snowstorm approaching and an emergency out-of-town trip on the day's horizon, Old Man worked fast to gather provisions. He had four hours to do what was needed before he had to leave for a three-day trip. Mr. Fox would then be on his own. On a legal pad, Old Man scribbled stratagems from a survival course he had once taken at a corporate team-building retreat. Could it be that

Corporate World—of all places—might contribute an idea to save the king of Fox World? Old Man smiled at the irony. And continued with his to-do list. To survive the winter storm, Mr. Fox needed pure clean water, high density calories, a waterproof shelter, terrain to block the wind, an insulation layer on top of the frozen ground, campfire, and hope … lots of hope.

N. Oldman decided that the best place to build the shelter was on high ground under a thick holly tree by Fox River. Mr. Fox liked this spot, so it was likely he would enter the shelter. The location provided a water source and an overhanging tree limb for shelter from snow. On high ground, the shelter was exposed to the forecasted stiff winds. This was a problem. Old Man solved the wind chill issue with two ideas. A third later came unexpectedly in a UPS box.

He addressed the insulation problem first. He covered the ground with ten inches of thick-matted timothy hay. The green hay would elevate Mr. Fox, keep him dry, and protect his bare belly. Old Man drove to a local pet store and purchased a triangular-shaped, waterproof cat house. It looked like a ski chalet. Old Man hoped Mr. Fox would use it, though the human knew that most wild foxes would fear it. The chalet was Mr. Fox's lone hope to survive the approaching snowstorm, so Old Man said a prayer. With the cat house angled away from the prevailing wind patterns, an adequate wind fort was finished.

When Old Man returned from the pet shore, there was a surprise UPS box on his red brick front porch. It was addressed to "Mr. Fox" and was from a wonderful friend in Mississippi. Old Man had told her of Mr. Fox's mange plight a week or so ago. In the UPS box was a wool fox blanket for his hay bed. It would make a toasty, fluffy floor for his wind fort, and Mr. Fox would be able to burrow into it when the nighttime temperatures dropped. An hour before dark, Old Man returned to Fox World with the remainder of the survival kit supplies. He re-fluffed the haybed and formed mounds of hay around the cat chalet so that only the small front opening of the chalet was exposed. Inside, he placed handwarmer packs wrapped in tin foil on the floor of the small shelter. These would provide eight to ten hours of warmth. He covered the heat packs with the fox blanket gift. And then he gathered Mr. Fox's loose hair and scat from the nearby hay bed and placed it in the corner of the wind fort. The familiar smells would encourage Mr. Fox to use the shelter.

Old Man poured hot bone broth with dissolved antibiotics, honey, and plump blueberries into Mr. Fox's rock bowl. He had heated the rock on the gas grill at home so that it would hold the heat in a bit longer and keep the broth warm. He added an assortment of fresh meats and fish proteins, including organs like liver for vitamins. He sprinkled bison treats inside the ski house and hid six boiled eggs in the corners. This was Mr. Fox's food cache. He would have sufficient calories with which to generate internal body heat until Old Man returned in three days.

Old Man stepped back and took a deep, hopeful breath. He checked his list, and one by one, he checked off the guidelines from the survival course. Before him was the best that a human could offer an ill, aging fox. There was one thing left to do—talk to Mr. Fox. He was thirty yards away behind a large log. It was blocking the wind, but it provided little else in the form of cover as heavy snowflakes swirled in the wind.

"Mr. Fox, this is your home during the storm. The shelter and the blanket will keep you warm until the cold front passes. I will be back in three days. Come and eat your nutritious soup. It will fill your tummy and make you sleepy. I know this is unusual and strange to you, but please trust me. I am your friend and would never hurt you," Old Man said. He signed the "one-two-three-for-you-and-me" buddy mantra to his friend and backed away a few steps.

Mr. Fox stood and stretched the ache from his tired bones. He was low on options in Fox World. The game was not over, though. N. Oldman had brought a bountiful blessing. Trust was the currency that connected the two sentient beings and Mr. Fox decided to make another big bet on Old Man. He approached the winter shelter confidently, devoured the delicious soup, and ducked into the toasty teepee. He heard Old Man's boots crunching in the snow as he left. He said a prayer for his buddy. His fox heart hurt as he thought of his human friend's long walk alone in the snow.

Mr. Fox looked out of the small door of his fox teepee. The forest was a snow globe—beautiful to his eyes, chilling to his bones. He snuggled deep into the fleece blanket. His tummy was full of nourishment, and his belly and paws, thinned by mange, were warm. The handwarmer packs felt like a campfire inside his tent. He counted snowflakes landing on Fox River until he was sleepy. He exhaled a canine sigh of contentment. He was going to make it through the storm, he reassured himself. As his eyes closed, he whispered, *much love to you, N. Oldman – talk to you in three moons.*

MILE MARKER 133.3
TURNING THE CORNER

Old Man liked to drive and think. He motored up the onramp to the interstate, set the cruise control on the Range Rover SUV, adjusted his seat a bit, and settled into the one-hundred-mile drive back to Washington, D.C. Secluded in his thoughts, he ran a sitrep on his life.

He was fifty-nine years old and had a mid-level executive job for a large international company. He had been happily married for seventeen years and had two lovable terriers. He was also known as the nutty guy who walked with the fox. Odd how an item is seen as a liability by some people and an asset by others. He had a few bucks in the bank—not a lot, but enough to treat himself to a porterhouse steak or a dozen new golf balls on occasion. His health was a wild card. He had died, they said, and after eleven hours of surgeries, he had new hardware and bridges in his heart to keep him alive. Thirteen weeks of cardiac rehabilitation were scheduled to commence soon. He was depressing himself, he decided. He changed the soundtrack. Things were as good, as good as they could get. Just win the moment and turn the corner.

He glanced at the orange logbook on the passenger seat and flipped to the last entry. It read: 133 miles. Old Man and Mr. Fox had walked a lot of miles on their four-month journey. Not bad for a couple of old nuts, the judgmental would say. His legs and chest registered sympathy pains as Old Man thought about it. More so, he grimaced when he thought of the pain, injury, and challenge that Mr. Fox had faced. What was next for the old lions? Whatever it was, they would square their shoulders and stare it down.

The bucolics of the passing Shenandoah countryside were hypnotic. Apple orchards, rippling white-water rivers, and the green grass of dairy farms whizzed by in the side window. Thoroughbreds stood in the fields, warm wool blankets across their shoulders. Old Man's mind drifted, exploring deep recesses. Questions were buried there. Had he died when his heart stopped for thirty seconds? Why had his heart restarted after thirty seconds? What about the beautiful things that he "experienced" on the "other side"? An illusion or a preview? Why was he back here "on Earth"? Why was an aging fox, whose life he had saved as a pup, back in his life? Was the old fox a guide on an eye-opening journey for a calloused old man? Or was the explanation less sanguine. Was this nothing more than a hungry little fox who followed Old Man around for food and Old Man had made a big deal about it? That reality, if true, had a razor's edge to it.

The hum of the tires on the pebbled asphalt road was a steady theme song for his theta state. He kept thinking. And driving. And thinking. What was going on in his life? If Old Man believed one thing it was this: belief was the origin of all success. He believed that both he and Mr. Fox had turned the corner. He would know the answer when he arrived back at Fox World. "Turning the corner" was a phrase that made Old Man smile. The words suggested that a simple right or left turn around the corner of a building could change one's luck. Old Man thought the trick to the phrase was to believe that what was around the corner was better than what was being left behind. Thoughts create energy, which when channeled, govern intentions and drive action. As hard as this was for Old Man or any resident of Human World to practice, it was second nature for Mr. Fox. He believed a good day was one that ended with you watching a sunset. Nothing more was needed. It was a lesson that Old Man would never forget for the rest of his life—be it a day or a decade.

Old Man's sports utility vehicle turned down the lane to Fox World. Had Mr. Fox made it through the winter storm? Old Man eased the truck into the Corporate World parking lot adjacent to Fox World. He put the lever into PARK and unfastened his seatbelt. He retrieved the orange journal and a small plastic pouch of dried organic cherries from the camel-leather car seat. He stepped into the forest and headed to Fox River. The forest floor was a mosaic of acorn-brown colored leaves and patches of crusted white snow pricked with blown debris from the storm. He moved forward with crunchy footsteps. Old Man turned the sharp left corner by Cherry Candies Table and then the second turn, a ninety-degree right to Mr. Fox's haybed, he clicked a positive thought into his mind. Belief is the origin of all success. Turn the corner. Life wants Mr. Fox and Old Man to turn the corner.

Mr. Fox was propped up in his timothy haybed nibbling on a boiled egg that he held between his silky, black front paws. It was his sunset-watching snack. He looked west. This was the first post-storm sunset, and it brought bright-orange fiery hope and extra degrees of warmth. Mr. Fox wiggled deeper into the haybed. He, too, took stock of his life. He was nine years old, and he lived in the best forest in the world. He had a beautiful and loving wife named Buttons. No one knew yet, but Buttons was pregnant, and he would have a family soon. He had many close animal friends, and he had a human buddy. He no longer felt ill, and he no longer itched. Sleep had come for days, and his batteries were re-charged. It was spring. He had survived mange during the winter, a near impossibility. *He had a bright future*, he smiled.

Mr. Fox watched N. Oldman turn the corner in the forest and walk toward him. Both boys smiled and released the stress of fear with an exhale. They had kicked a tough ole winter out of town. *They had won one more than they had lost.* Behind them was the cold, barren forest. Ahead of them was a sunset with the promise of warmth and light. What was ahead of them was better than what was behind.

The old boys had turned the corner.

MILE MARKER 137.2
BLUEBERRIES, HONEY,
AND BUTTONS

Spring brings the inevitable promise of love, it is said. Old Man laughed; most people would settle for a semi-guarantee of mild infatuation. Never settle, Mr. Fox would say. Go for love; form a dream and get who and what you want.

Mr. Fox looked at his reflection in Fox River as he sipped an early morning wake-up drink. Gone were the dashing looks of the king of the forest. His orange coat was mottled with bare spots and gray patches. His tail, once the largest and most luxuriant in the forest, was stick thin. The mange-fueled, blistered red welts on his chest had sealed, but gobs of white hair had fallen. Mange chew marks on his forelegs were scarred over. His face was nicked by coyote bites. But he was alive, and that glorious fact filled his heart with love.

From a nearby holly bush, Buttons looked at her mate, the dear and wonderful Mr. Fox, and she did not see scars. Instead, she saw a powerful aura, one expanded exponentially by kindness and wisdom. She felt viscerally the character honed by his endless deeds to help fellow Fox World residents. Before her was a prince that would defend her to the death and walk miles in snow to feed their family. She admired his ability to speak with his human buddy. And while Mr. Fox might need a comb-over here and there, he was ruggedly handsome, she blushed.

For months, life had been day-to-day survival drudgery. Mr. Fox decided to change the script. He finished his morning drink and smiled a clever fox thought. *Suspend for a day the challenge of the urban wild and the horrid advances of age and aches and introduce a love story*, Mr. Fox posited. Yes, he planned to direct and co-star in a one-act play punctuated by the oldest hook in theater—love.

Mr. Fox, with a bit of assistance from his buddy, packed a picnic basket with treats that he had cached around the woods. Chicken thighs, livers, bison jerky, strawberries, blueberries, and honey. Nothing but the best for Buttons. He finished his date prep by dipping his noggin in the water and running a paw through his orange locks. *Spiffy*, he observed when he took a second look in the stream's reflection. He skipped along the path to Foxville to find Buttons. His pace was brisk, and his gait was sure. No limp. No stiffness. There was spring in his step; he laughed at the seasonal pun. Yet no doubt the sun and the warmth of spring made the old field general feel better. Being in love with Buttons was a healing balm also.

How many ills had love cured, Old Man pondered? His mind rolled back forty years to high school when he was a cast member in Thornton Wilder's one-act play, *Love and How to Cure It*. Their ensemble had won a gold championship ribbon at the state one-act play championship in Charlottesville. It had been spring. There had been love and hope in the air. The championship had brightened an otherwise painful chapter in his younger days. His parents had divorced when he was fifteen. In the next thirty years, he saw his father four times. The one-act play might have well been renamed *What Love Cured* in his dismal teenage life. Love was about to do the same in Mr. Fox's.

Mr. Fox selected a small mound covered in moss and fragrant pine needles. Daffodils in sparkly yellow ringed the mound. Mr. Fox was a details man, and he missed none. He set up the picnic and fluffed a pine needle seat for Buttons. *There, all ready.*

Leaves crinkled in the woods behind Mr. Fox, and he stopped, frozen like a statue, his silky black ears pricked. He barked softly. Once. Twice. A longer third. A calling—fox to loving fox. She emerged from the brush and glided gently to the moss. He walked to her, and she whimpered. She wrapped her thick tail around his bare legs, giving warmth to the old warrior's arthritic knees. Buttons complimented his short haircut graciously and invited him to dance, and they did so under the sun. They nuzzled and conversed lightly in their gekkering language. Old Man imagined that Mr. Fox shared a fox secret with her. *"We can nap peacefully. N. Oldman will watch over us. We are safe."*

Under the afternoon's warmth, Buttons chinned the back of Mr. Fox's neck and gekkered, *"Rest easy, old warrior. I love you. You are the most handsome fox in the whole forest."* Old Man watched their chests rise and fall in unison. He was happy to see the old fox have peace.

Old Man realized that he, too, had found solace. His trail buddy, Mr. Fox, had led him into the hardest winter of his life and, through the mental pain, Old Man had softened and evolved. There was no going back; the road to redemption is one way, fortunately. Old Man accepted that as he leaned back against the tree trunk, admiring the romantic fox couple across Fox River, and accepting lthe blessed rhythm of another "be here now" moment. Soon, three chests were synchronized in the cadence of deep sleep. Halcyon days were here.

MILE MARKER 141.3
SHINY AIRPLANES

From Reagan National Airport to a western U.S. destination, a plane flies directly over Fox World on take-off. The flight begins on Reagan's short north lane, followed by a sharp low altitude bank left on a northwestern heading along the Potomac River. Within a few minutes at five thousand feet altitude, the forest's green oasis appears amidst the bland concrete canyons. With the midday sun shining down vertically, the stream that separates Fox World and Human World shines like a gold ribbon below. The stream's shiny gold, the forest's green, the red glowing taillights of commuter cars, and the drab-gray asphalt of the office parks paint the snow globe below called Fox World.

Old Man often looked out the airplane window and whispered, "Hello down there, Mr. Fox. Hello, Bucky the deer. Hello, Professor

Owl, Colonel Hawk, and Deja Blue the heron. Hello, Beacon and Bounce." The menagerie was the last calm (and sane) checkpoint before heading on to business meetings in Dallas, Phoenix, and Los Angeles.

What Old Man did not know was that Mr. Fox was often looking back. On this Saturday morning, Old Man sipped a coffee and watched Mr. Fox across the meadow, tracking silver jets and their white contrails against the cobalt sky. Old Man laughed at the oddity and uniqueness of a wild animal watching airplane flyovers. He had once read in a book that Secretariat, the Triple Crown champion, did the same in his retirement in a Kentucky horse farm pasture. There, the horse had often tracked jets across the sky until his passing at age twenty-nine.

From the meadow, Mr. Fox turned to look at his buddy, N. Oldman. *You've been up there in the sky. What is it like?*

"It is too far from down here, fox buddy," Old Man replied.

Mr. Fox agreed with that, but he wished that he could fly—just once. He wanted to see other places and fly in the sky like a bird. The closest that he had come to the sky was when he and N. Oldman had climbed Fox Mountain months ago. Mr. Fox loved Fox World and his animal friends, but just once, he wanted to climb inside one of these shiny steel birds with N. Oldman and sail into the sky, because *a good life is part paw on the ground and part heart in the sky.*

MILE MARKER 145.8
WHEN LIFE IS TURBULENT,
GO FLY A KITE

Industry conferences, sales seminars, and distribution channel meetings had piled up while Old Man was recovering. He needed to get out of the office and get on the road. "You can't sell 'em if you don't see 'em," a sales manager of decades ago had said. Old Man laughed. The manager had been right.

Old Man felt well enough physically to travel. The issue was his dark, well-kept secret. He was fearful of flying on airplanes. More specifically, clear-air turbulence frightened him unmercifully. Sometimes panic attacks ensued—and they were suffered silently in an Economy Plus seat on United Airlines. Old Man swallowed hard as he thought about the prospects of a panic attack vis-a-vis his newfound arrythmia.

He sat at his desk on Connecticut Avenue and plotted a sales trip itinerary. He would do a two-day trip to Chicagoland first—as a test. Then he would attend a weeklong sales conference in Phoenix. From there, he would reassess and make more travel plans. Translation: Old Man would make more trips if the clear air turbulence panic attacks and arrythmia did not kill him in the first round—a spot of macabre humor always helps, Old Man laughed to himself. He pressed the BUY button and printed the airline tickets. Time to find out whether he was healed or not.

Chicago was uneventful, made consistently wonderful by undertones of good pizza and great people. It was an in-and-out overnighter—a perfect business-trip icebreaker after his four-month illness. The taxi drive back to the airport was surprisingly free of afternoon commuter traffic blockages. He relaxed, sat back, and watched the spring season warm Chicago through the taxi window. The comeback road trip was going smoothly, Old Man noted with short-lived relief. His smartphone flashed a weather update. Severe windstorm in the Washington, DC area. Old Man felt his pulse rate quicken. His heart rate monitor wristwatch confirmed the high numbers.

The wind shear hit halfway into the flight. Old Man had flown one million air miles in three decades. This was the second worst turbulence that he had ever experienced. The gold medal in scary flights had been won by an emergency landing in Newark, NJ years ago. Today, the airplane shook like a clothes dryer with a missing leg leveler. There were screams for twenty minutes and in the seat next to Old Man, a former military officer, fit and young, was catatonic. His stare was frozen in a mask of fright. Old Man gave him a hang-in-there pat on the shoulder and then braced himself. The noise of the wind shear slamming the hull sounded like a rubber hammer crunching the aircraft's metal skin. These were perfect panic attack generating conditions.

Old Man tightened his lap belt and loosened his mental grip. He searched for a calming mantra. He scanned random thoughts about wind. Blustery wind. What is wind really? Is it real? No one sees it. Just its effects—swirling leaves, misty whitecaps, flapping shingles, banging shutters, errant golf shots. Wind dries the eyes and musses the hair. And yes, wind does create horrific damage. Hurricanes destroy homes and lives. Wind can shake an airliner at thirty thousand feet like a toy in a terrier's mouth.

Wind—friend or foe? A day or two earlier, Mr. Fox and Buttons had offered a balanced answer, subtle and intuitive as always. Mr. Fox and Buttons were playing at the edge of the forest. N. Oldman offered them meaty snacks, but they declined politely. Their fox tummies growled, but their gaze was fixated on a one thousand square meter green grass field near the forest. Food ignored and ears pricked, Buttons and Mr. Fox detected the tiniest speck of a child's scream of delight and their eyes went upward to a kite, lifted by the wind and when tugged by a running joyful child, it climbed the horizon. Mr. Fox and Buttons cocked their heads in fascination. Mesmerized by the colorful kite, they squinted through swirling leaves and debris. They watched and watched, wagged their tails, and gekkered with delight. They loved the kite.

The clock dial in Old Man's mind spun back a half century. He was a boy running across the empty Little League outfield grass, and as the string unraveled from the kite's spool, the words "more wind, more wind," were screamed. His cheap paper kite, purchased at the five & dime store, had lasted but one afternoon, yet the memory of that day and the kite purchased with a newspaper carrier's payday had spanned half a century.

The plane banked sharp right into Reagan National Airport and fluttered to the runway. Passengers clapped. Old Man smiled and digested the lesson. Fox World always had a memorable way of unearthing joy and re-coding the needed lesson.

The same wind that shakes the plane also lifts the kite.

MILE MARKER 149.8
BLANKET OF QUIETNESS

Old Man was drawn to the old fox's calmness on this day. After all the maladies that Mr. Fox had faced and conquered, he found the most pleasure in escaping into the world of Be Here Now and today, his posture was "fox chill" perfected, Old Man marveled. Mr. Fox approached closely, stretched out on his moss mat, closed his eyes lightly, and became eerily still. He invited Old Man to achieve and savor the stillness. *From the space of inner quiet, all energy flows and multiplies,* his fox calm face proved.

Mr. Fox saw through Old Man's fake tough façade. The remnants of a pressing day in Corporate World were evident. Old Man was haggard, worn thin by long, shapeless meetings and endless teleconferences. Mr. Fox could see N. Oldman's ailing aura; his resolve was dissolving.

Come and sit. Pull up the blanket of quietness. Hear only the wind. Feel the spitting rain. Smell the blooming buttercups. Be still, N. Oldman.

MILE MARKER 153.9
SATURDAY EVENING
REDUX

Old Man and his father, Silvin, were apart for twenty years at one stretch. It was not planned and most likely, neither of them wanted the exile. It just happened. A broken family and lots of career-related relocations advanced the father-son fissure into a wide chasm. A birthday card would arrive and there would be an echo-filled phone call placed on Christmas from two bad cell phone areas. Other than that, life moved on. The pain didn't; it found a deep crevasse in which to hide. His father would say later that they were never apart; they were just exiled and destined to be together again. How far apart? Four hundred and forty-five miles to be exact, the kind of exactness that comes from staring at a United States road atlas and noting that on a 1:50 scale map, he and his father were less than ten inches apart.

A decade ago, Old Man decided, out of the blue, to end the divide. With his wife and dog, both of four years, he drove to Cherokee Lake, Tennessee. Old Man had never seen his father's house there, not even a photo. That would change in more ways than he would know.

He imagined what the knock on the door would be like, but he did not find out. There was no knock. While Old Man and his family drove hundreds of miles to Cherokee Lake, Silvin waited on his porch all day with a glass bottle of his favorite soft drink, Dr. Enuf. He had waited nine hours, and he stepped off the porch of his fishing cabin into son's heart. They hugged and became best friends for the next five and a half years, the remainder of Silvin's life. Old Man returned to Tennessee twenty-three times in the next five years. They passed time quietly. Bass fishing. Tennessee Smokies minor league baseball games. NASCAR auto racing on TV. And they dined like conquering kings at Golden Corral on Saturday evenings.

Silvin's house was not expensive or fancy. It was a tiny, three-room fishing cabin, immaculately clean and obsessively neat. It was a warm home—every wall in the fishing cabin was covered with 5" x 7" inch photo frames that Silvin had assembled in his exile. The best part of the house was the small, fifty-square-foot porch decorated with three white plastic Adirondack chairs and a "No Spin Zone" straw mat. His father often said, "All you need when you get old is a place to lay your head and a porch upon which to sit and drink sweet tea." Gospel truth, Old Man would come to know.

In their front porch talks, they vowed that they would always try to be together on Saturday evenings—if not physically—in spirit. Old Man honored that promise. During auto racing season, he sent a large, extra crispy, meat lover's supreme pizza to his father's house every Saturday night. With a slice of pizza on a paper plate on his lap, Silvin would sit on his porch, drink iced tea or Dr. Enuf, and talk to his son on the phone about the auto race. There were race conspiracies to figure out, of course. Which car was technically cheating to gain an extra mile per hour? Who was the roughest, meanest driver to have on your bumper?

Old Man had a ritual that he kept secret. In his wallet was a Google Earth aerial photo of his father's fishing cabin. While they talked by phone on Saturday evening, he would light his weekly cigar and look at the photo. He would imagine that they were together on his father's porch watching the sun set over Cherokee Lake. It made him ache for their twenty lost years.

These thoughts transited his mind as he walked into Fox World on this Saturday evening. There is a sacredness to the thirty minutes before sunset on Saturdays. He had Silvin to thank for that. He pulled the Google Earth aerial photo of Silvin's cabin from his pocket as a reminder. As he did, he heard a bark. Looking left, he saw Mr. Fox sitting on a log by the stream—his front porch by the water. Mr. Fox beckoned Old Man to pull up a stump and sit for a sunset. N. Oldman shared stories about his father, pizza, stock car racing, sunsets, and fishing. He poured Mr. Fox a bone broth and pulled a Dr. Enuf soda from a Ziploc bag of ice for himself. They looked southwest to the setting sun. To Tennessee. They listened to Fox Creek flow and ripple like the waves on a lake caused by a bass boat's wake. Old Man drew a cigar from his pocket—a Saturday tradition. He looked at the aging fox. Mr. Fox had not known his own father before he had passed a decade ago. The human and the canine were kindred in that both had no father for most of their lives. Old Man grimaced at that thought. Silently, Mr. Fox looked at N. Oldman and thought differently. He was sitting with his father on a Saturday evening, and nothing could be better.

Exile is a self-built island. Build a boat instead, Mr. Fox whispered quietly.

MILE MARKER 157.5
MR. FOX LIVES ON
DO AVENUE

There is a house on Try Street called Excuses. The house is full of guests; some are permanent residents. Old Man had stopped by that metaphorical house for a meal or two over the course of his life. It is a comfy place—that is, if you have given up on the concepts of winning and succeeding. Mr. Fox, a natural born winner, never found the Excuses residence cozy. Failure has a harsh price in the wild, and it judges harshly <u>those who try vs. those who do</u>. The right answer is across town, Mr. Fox would say. It is a neighborhood called Do Avenue. Mr. Fox did not *try* to swim Fox River to get food and medicine; he did it. He did not *try* to save a young fox from a coyote; he did it. He did not *try* to sleep on the beach rocks away so he would not spread mange; he did it. Mr. Fox would have no part of the concept of "try." He championed the word "do" in his warrior-tough spirit.

It was week three of his thirteen-week cardiac rehabilitation plan at the Mayo Clinic. Every morning, he awoke at 5:45 a.m., drove to the hospital, put on the EKG harness, did a monitored workout for fifty minutes and then drove to his downtown D.C. office to work until 5:30 pm. Aching, Old Man heard a steady rain on the bedroom window. It was 5:40 a.m. and he had five minutes to get up and get dressed for another week of cardiac rehab. His left arm and chest were healing from six DVT blood clots and surgical scars. A plantar fasciitis tear had formed in his right foot because he was unable at this point to get elective surgery on an injured left foot. Overcompensation had caused the tear in the uninjured foot. It would be difficult to get his shoe on, he grimaced. Would the world forgive him if he gave up—just for one morning? Old Man remembered what he had seen in the binocular lens the evening before—the old warrior smiling bravely from across Fox River as he hunted for dinner. The image was motivating: "do, don't try."

Old Man swung his feet over the edge of the bed onto the rug. His right foot lit up in pain. Deal with it, he thought. He added running shorts and an Orioles t-shirt and laced up his fluorescent blue Brooks. One minute later, he was driving past Fox World in the intermittent rain to the Mayo Clinic cardiac center. He hit the down button for the right passenger window, tipped his coffee thermos to the forest, and yelled, "Time to go 'do,' Mr. Fox!"

From atop Fox Mountain, Mr. Fox watched the SUV drive east in Human World. He smiled. *N. Oldman was a tough cookie*, he concluded. Then, the old fox walked down the mountain and began his day—as always, on Do Avenue.

MILE MARKER 160.2
THE LIGHTHOUSE'S
BEACON

Trusted friends never go away or give up their watch. They wait patiently without expectation or reward like the lighthouse upon a rocky outcropping. Their beacon of light calls you home.

These were Old Man's thoughts as he saw his fox buddy under the sunset on Fox River. Old Man had been away at a sales conference in Arizona; the old lions had not "walked and talked" for five days and still, Mr. Fox waited on the rocks of Fox River's shore. Old Man's heart ached as he thought about Mr. Fox visiting daily, waiting, giving up hope, and walking back to Foxville at dark when his Human World friend did not show up. Old Man mouthed the word faithful. Was he worthy of such faithful devotion? What human was?

Mr. Fox saw Old Man approaching. It was late, a few minutes before dark. Mr. Fox was excited and thankful to see him. They hurriedly shared a drink and told a few stories. The sun kissed the treetops, and they said their buddy goodbyes. Mr. Fox could not wait to show N. Oldman a surprise, but the gift would have to wait one more fox moonrise. He bid N. Oldman a good evening and turned east to Foxville with a skip in his four-legged fox step.

MILE MARKER 165.3
THE SECRET GARDEN
OF "BE HERE NOW"

Old Man awoke on the beautiful early April morning with a touch of spring fever. A Carolina wren was raising the roof outside his window, so much volume from such a tiny bird's lungs. The window was slightly ajar, and the smell of the landscaper's turned earth wafted in from the freshened-up flower boxes. The light breeze carried a hint of warmth that whispered "mid-seventies today." The golf clubs, leaning in the Callaway bag in the corner, called seductively to him. Golf was a tempting mistress on a spring day, but Old Man declined golf in his head. Scar tissue in his healing chest wounds helped with the decision. The pain and tightness would end any golfing endeavor by the ninth green. Gone for a week at a conference, he was weeks behind in paperwork (an antiquated term that he laughed at as soon as he said it). He was certain that Corporate World did not care about his mild tardiness. He was a declining asset—an end of his career old guy with a waning heart. He was Joe Namath on the Los Angeles Rams or Johnny Unitas on the San Diego Chargers. It is called the golden years by people who have not experienced it. Nothing golden about them. Tin maybe; bronze at best.

Old Man spent the coffee-fueled Saturday morning plowing through emails, expense accounts, client contact reports, and business development plans for new prospects. He ended with the activity he cherished most—thank you letters to business friends penned on cream-colored thick stock vellum. He spread the eight notes across the desktop so that the indigo ink from the fountain pen could dry. He opened the desk drawer and withdrew a plastic snap-top box which contained US postage stamps, a big variety; he liked to match a fun stamp to each handwritten note. Good manners or a touch of obsessive-compulsive disorder, he pondered and laughed. Customer notes finished; Old Man focused on an urgent task—wrapping birthday gifts. His wife's birthday was in two days. He dug into another box for scissors, tape, and bows and began wrapping. He smiled when he thought of the only gift that she had requested. Smiling Wife's only wish was to see the Mr. Fox and Button's babies.

Buttons had planted the "I'm pregnant" seed weeks earlier. She gained weight rapidly and exhibited standoffish behavior before she disappeared for three weeks (the amount of time after birth that a vixen will not leave the den). Even if the clues did add up to the birth of fox kits, there was one big problem. Old Man had no idea of where Buttons and the kits were.

Mr. Fox and Old Man were caked with almost two hundred miles of road dust and trail mud at this juncture. Trust grows well in this type of well-tilled soil and Mr. Fox decided it was time to be all in with his trail buddy. Mr. Fox stood creek-side on the green moss mounds called Ireland. It might be a long wait and, sitting would be more comfortable, but if he stood, he could see who or what was coming down the trail better. So, Mr. Fox stood up. Real tall.

Old Man and the lady with the sweet smile brought bison sliders and dried cherries mixed with whipped cream. It was Smiling Wife's birthday party, and they celebrated al fresco in grand style. Mr. Fox had a burger and pushed two more to the side of the plate. He would need those later. Over a couple hundred miles of hiking, Old Man had learned Mr. Fox's moods and moves. If he wanted a nap, he would twirl three times to the right and recline on his brushy tail as a pillow. If he wanted Old Man to follow him, he would walk five steps, stop, and look over his left shoulder. He would repeat this until Old Man picked up on the message. Mr. Fox mouthed the two burger sliders and did the latter move. *Follow me,* he hinted.

Brushy, ankle-twisting terrain filled their path on the hike to the not yet revealed destination. Mr. Fox with four-paw drive managed better than the two following humans. The trio crossed the widest, deepest part of the chilly Fox River, eliciting squeals from the birthday girl. Mr. Fox crossed on Fox Bridge II, a wide tree log that had fallen across the river years before. Old Man, banned from Fox Bridge after he'd slipped on the icy log span and fallen into the creek with his Nikon camera, nodded to the bridge and was immediately chastised with a curt look from his wife. Ok, water it is, and Mr. Fox, his mouth stuffed with two birthday beef patties, winced as he watched N. Oldman and Smiling Wife splashed through the spring-fed, chilled stream.

Their eyes adjusted. It was like moving from light to dark. The other side of the stream was the wild, unexplored part of Fox World. The forest floor was covered in thick ferns and fallen rotting tree trunks dotted the landscape. It was sure to be known as "watch out for snakes" country as the weather warmed. It was slow slogging, led thankfully by the sure-footed Mr. Fox, who paused every twenty steps to allow the two Human World emissaries to keep pace. He disappeared into a stand of tall, wispy wheat grass. It looked like waist-high golden grass in an African Sahara documentary.

Where was Mr. Fox? He went into the grass and gone. Old Man and his wife exchanged anxious glances. Deep in an uncharted part of the forest and most likely in snake country, they had lost their sentry. It was a serenely quiet spot. It stopped their thoughts and heightened their auditory sense. There was a sound—a twigs-scratching-on-concrete kind of sound. They pivoted right.

Up ahead, burgers in mouth, Mr. Fox had hopped atop a five-foot-high drainage culvert, his nails skidding across the concrete. His warrior face was softened by a father's pride. He stared at an empty house—one with a cared-for lawn but with no apparent occupants. A labyrinth of wooden flower boxes and grass tiers, walled by railroad ties, filled the backyard. This garden had been someone's devotion, their passion, their love spot that filled their after-work hours or retirement days. It was a secret oasis—known now only by Mr. Fox and Buttons.

Three orange and gray puffballs crawled out of a dirt tunnel dug under the abandoned house's deck. "Be," "Here," and "Now" saw Daddy on his perch. They smelled the juicy bison burger. They began growling like lion cubs. Dad Fox jumped down and fed the cute puff pups the two bison burgers. They mauled him with fox licks. If there ever was a time and place called the land of Be Here Now, this was it. Just that quickly, the three fox kits had names. *Be, Here, and Now.*

"Happy birthday, sweetheart," Old Man said to his wife.

"Best gift ever," she smiled. They hugged a deep I-love-you embrace.

Old Man watched the senior fox play with his kits as they wrestled and tumbled in the grass. Mr. Fox was elated to share this gift with N. Oldman and his wife. *This is the best of the best, I'm here with both of my families*, the old fox smiled. Smiling Wife's face was beaming with raw joy and her cheeks glistened with tears as her birthday wish materialized in front of her. The pups tugged at their father's tail and at the human's hearts. *It is a miracle to be here now*, Old Man and Mr. Fox thought simultaneously. N. Oldman and his fox buddy had walked through the valley of death during the winter and every time they had shaken death off their backs, misery had knocked at the forest door again the next morning. Enemies and illness were gone for now. The road to redemption would have no curves for a while. The Secret Garden was filled with magic, joy, innocence, and wonderment. Buttons joined Mr. Fox and they nuzzled. The pups played until exhausted, and Mr. Fox tucked Be, Here, and Now into their beds. He kissed Buttons and whispered to her, *I want to walk N. Oldman and his wife home. They are lost in this part of the forest and the sun will set soon.*

Old Man nodded at the old fox. "I've been lost most of my life's travels, old buddy, but today I've never been more found or centered. Thank you for leading us to the Secret Garden. Thank you and Buttons for sharing Be, Here, and Now with us. It was my wife's best birthday ever. Thank you."

Mr. Fox dipped his head modestly. *I owe you much, N. Oldman. I'm alive today to see my pups because of you.* Old Man returned a respectful look, one that said I'm pretty darn sure that we're both alive because of a gift the universe wanted us to share—trust.

Old Man and Smiling Wife left a cup of birthday cherry parfait for the always appreciative Buttons and blew air kisses to the pups. The trusting trail buddies saddled up and began the long walk back through snake country to Human World with Mr. Fox, the loyal sentry, on point and Old Man, the ever-protective Practorian, on the fox's six. Smiling Wife watched the old lions walk together and more happy tears misted. No one would believe this "man and animal become best friends" story and that is why it touched her heart's core—it was true and unfolding today on her birthday and every day for the past four or five months. Every story has a beginning, a middle, and an end. Where was this story in the book, Smiling Wife wondered? Where were her husband and the little fox headed ultimately?

Up ahead, Mr. Fox traversed the log-strewn landscape with canine precision. He paused and looked over his shoulder to Smiling Wife. *Be here now. Let it all go, all of it. This is how the animals think in Fox World, ma'am. Tomorrow will come or it won't, but for today, be here now.*

MILE MARKER 168.9
"FOREVER" GROWS
THE GARDEN

A week later, Old Man bumped into Skateboard Guy.

"Whazzup, Fox Man?"

"Nothing but the rent, Silver Surfer. How are you?"

"I saw your cool old fox last night. Man, I love seeing that dude. Chills out my day. Funny thing—he was carrying a tiny baby fox in his mouth, and the pup was crying."

Mystery solved—partially. Old Man had heard an odd noise the evening before. It sounded like a young lion cub deep in the briar brush—a mile from Secret Garden. With Skateboarder Guy's update, Old Man had a hunch and he decided to check it out after his workday ended. Following nine hours of teleconferences in Corporate World, Old Man grabbed his dash bag and made the arduous walk through the sticky briar bushes, which tore scratches into his ankles and arms, to Secret Garden. After patching his profuse, blood thinner medication - driven bleeding with a dozen tiny Band-Aids, he climbed onto the concrete culvert, Mr. Fox's perch near the former flower garden, and opened a pack of peanuts for himself and a baggy filled with dried cherries. He sprinkled the cherry candies on top of the culvert's flat top and smiled; Old Man loved surprising Mr. Fox.

He thumbed the focus button on his binoculars. In a few minutes, Be, Here, and Now raced out of their den and were soon a tri-ball of orange fur wrestling in the garden's wood chips. There was no winner except the sandman, as all three were soon napping in a clumped heap.

Old Man heard the meek growl-meow that he had the day before in another part of Fox World. He shifted the binocular lens twenty feet to the left. There she was. She was very petite, half the size of Be, Here, and Now. The fourth fox had a puffy (one could say, "over-puffed") white chest, which along with diminutive size were her signature marks of differentiation. The other three fox kits ignored her. She was alone—almost. Old Man raised his lens two degrees. Behind the tiny pup was Buttons, who had a look of pure love on her face. Buttons was smitten with the orphan. "Forever" had found a home. She would be warm, she would be fed, and Button's adoring look ensured that Forever would be forever loved. The Secret Garden would now be the land of Be Here Now and Forever. Enchanted in all respects, Old Man declared.

The answer to the next question was only a guess—hopeful and wistful. Had the aging fox warrior returned to a spot in Fox World near his birthplace and saved a lost kit? Most likely so, Old Man concluded. Mr. Fox had lost his mother, Buttercup, when he was six months old. Forever had lost hers at eight weeks of age. The two orphans, star-crossed by chance and challenge, were now bonded. Forever loved her new dad and mom. The garden had grown.

Be here now and forever. Old Man planned on it.

MILE MARKER 173.3
ST. FOX AND HIS PURPOSE

Old Man sat in Fox World on a breezy afternoon. He was numb after a tiring workday, his stamina drained by a waning desire to be in Corporate World. Alone in the forest, he was letting a whole lot of nothing happen. He was accepting—just accepting what was. He had seen Mr. Fox do it dozens of times.

Six months ago, he had been healthy. A few minutes later, he'd had emergency heart surgery. Just that quick, life had changed. Since then, there had been good days and ones that resembled a mule kick. This day was in-between. Happy to be alive, Old Man was confused as what to do with the bonus time. There was one thing that he could rule out—life was never going to be the same again. The road to redemption had no U-turns.

Old Man cleared his throat with a what-the-heck cough. He felt himself taking the exit ramp to the City of Self Pity. Better find a filling station, gas up, get a map, and get out of there pronto. Well, maybe take an extra minute to grab a Slim Jim and a Mountain Dew for road trip fuel. Old Man laughed. A drink and a snack always made the world better, he laughed. Navigating adversity is fungible. Success is found somewhere in the willingness to find a purpose. A purpose births a plan. His purpose? It was simple and rather silly in many people's eyes. Old Man had decided to get up, stand up, go walking, and help Mr. Fox live one more winter, see one more Christmas, experience one more birthday, have a few months of an easier life, and to die with dignity deserved.

Mr. Fox had rewarded his friend's faith. He had struggled, endured, and recovered. Every day, they met at the head of the trail and set off on a walking adventure. Old Man, when pressed by his wife, would admit that they talked to each other a bit too. And during some of the best times, they did not. They chose instead to savor the silence of Fox World while they napped in the sun together.

Old Man looked at the elmwood cane at his feet. A walk to save a fox had saved Old Man as well. Old Man breathed a deep sigh with that thought. A purpose has a plan. A plan fosters action. Actions have consequences—but better yet, purposeful actions drive benefits. He focused the telephoto lens. Framed in the lens was an unforeseen benefit. Mr. Fox had lived to see one more thing—Be, Here, Now, and Forever. As the pups played with their father, the lens noted one unexpected find. The lady who had planted the beautiful backyard garden had centered it with a concrete statue. It rose tall over Mr. Fox. It was a saint. A saint who watched over the old boy. Secret Garden was blessed, Old Man whispered through the lens. And so was N. Oldman, for he had found a purpose.

MILE MARKER 177.6
THE TALLEST OAK IN
FOX WORLD FALLS

The Great Oak towered over its fellow trees in Fox World. If the lesser oaks were majestic, The Great Oak was gigantic in its majesty. It stood six stories high, its heights rising well above the four-story, red brick, class A construction office buildings in nearby Corporate World. The Great Oak was a treasured play spot for Mr. Fox with cushy leaves underneath, a massively wide trunk that shielded the wind, and a blanketing tree canopy that shaded him on hot days. It was also near Fox Creek, where he could drink from the creek's spring-fed waters. The Great Oak's height fascinated Mr. Fox. It epitomized his "paws on the ground; big dreams in the sky" life credo. He was a little fox, but someday he dreamed of climbing The

Great Oak. Sadly, the dream was over, The Great Oak had fallen in the spring windstorm.

Old Man walked into the calm, still forest. The thermometer had clicked from fifty to eighty degrees in one day, typical of Virginia. It was not the quiet-before-a-storm type of quiet; it was the deadly quiet after a storm's brutal destruction type of quiet. Too silent, Old Man lamented. There had been no Mr. Fox sightings for days. It pained Old Man to the core to think it, but the thought was present. The tall oak had tumbled near the spot where Mr. Fox had been playing five days ago. Could it be? Buttons had appeared twice and sat in the field across the creek, looking longingly at The Great Oak on the ground. She would not come to food, and the bison jerky left by his haybed remained there until dark. There was a glimmer of hope in that the morsels were gone by morning, but Russell Raccoon could have stopped by for a midnight snack.

Old Man went back home, taped up his plantar fasciitis, put on his hiking boots, filled his camelback, found his homemade elmwood staff in the garage, and hiked the perimeter of Mr. Fox's forest. Seven miles in total. He whistled until he was raspy. No luck. Old Man went to the fox family den. No sign of any of the foxes—Mr. Fox, Buttons, or the four kits. Likely they had moved to a new underground den, one air-conditioned by the cool earth. The weather had been unexpectedly hot. Old Man looked to the sky and telegraphed, *Mr. Fox, wherever you are, come home.*

MILE MARKER 181.3
WATERPROOF FOX

Rain moved in like it had bought a house on the block. It rained, rained, and rained. Old Man launched search parties during the intermittent storms. Deep puddles had sprouted everywhere on the forest floor. Would the river overflow its banks again? The waterlogged oaks creaked in the light winds. Would another one fall? Five more inches of rain were forecast to pelt the forest the next day.

Mr. Fox broke his absence and was waiting across the waters of Fox River on the fifth day. Old Man released the tense breaths held for days; he was overjoyed to see his buddy. The old lion looked weary. Fatherhood was exhausting the elderly fox, and he was soaking wet from the omnipresent rain showers. He looked anxious—a busy father, lots of mouths to feed, and shelter to seek before the next gully washer. Old Man signed their 1-2-3-For-You-And-Me greeting. Mr. Fox looked at Old Man, gave a quick yip, and gazed at the creek turned raging river. "No, Mr. Fox, don't. Do not swim the river. You will never make it this time," Old Man called out.

Mr. Fox was hungry. Hunting had been poor in the flooding conditions. He waded into the river. The raging whitecaps swept by threateningly, and he was forced to retreat when the swift current almost bowled him over. Mr. Fox could not cross the swollen river. Old Man was taller, and he could—and he would. He loaded the fox's emergency food cache into his backpack and hoisted it onto his right shoulder. He left his camera, mobile phone, and wallet behind on a dry spot. He gauged the depth of the white rapids with his walking staff and plunged in. With water depth at mid-thigh level, his special edition Russell Raccoon-carved walking staff centered him. Fortunately, it was a short cross with limited peril for a two-legged human and he emerged on the Foxville side of the river, elated to see his fox friend up close after a five -day worry. Mr. Fox returned the thankful look. Both paused and exchanged how-are-you-buddy's and where-have-you-been's, and then they sat. Gratitude filled Mr. Fox's features. There was silence—broken only by the squish of Old Man's sneakers.

Mr. Fox needed nourishment. Medicine meatball first. The sour booster med was masked with the flavor of South Carolina honey. Paw licking tasty. Then came a bowl of meaty stew and a handful of blueberries. And lastly, Mr. Fox nibbled on the tasty, high-energy offerings of sunflower seeds and cherry candies. Old Man pulled another package from the green backpack. It contained five steamed chicken breasts. "This meat is for your family. Times are hard during this flood. I respect your wild nature and do not want to disrespect you and your ability to feed your family. Accept my gift. Truth be told, I owe you much more," Old Man said to his buddy.

Mr. Fox nodded. *A leg up is not a hand-out, the old fox knew. He did not decline Old Man's generosity. The best gift to give someone is to accept their gift of love.*

The weight of the meat made his head hang low as he gathered it for the long walk home. However, with more flooding coming, the heavy burden of feeding his starving family was lifted. They would eat, replenish their energy, and huddle together for nature's next blast. Mr. Fox headed up the trail. Behind him, he heard a splash. N. Oldman was back in Fox River. Mr. Fox stopped and watched closely until the old man crawled onto the riverbank on the Human World side. The river, which divided the two worlds on the map on all days, united them on this one. Mr. Fox was grateful for the chicken dinner for his starving family and even more so for the man who had delivered it.

I appreciate you, N. Oldman. You are a champion. Thank you for the sustenance; for the gift of life.

MILE MARKER 188.8
BRAVO, BRAVO

Old Man and Mr. Fox's next few miles were muddy ones. Midway through the year's calendar, the state of Virginia was considerably ahead of the pace to break an annual rainfall record. The deluge had turned the nontidal Fox World into a perpetual mudflat. As Old Man stepped into Fox World on a Saturday evening, he said "Bravo" in two respects. First, the rainclouds and chilly breezes had packed up and departed. Buh-bye—thankfully. Secondly, the real-life Bravo was in Fox Forest.

Old Man spotted Bravo running loose through the woods, and his thoughts were immediately brightened by the mega-friendly Australian shepherd mix dog. Bravo often jumped the fence at his house and joined in Fox World adventure hikes. The questions that crossed Old Man's mind were—*is Bravo just up for some hiking fun or is he lonely?* Lonely, most likely. From a broken home, he didn't get much attention. His single mom loved him and tried hard, but she was overtaxed in a stressful life. Bravo, an only dog, was sometimes left to entertain himself.

Bravo was many good things and at the top of the list: world class hiking companion. He stayed close by Old Man, always coveting a head rub and a kind word, and best of all, Bravo did not chase the wild animals in the forest. Instead, he looked at them with a longing, begging look—*will you be my friend?*

Old Man made a let's-mount-up finger point and he, Smiling Wife, and Bravo trudged forward in the post-storm muddy expanse of Fox World. Bravo digested the invitation, along with a bite of bison burger, and returned an ever-present smile. Clad in knee-high rubber Wellingtons, Old Man and the gang gripped the mud and moved forward as the official Mr. Fox family search party. They forded the stream in the misty fog, Bravo in the lead, and penetrated Fox World's hardest terrain with their compass centered on Secret Garden. Ghostly eighth-of-a-mile visibility engulfed them.

Squish, squish, squish. Bravo, Smiling Wife, and Old Man sloshed through the still forest in their quest for the majestic foxes. The *Gorillas In The Mist* fog banks added suspense to their search for the water-logged, hungry foxes, but Bravo broke the tension with an over his shoulder glance of a humorous *ain't this fun, Old Man?* look on his face. Bravo liked having a mission. Better, he relished having a friend and, with this mission; he did not feel alone and abandoned any longer.

Up ahead, the beautiful Buttons, the rough-hewn handsome Mr. Fox, and the four fox pups heard the Bravo search party approaching. They were thinking (correctly) the adorable fools are ankle deep in mud and lost in the fog. *It sounds like elephants approaching*, Mr. Fox laughed. The scent of steamed nutrient-rich food bespoke the purpose—a flood rescue team on patrol with provisions. Little fox paws danced with the anticipation of a burger delivery. In the rain and fog, in the simplest of ways, nine souls (six fox, one dog, two human) were connected by the oldest of fox principles—find a purpose and help others.

Bravo, Susan, and Old Man broke into the clearing near Foxville. Buttons called out, *Bravo, over here!* His ears pricked and tuned into Buttons' cry, and he whined back to her. Old Man realized in a moment of heartfelt observing that Bravo and the foxes were not adversaries—they were friends. The foxes enjoyed playing with Bravo when he jumped his fence. He was a friendly dog with a kind spirit.

The six foxes were beleaguered by the floods, as exhaustion and hunger were evident on their faces. Seven days and twelve inches of rain had flooded their den and boxed them into a small area atop a crested mound. Deep, almost impassable, pools of water surrounded them on three sides. Old Man and Bravo distributed the care packages. The foxes ate and Old Man petted Bravo, the divorce dog. Old Man's heart twinged as he sat in the ring of nine souls. Old Man had once been Bravo, the kid from a broken home. Long ago, he too had jumped the fence as a young boy and walked without friends in the seven-acre forest behind his house. There fifty years ago, he had talked to the animals, invented hiking adventures to magic kingdoms, and fantasized about faraway dream golf courses. Half a century later, he was doing the same again. Mr. Fox would call it *"full circle closure"*.

Old Man and Smiling Wife bowed goodbye to the fox family and walked Bravo home. Old Man hugged Bravo, and then fed him a generous handful of snacks and lifted him over the fence. He pulled a dry fleece blanket from his backpack and shoved it deep into Bravo's doghouse. Bravo shook his fur dry, crawled in, circled into the blanket, and whined appreciatively. He was full, he was warm, and he had friends. Contentment is a quick-fire sedative; Bravo was asleep in minutes.

Back home, Old Man washed the Wellingtons and hung them to dry. He leaned his walking stick in the corner and tossed his rain jacket on the peg on the back of the garage door. Before pressing the garage door's CLOSE button, he looked to the forest on the distant horizon. The pawprints on the muddy forest trail would have dissolved by now; the ones in his heart would last forever.

MILE MARKER 192.5
TREASURE CHEST

M r. Fox led the walking expedition on this delightfully dry summer morning. With the rain gone, color came. Fox Forest was ablaze with color; the forest floor carpeted with green grasses and flowers. Fig buttercups glowed a sunshiny yellow. Virginia spring beauties were the pink hue of a pastel-colored Easter egg; Missouri violets added velvety purple with their contribution.

In Virginia, summer does not always deliver on the hope it promises. In fact, Old Man reflected, temperamental summer often had the dubious standing of a third party, unendorsed, out-of-state personal check. But when summer gets it right, it is glorious. Today it was righteous.

Old Man let the elder fox lead. Six months ago, he would have been thumbing through his smartphone and half paying attention—a forest hike would have been fun but half-ignored. He was asleep then, awakened later by death's scrape. That's irony, Old Man laughed, he spent fifty years numb and dulled, and then darn near died, and only to wake up with the secret patent to living life fully. The irony double downed when Old Man realized that the clock's hands of his life were approaching midnight. Put simply, he should have started his wake-up journey earlier.

Today he was fascinated by all around him. The little fox, the quintessential survivor, was treasure hunting with his nose and paws—a handful of blueberries, a golden warm sunset to watch, a mattress topper of lush green grasses to relax in, and a bouquet of 1-800-foxflowers. The doubloons of summer's bounty filled Mr. Fox's treasure chest. Old Man's nephew had once observed, "The Fox World map is like a treasure map, and Mr. Fox is the X."

Follow the X, the young man had said. And start early in life, Old Man added. Mr. Fox looked up from a field of flowers and posed with a toothy smile. *The best treasure hunts are with friends; because best friends are the treasure and I found mine.*

Follow the X.

MILE MARKER 197.2
SKY TOP LOUNGE

Old Man walked as fast as his old legs and heart would propel him. He had good news to share, and every fiber of his being was alive and happy. He heard a low-tone, raspy bark. "Huh? What? Where did that come from?" Old Man asked. *Up here,* Mr. Fox said with a grin. Mr. Fox was in a tree—twenty feet up. He had climbed the ascending diagonal tree branch of The Great Fallen Oak which had fallen two weeks ago. Old Man was surprised (and startled) to see Mr. Fox so high in the air. *Been up here in the tree waiting and doing some talking to the Great Fox Upstairs. What did your medicine man say?*

Mr. Fox was referring to Old Man's surgery follow-up meeting. "All better, Mr. Fox. My heart check-up was quick and mostly successful. I have been released. No more hospital visits or weeks of cardiac rehabilitation. Thank you, Mr. Fox. The last two hundred days in these woods with you have been life-enhancing. I owe you tons. By the way, what are doing up there twenty feet in the air, Mr. Fox?"

Believing, N. Oldman. I am focusing on believing. When I was a little fox, I dreamed of climbing The Great Oak. I thought about it every day. I believed if a little fox could climb the tallest oak in the forest, then no other challenge or trouble could ever defeat me. It took almost a decade, but here I am. I am high atop The Great Oak.

N. Oldman nodded, "Yes, you are, Mr. Fox, you rose to meet every challenge and stared down the longest odds. You surely did. You had faith in yourself. And, accordingly, The Great Oak believed in you so much that it reached down to lift you up."

Believing really works, N. Oldman. I believed that your medicine man would fix your heart. Now come on up here and let's celebrate your great news! Old Man sat on a stump and looked up. A fox in the sky? This walkabout was becoming more unbelievable with every step. Smiling Wife would veto tree climbing, but she was not here, and it was a day to celebrate. Old Man gave the our-lips-are-sealed sign to his fox friend and began climbing an alternate branch. Moments later, the boys sat comfortably in their sky top lounge, sipped a bone broth rocks with a cherry-blueberry garnish, and toasted the sunset.

Nearby, Colonel Hawk and Professor Owl, their kids asleep in the nest, poured a shaker of Sidecars, and dealt another hand of gin rummy. Both glanced over their reading glasses to behold the healing miracle of the man and the fox in the tree. *Mm-hmm, guess the boys are feeling better.*

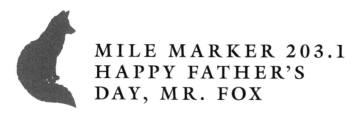

MILE MARKER 203.1
HAPPY FATHER'S
DAY, MR. FOX

A father's job is to provide sustenance, shelter, and comfort. For weeks, Old Man had watched Mr. Fox walk miles twice daily to hunt and feed his family. A hip injury that had healed slightly crooked and arthritis in his front shoulder made his gait wobbly. Yet he walked and walked and walked to complete his paternal chores. A father leaves footsteps in life called lessons. And in this regard, Mr. Fox had fed his progeny well. He was a living and courageous illustration of the adage, "throw me to the wolves and I will come back the leader of the pack."

Dutiful as ever, he made the two-mile trip to feed his family with the morsels provided. Piece by piece, he carried the heavy load on a "summer's damn well here" humid evening. He returned and sprawled out on the cooling sands of Fox Beach. "Why isn't he spending the evening with his pups?", Old Man wondered. Smiling Wife smiled in her all-knowing fashion, reached for her husband's hand and responded soothingly. "You found him starving eight years ago. You fed him until he was strong. In his eyes, you are his dad. Where else would he want to be on Father's Day?"

Epiphany … the wonderful wife kind.

MILE MARKER 207.1
"GROWBACKS"

In Old Man's youth, Saturdays entailed a once-a-month trip to the barber shop. There, Old Man and his brothers would get "crew cuts." Old Man laughed at the term—it is worth an internet search. In the olden days, money was short and so were the haircuts. A single mom had to get her money's worth from the barber for three sons' haircuts. A stylish coiffure was not an option. The barber stiffened the freshly cropped hair with a gummy wax substance called butch crème (which hardened the experience visually and emotionally) and then stifled a child's complaints with a bribe—a piece of bubble gum. The best part of the ordeal, if there was one, was chewing a big piece of pink bubble gum and reading the miniature comic book inside the gum wrapper. Afterwards, Old Man recalled, the brothers were solemn as they rode in the car to the Little League baseball field where ridicule from their friends awaited. Their mom would look at their crestfallen faces in the rearview mirror and say sweetly, "It will grow back."

Thus, "growbacks" begat comebacks. Old Man learned early in life to toughen up, hunker down, swallow the perceived indignation, and plot your return to victory lane. Comebacks are all that counts; growbacks are just the inconvenient roadblocks. He looked across Fox Forest and saw Mr. Fox atop his log. Mr. Fox had lost most of his hair during winter due to his illness. He was never ashamed of it; he was just thrilled to have survived the endless cold winter. There are real problems in life and there are ones that are simply perceived, and there is a wide chasm between the two.

Three months ago, in the dead of winter, Mr. Fox's tail had looked like a strand of jump rope, providing no protection from frostbite temperatures. He had a mange-induced bald spot on his forehead, a semi-permanent mark of Ash Wednesday. For the zillionth time in recent weeks, Old Man looked at the courageous fox with immense admiration. Mr. Fox's emerging "growback" was promising. New silky hair lined his tail. Orange hair thickened on his forehead and belly. His black leg stockings were returning. Old Man shouted with glee, "Your crew cut is not only edgy and stylish in today's world, Mr. Fox, but it is also spot-on in this humid weather. You lend the trend to all of us. Rock the fox hairdo, buddy!"

There are no comebacks in life without growbacks, Mr. Fox confirmed.

MILE MARKER 212.0
VANDERBILT TEA PARTY

Mr. Fox waited in the steady cold rain. The temperatures had dropped thirty degrees. With four pups to feed and his hunting grounds turned into a muddy quagmire, he was resigned to two things—enduring the fifty-degree rain showers and accepting a handout. No doubt the latter singed his warrior soul. Mr. Fox swallowed hard and acquiesced to the pelting rain. *His pack before his pride was his guiding principle and you need to do what needs to be done.*

Old Man poured hot chicken soup in Mr. Fox's rock bowl and beckoned Mr. Fox to warm his rain-chilled innards. Old Man signed their one-two-three-for-you-and-me mantra. Mr. Fox understood and relaxed, the indignity of begging for a meal draining from his face. "Salute to you, fox warrior. When it comes from a friend, it is not a hand-out. It is a loving gift."

Buttons looked on from a nearby patch of shrubs. Timidly, she approached, land Mr. Fox pointed to the chicken bounty with his nose, beckoning her to eat. She opted instead to kiss the old boy on the top of his rain-soaked head. She must have whispered, *get back to the den before you catch a cold.* He picked up a kit's share of the food for Be, Here, Now, and Forever and began the mile hike back to their den in Secret Garden. Lovingly, she watched him walk away, then turned and shy no longer, she locked eyes with Old Man—the look of a tired but grateful mother. In any language, the translation was true: *Hope we're no trouble. This flood has been painful. Thank you for helping us until we get back on our paws.*

Old Man fixed her a cup of meaty stew and added two quail on the side and hung his umbrella in a bush to create a rain shelter. Buttons sniffed the steam and licked her fox lips hungrily. Her stomach quivered as she thought about eating a meal for the first time in days. Buttons had a look on her face that was familiar; Old Man had seen it as a child. It is the painful recognition that the cupboard-is-bare-between-paychecks. Old Man had seen it many years ago when his single mom offered PB&J sandwiches to three hungry boys. She cut the thinly spread sandwiches into triangles, made them a cup of hot sweet tea, and told the boys that they were having a Vanderbilt tea party. It worked. To this day, Old Man still thought triangular-cut finger sandwiches were highbrow. You do what you need to do, he reminisced.

Buttons drank the steamy soup and nibbled the quail. Her hunger pangs eased, and the warm liquid elevated her spirits. She shook vigorously to release the rain from her fur and dug deep in the rock bowl to pull cherries and blueberries from the stew. The vitamin C would stave off any maladies brought on by the chilling rain. By all measures, it was a quality meal and she shared a grateful smile. *Bless you, N. Oldman, we are struggling so hard in these rainstorms. Your kindness is helping us keep enough calories on the table for the six of us to survive. When the floods subside, my mate, Mr. Fox, will be able to hunt and provide.*

"You're most welcome, Buttons. May I ask you a question? Would you and Mr. Fox be available again tomorrow? Say, ah, about 5 pm? If so, maybe we could have another Vanderbilt tea party."

She curtsied and turned to leave. *Bring Smiling Wife. Eight is the perfect number for a tea party.*

MILE MARKER 217.4
FOX TONIC

Too tired to attempt a hike after a long week in Corporate World, Old Man pulled up a folding camp chair beside the creek, unpacked his camera and binoculars, and melted into the chair's embracing comfort. Feet up on a log and a cup of organic Blue Sky root beer on ice, he assumed the exhausted corporate worker pose at 5:15 p.m. Seventy-three degrees of pure sunlight filtered through the canopy of Fox World and shouted, "Weekend!".

An animal menagerie unfolded; a pair of pileated woodpeckers drilled termites out of a log nearby. A great photograph, but not what Old Man wanted to hear after two hours in the dentist chair. Drill, drill, drill. Bluebirds came by and sang in the tree limbs overhanging the stream, their sweet tweet softening the pileated woodpecker percussion ensemble. The birds fell into rhythm. Not a bad band, guys. Cue stage left, Mr. Fox entered and assumed the position of lookout on high ground by a tree trunk. Confident the coast was clear, he summoned his clan, who had walked one mile from the Secret Garden to sunbathe in a clearing down the stream. Old Man laughed off the workday's pressure as he imagined the pups in swimsuits with flip flops on their paws.

Forever was with the clan—so tiny compared to the others. Once again, she sat alone as the other three pups played and ignored her. Sometimes, the most brutal bullying tactic is the one of exclusion. Thin twigs partially hid her angelic face, but she strained to peer through a gap in the trees and look at N. Oldman. He mouthed the words, "You are beautiful, Forever, and you are not alone." The pups kicked up sand as they wrestled, creating a rolling orange fur ball of fun. Fox World's relaxing tonic oozed into Old Man's soul—fresh squeezed, not available in stores.

Buttons and the pups retired an hour later to their alternate digs on a hill overlooking the creek. Waterfront, Old Man observed. That Mr. Fox guy goes first class. Old Man expected Mr. Fox to say goodbye too but he did not. He eyed N. Oldman's iced root beer until the inattentive human picked up on the hint and poured Mr. Fox a bone broth rocks. Hearts joyed, they adjusted their heads for a direct hit by the sun and the soothing breezes. Old Man and Mr. Fox, one trusting the other, fell into nap land and Fox World's embrace.

MILE MARKER 222.2
A FOX, A MAN, AND
A MISSING BAND

Mr. Fox and Old Man took in the beautiful summer evening—
sunny, low humidity, mid-seventies. Perfect evening for a
concert and an evening on the town, and this thought saddened him.
He had purchased tickets to a country music star's stadium concert.
Old Man liked Kenny Chesney; he was from a town near his dad's old
fishing cabin. The idea of a lazy evening of khaki shorts, flip-flops,
and a frosty beer had been on Old Man's mind the entire work week.
More than that, he owed his wife a special evening. His illness had
been an unspoken burden on her. She needed some light fun.

Human World had other plans when an eye doctor appointment
went poorly. The diagnosis was unexpected. Old Man had developed shingles on his cornea according to the eye specialist. A strong

prescription medicine and an order for eye rest crimped their concert plans. His wife unloaded the tickets online to stem the financial hurt, but her disappointment had no remedy. Old Man and his health had betrayed her again and his heart was broken. Old Man was sure that he could not repair things, but he was determined to bring some R&R to his wife's spirit.

Mr. Fox had a solution. Relaxing in the sand on the creek's beach, hind legs kicked out like a frog, the old fox telegraphed *it is Friday and I need a cold one and better yet, let's have a beach party*. It was dubbed "Mr. Fox's Plan B" and they huddled and compared notes on what Mr. Fox called *getting into the fox flow*. Call Smiling Wife and ask her to join the party. Start with a burger fry. Check. Fill the Yeti cooler with ice and Blue Sky root beer (not real beer - to be compatible with the antibiotics). Check. Kick off your shoes, wiggle your toes in the sand, find No Shoes Radio on Sirius radio, and chill, foxy, chill. Check, check, and check. By sunset, Old Man (looking pirate-like in his eye patch), Smiling Wife, Mr. Fox, and Buttons were beaching with burgers, quaffing root beer and bone broth, and dancing on the warm squishy sands of Fox Beach. No, it was not a stadium filled with fifty thousand fans singing "Beer In Mexico".

It was better. It was Root Beer In Fox World.

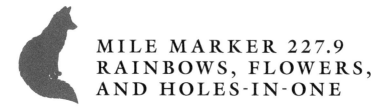

MILE MARKER 227.9
RAINBOWS, FLOWERS,
AND HOLES-IN-ONE

Old Man and his wife planned a week-long seashore vacation for June, the mid-point for the boys' five-hundred-mile walkabout. Old Man was still weak at times, so this getaway was structured as a low-key "let's get away and be thankful for our blessings" escape. Old Man visited Mr. Fox to say goodbye. The fox was not in his usual summer spot on Fox Beach. Instead, in his sitting spot, there was a golf ball and ir was a special golf ball to Old Man. He knew it when he picked it up. It was the same type of golf ball that Old Man had used to make a hole-in-one four decades ago. It was a Top-Flite—early '80s vintage, an exact match to the one in a wooden display case on a shelf in Old Man's loft office. The golf ball was aged yellow by decades in the sun and covered with fox tooth marks. The golf ball sat atop the sand like an errant shot into a pot bunker at St. Andrews. Next to the ball was a single fox paw track. It was an awesome fox gift, handed down through ten fox generations probably.

After a light rain shower, Mr. Fox circled the woods, sniffing flowers and licking water droplets from the leaves. He breathed in deep the floral fragrances of the damp forest. Sunlight patches sparked the orange in his fur, highlighting the new hair growth. As he wormed his way through the thick grass on the forest's edge, he could smell Old Man's cigar. N. Oldman must have snuck away for a walk and a talk … and a cigar. Mr. Fox smiled as he had a mischievous idea and he barked in fox language: *Fore!* He did not know what that meant but he heard humans yell it on the nearby golf course. Mr. Fox barked again as he poked his cute fox snout through the brush.

Startled, Old Man jumped two feet in the air and laughed. He loved the fox's humor and sense of mischief. Old Man thanked Mr. Fox for the golf ball gift and explained its history and significance. Mr. Fox tipped his head in rhythm with the story. He knew the story already—Old Man told good stories and repeated some of them too often, but Mr. Fox let on like he had not heard it before. Old Man was happy, and that made Mr. Fox happy.

Mr. Fox ambled on to the north side of Fox Forest and Old Man followed. Corporate World had cleared the tree canopy for a building and a parking lot there long ago. The animals in Fox World, as always, had gritted through it. Mr. Fox continued flower sniffing and fox smiling. He was at peace when he was with his human friend. When he reached the edge of the forest to the clear space near the parking lot, he looked up. Old Man's eyes followed.

The sky was mottled gray and bright blue—with gray winning. As Old Man's mother would have said when she was alive, there was just enough blue to make a Dutch boy's pants. Across the sky was a bright arc. The curve was comprised of seven colors—red, orange, yellow, green, blue, indigo, and violet. It glowed against the Dutch blue background and the breathtaking kaleidoscope bridged all worlds— Human, Fox, and Corporate. Mr. Fox and N. Oldman savored it together. "A golf ball and a rainbow, Mr. Fox? Wow, thank you!".

Mr. Fox looked down and scratched the dirt with his paw. *Aw shucks, hope you like it. The golf ball is a prompt for you to return to your love of golfing. Go golf now; you are healed. Maybe you could go to that magic golfing place in Pennsylvania that you told me about on our walks.* He turned for Fox Bridge and paused. He looked over his shoulder. It was a loving stare, one from a caring mentor.

Holes-in-one are rare, I hear guys on the nearby golf course say that. They are spectacular, never to be forgotten events, I imagine. The rainbow is uncommon too and is easily missed. Finding and enjoying the smaller things on one's walk is a purposeful choice. Those are the deep grooves, the crevices, that life lives in. Make that small choice every day, N. Oldman. The ROI, as you say in Corporate World, is infinitesimal—possibly incalculable. It is why I smell the flowers when they bloom. In a fox's life, there are only five or six seasons of colorful, fragrant blooms.

Old Man digested the lesson—enjoy the flowers while they last— and watched Mr. Fox walk west to his family. His gait might be impinged by old age, but his heart was as light and young as the pups on the horizon. "See you in a week, little buddy."

I'll be here watching rainbows, Mr. Fox responded cheerfully.

MILE MARKER 229.8
99 DEGREES AND THE
WARRIOR WAITS

After seven days of steamed blue crab dinners, evening ice cream cones, oceanside sand walks, and photographing wild ponies at Assateague Island, Old Man packed the SUV in the hotel parking lot. The heat, even in the early morning hours, had been stifling all week and he was perspiring from ten minutes of suitcase loading. His smartphone had beeped heat advisories several times for back home in Fox World. A handful of days, the heat index (i.e., "feels like") gauge registered 110 degrees back home. Old Man looked to the east and worried about his aging buddy.

Four hours later (in hotter afternoon temps), Old Man unpacked the sports utility vehicle at home. Car unloaded, beach gear stowed, and washing machine filled with laundry, Old Man tucked the terriers,

Beacon and Bounce, in their home beds after an "extra helping" meal. It was the last day of vacation, and he thought about squeezing in another blissful nap. Instead, he walked to the kitchen and packed a small Yeti cooler, a prize won in a golf tournament raffle, with ice water, chicken filet popsicles, and juicy apple cubes. He added an emergency Diet Pepsi for himself. Clad in flip flops and a wide brim hat, he began walking. When he crossed the narrower of the two branches of Fox River, he was reminded of the heat wave. The water in the shallow stream was not chilly as usual; it was lukewarm. He adjusted his eyes to the horizon to scan for Mr. Fox. It was probably too hot for him to be out and about; he was likely deeper in the shade of the forest or underground in his earth-cooled cave.

Mr. Fox was asleep on the Ireland moss mounds. He had not left his post. Even in triple digit weather, he was a loyal sentry. Old Man distributed the icy picnic goods. Mr. Fox awoke and smiled. *I waited,* his beaming face said. He drank the icy filtered water. Usually, he was ok with creek water, but he had to admit that the cold, filtered water refreshed his parched throat. His panting stopped and the heat stress subsided. He snacked on a chicken popsicle, held upright by his two black-socked paws, and licked his lips where apple juice lingered from the melting cubes. The chilled apple treats cooled his core temperatures. Refreshed by the treats and the first visit from N. Oldman in a week, he was happy, and his eyelids grew heavy. He had hunted the baking hot forest with his pups for a week and he was gut-wrenching tired. His buddy back, it was ok to rest. Mr. Fox returned to the center of the cool, green moss and flopped over, legs akimbo. Exhausted and relieved, his eyes spoke, *watch over me, N. Oldman. I am tired.*

Old Man did—until the forest cooled into the night under the full moon. Tomorrow, the second semester of their trail adventures in Fox World would commence. The old lions would be rested and well provisioned and they would need to be for the challenges ahead.

MILE MARKER 237.6
AMERICAN-MADE HERO

D awn unfurled on the Fourth of July. It was a no-traffic quiet day near the forest, but this was likely short-lived. If precedent were an indicator, an illegal cache of bottle rockets and firecrackers would interrupt in seventeen hours. For now, Old Man enjoyed a quiet morning coffee and studied the old fox reclining on the sand. For nine years, he had guided (not ruled) Fox World fairly and bravely. When he was ill, he slept on beach rocks for weeks so that he would not infect others. When a young fox was threatened by a coyote, he threw himself into the fight on the rocks. As a result, he had bled on these rocks. Beyond his tattered ears, mottled coat, hitched gait, and brave heart, his best attribute was his fox wisdom. *Steppingstones and stumbling blocks are just rocks used differently.*

Old Man felt safe with Mr. Fox on watch, not only from danger, but from the negativity of the world. The old fox projected an uncommon level of good onto an agitated world. Old Man felt privileged to be here, in an alternate dimension where the good and the kind prevailed.

The grand old fox approached the Fourth of July flag, intrigued by its vivid colors fluttering in the mild breeze. Mr. Fox quietly bowed in awe of Old Glory. Happy Independence Day, old warrior.

MILE MARKER 241.3
WHEN YOU THINK YOU
KNOW EVERYTHING

Old Man always tried hard (but was not always successfully) to maintain a modicum of self-awareness in his life. That said, like many in the Corporate World zombie state, he had ambled aimlessly and oafishly through life at times. Due to either good fortune or painful lessons, he had managed to stumble over, and absorb, one lesson of self-awareness—it is what you learn after you think you know everything that is "the really good stuff." Fox World was about to reinforce the lesson.

By late summer, Old Man and Mr. Fox had banked two hundred fifty miles. Based on his drawn map, thousands of photographs, and lots of worn shoe leather, the part-time hiker from Human-Corporate World began to feel like an expert on all things regarding Fox World.

With self-proclaimed expertness comes hubris, and Old Man fell victim to it. He boldly asserted that he knew every inch of Fox World—no, not really. He was confident that he knew all its contours and nooks and crannies like the back of his hand—no, he did not know them all. Likely, there was nothing left for the fox to teach him—yes, there was.

Mr. Fox was fidgety on this mid-July day. Restless, he had something on his mind. He kept staring east with his ears pricked. Old Man had learned to interpret this behavior; Mr. Fox wanted him to follow. Mr. Fox walked east, looking back over his shoulder, beckoning, and led Old Man to a never-before-discovered part of Fox World. How could that possibly happen? Surely, the self-titled Christopher Columbus of the forest (aka the big ego from Human-Corporate World) would have discovered it, no?

No, because the Secret Oasis had not existed before the intense summer storms. The area, and access to it, had been opened by the floods in May. The flash floods re-routed Fox Creek across a small underground spring, and the flood waters had knocked down gnarly brush and vines that covered the entrance to this secret spot. The raging flood waters had also dug sugary soft sand from the bottom of the creek bed and deposited it on the shore. Now dry, the fresh sand was bleached white by the sun and flour-powder soft to the toes. It was Tahiti-like.

The white sand beach bordered a spring-fed, crystal clear pool. The spring's waters oozed through the sandy mud, creating a permanent cool sand patch. Hmmm, so that was how the foxes were staying cool in the one-hundred-degree heat, Old Man concluded. On the beach, there were toys "borrowed" from Human World, and others found in nature—a spiky red ball, a blue jay feather. The most soul-touching sight was hundreds of little fox paw prints in the sand. And, on the creek's edge, there were six (Mr. Fox, Buttons, Be, Here, Now, and Forever) little belly scrapes, side by side, in the wet sand, their beach chairs, so to speak. This was their Secret Oasis, their hidden paradise. Old Man was as touched by this site as much as he was by the discovery of Secret Garden where the pups were born. Mr. Fox had led N. Oldman to both locations, proud of his family's home and secret hideaways. Old Man was humbled by Mr. Fox's trust and by the fox-taught lesson: *do not ever stop your journey because you think that you know it all.* Before him was Exhibit A in the airtight "Humans don't know everything" indictment. The gavel descended, and the lesson was imparted.

Mr. Fox just winked, *don't be hard on yourself, buddy, it is what you learn after you think you know everything ...*

N. Oldman finished his sentence, "... that's the really cool stuff."

MILE MARKER 249.7
STONE CRABS AND
FOX TAILS

Stone Crabs are a highly pursued, ridiculously priced delicacy found in the waters of Key West. The crab is also a Houdini of sorts in its escape capabilities to sacrifice a limb to escape predators or tight spaces. The Stone Crab was also granted one other magic evolutionary power—their lost claws grow back. When a claw is broken, the diaphragm at the body-claw joint is left intact. This allows the wound to heal quickly and regenerate a new claw with which to swim and hunt.

Mr. Fox was excited to see Old Man when he returned from a short business trip to Florida. Relaxing in the tall green grasses, he arched his head high to see N. Oldman, and followed with a little yip: *I'm over here*. Mr. Fox forded Fox River, which had been made shallow by the extended heat dome. He approached within five paces—setting a new intimacy record. His orange coat, now regenerating, was illuminated rust orange by the summer sun. His new fur spoke hope and recovery. Particularly proud of his tail, he wagged it repeatedly. No longer rope thin, it was resplendent with silky regrowth.

Old Man smiled as he looked at his friend playing in the sun. A good, warm, familiar feeling rose in his chest. Stone Crabs had won evolution's lottery—their claws grow back. Life had rewarded the faithful fox with a regeneration of another kind—a fluffy new tail. A surgeon had given Old Man life with a new steady spark.

Crab claws, fox tails, and heart sparks—all renewed.

MILE MARKER 268.0
MAYBE THE ONLY FAIR
DEAL IS IN FOX WORLD

Fairness does not exist in Human World. Any sighting of it is usually an illusion. Midsummer, Smiling Wife had planned a special date night to recapture the magic of better, healthier times. The couple departed their home with fresh smiles, caught a cab, and headed to downtown Washington, DC. Holding hands like teenagers, they ordered a special drink at their favorite haunt. They circled the baseball stadium, took once-in-a-lifetime photos, shopped for All-Star Baseball souvenirs at kiosks, and sampled food cart offerings. The evening could not have been more perfect.

Perfect ended at 6:45 p.m. At the ticket gate, the attendant informed Old Man and Smiling Wife that their All-Star game tickets were counterfeit. Hundreds of dollars gone, the date night couple was re-routed, as a favor, into a stifling standing-room-only pavilion. Sadly, the ticket-faking criminal took more than Smiling Wife's money; he robbed her heart and she cried hysterically. Date night, their first in several months due to Old Man's health, was crushed. Unable to stand and watch the game because of Old Man's limited stamina, they left the game and drove home with souvenirs that would never be taken out of the bag.

The next evening, Old Man sat with his camera in hand and a Blue Sky root beer poured over ice in a Dixie Solo cup and waited for Mr. Fox to appear. His stomach felt hollow—like something had been lost and it was never coming back. Maybe that thing was fairness; maybe it was hope that was lost. Whichever, it was gone, and he was sad.

He sipped the soft drink and told himself to stop whining. On Mr. Fox's rock plate were grass-fed beef burgers steamed medium rare. It was a bountiful offering, an attempt at giving a fair deal to one less fortunate.

The fox nibbled the first burger patty, savoring it, licking the juices. He took small bites, not ravenous wolf gulps, to make the meal last. Eat slower and you will fill up, the diet gurus say. It does not work that way in Fox World. There is but one goal: consume enough calories to survive. Three burgers left. He circled the succulent meal three times, weighing his hunger with that of his pups. He could short the pups a burger—they would never know. He looked over his shoulder to the den. He opened his jaws wide and mouthed the three burgers gently and with a nod of thanks, he jumped the log and headed faithfully to his den where the famished pups waited in a rain-soaked den.

A fair deal delivered.

In Fox World.

By Mr. Fox.

MILE MARKER 273.4
HAIL YE JULIUS CAESAR

Old Man loved two things—rainy days and sports talk radio, especially in combination. On second thought, there were three things. He also liked to debate what he heard on sports talk radio. He cherished spending a rainy or snowy afternoon in his garage, door open, ceramic heater at his feet, and listen to sports talk radio. His ever-present companion in this secret pleasure was a chipmunk named Julius Caesar. Their sports talk radio banter unearthed memories of sitting on his father's fishing cabin porch, watching it rain, smoking a Julius Caesar cigar, and debating NASCAR. His father now gone; Julius Caesar the chipmunk had stepped in. He punched way above his weight as a sports-talking little guy.

Julius Caesar enjoyed social discourse. He would come around often, sit awhile, and he and Old Man would snack and engage in mano a mano sports talk. "What's wrong with the Orioles pitching?" "How you'd like the Packers' draft choices?" "Isn't the Jim Rome Radio Show cool?"

Occasionally, they went off topic. They discussed books, music, Roman and Greek philosophy. Julius Caesar liked Ovid poetry. Old Man countered with his interest in Cicero logic. Julius was a man of art and its freedom of expression; Old Man's mind was limited by the boundaries of reason. They were a well-matched pair in their ability to complement each other.

Mostly though, they just watched it rain in silence. Julius Caesar changed Old Man's diet. He scoffed at his favorite snack, corn chips. Too much salt, he said. He preferred peanuts in the shell and sunflower seeds. Much healthier, he exclaimed. Old Man caved and switched, and he became healthier. Old Man learned to "mouth" (aka chew) his cigars, not smoke them. Julius Caesar did not like the smoke, and Old Man liked his company—so, Julius Caesar won.

The beat of the rain and the hum of the radio always serenaded them to one ending—a nap. Julius Caesar would curl in the drink bottle pocket of Old Man's golf bag. Old Man had lined it with a small golf towel to make it cozy. Old Man would cock his head back in his rocker camp chair and snore. While they slept, Smiling Wife would quietly slip into the garage and refill their water bowl, peanut trays, and Mountain Dew cooler. Old Man always awoke first and he loved to watch the tiny chest of the chipmunk rise and fall rhythmically in peaceful bliss. He was grateful for moments like this. He was thankful that the walks with Mr. Fox had awakened him to the magic teachings of animals.

Julius came by on a Sunday for one last rain nap. He looked tired and old. Old Man and he shared peanuts and listened to sports pundits discuss the Bristol Night Race. Old Man and Julius Caesar discussed the year's historic rainfall in Virginia. It was annoying, but the extra rain had a silver lining—it gave them more opportunities to gather in the garage. They swerved into heavier topics like the plight of the animals in the forest, but they eventually retreated to lighter fare discussion topics. Theirs was a relationship founded in man cave gatherings and embodied by buddy talk, so they did not try to solve the world's problems. On this rainy Sunday, they talked into the night until they were talked out. Old Man clicked off the overhead light, thumbed the on button to the plugged-in nightlight and tucked in Julius Caesar—warm and dry from the thunderstorm outside.

Next morning, Old Man discovered that Julius Caesar had passed away. He had left the golf bag during the night and climbed into Old Man's camp chair. He was curled into the fleece pullover that Old Man had left on the seat of the rocker. Old Man was sad that he had not had the chance to say goodbye to his little buddy. He imagined Julius Caesar would have bid adieu in the prose of his favorite orator, Ovid. *I grabbed a pile of dust, and holding it up, foolishly asked for as many birthdays as the grains of dust. I forgot to ask that they be years of youth.*

Old Man patted the soft fur on his head. "Hail ye, my companion, Julius Caesar, for your lessons and your wisdom. You gave so much from your little heart."

MILE MARKER 279.9
SLEEPING IN IRELAND

O ld Man unpacked a snack and his rain jacket (for insurance) and curled the jacket into a pillow atop his backpack. He stretched out on Ireland Mounds, two hundred square feet of thick cushiony "putting-green like" moss. Ireland Mounds comforted Mr. Fox's old bones every day, and the moss fit Old Man's contour like one of those ten-thousand-dollar beds that he had seen on television. He had never tried one in a store—no need to be tempted by something that you cannot afford. The moss bed was free of charge and pre-formed by his fox buddy. Good fit, exactly right.

From space, Earth is a green and blue marble, the same is true when the view is inverted. Old Man reclined on the moss like a snow angel. Looking up, Old Man saw green leaves and blue sky, Earth in reverse. The late-afternoon sun rays took him quickly. Longer naps he had taken, none better. When he awoke, the watch-over-me roles had reversed. Mr. Fox was fifteen feet away, watching over him.

The scene was fittingly symbolic and concrete in its message. Mr. Fox was the guard on duty now. Truth be known, he always had been. Old Man was the well-cast understudy to Mr. Fox the grandmaster. On this day, they were simply two sleepy souls in "Ireland" as they cocked their heads to the sun-splashed sky, eyes closed tightly, trusting each other and the universe.

MILE MARKER 289.0
WHAT WOULD CHRISTMAS
BE WITHOUT SANTA?

Santa Claus is the fattest fox in Fox World and sports a large, white-fur chest that looks like Santa's coat—hence his moniker. Santa is a prankster, a pawful at times with his jokes, stories, and adventures. He is that friend who makes you belly laugh yet annoys you because he always shows up late or knocks on your den door unexpectedly at odd hours. He is an accomplished photobomber. He is frenetic, unorganized, and has no savings. Money comes in, and out it goes to adventure. He is a traveling man—often disappearing on unannounced road trips. Santa Claus is loved by all of Fox World. Put simply, Santa Claus has the "it" factor. And he is Mr. Fox's best friend.

Months earlier, when Mr. Fox was ill, Santa Claus would tease the old fox him and induce Mr. Fox to chase him daily. Old Man watched this spectacle in the winter months, and he concluded that Santa Claus knew Mr. Fox was sick and he needed the exercise to improve his stamina. In essence, Santa Claus became Mr. Fox's "personal trainer" and took delight in the job.

Mr. Fox was pacing back and forth when Old Man arrived for their daily walk. N. Oldman picked up on the *follow-me-look* immediately and Mr. Fox led him to a fox lying sick in a well shaded, secluded part of the woods. The fox was rail thin. It was Santa Claus. He was a shadow of his former rotund, jolly self. His ailment was evident; he was in the advanced stages of sarcoptic mange. Santa Claus never broke character as he employed comedy to cover his fear. *I'm ok. Just had some bad sushi. Couple of cheeseburgers and I will be up and back on the road.*

Mr. Fox and N. Oldman exchanged a knowing glance. Their buddy was gut shot with sickness. Possibly fatal. They divided duties—N. Oldman would fetch groceries and medicine; Mr. Fox would stand guard. Old Man returned an hour later with the magic mange potion and a bevy of clean organic calories to stabilize Santa Claus. The jolly fox ate heartily and thanked his human and canine friends and retired to bed, but not before sharing a couple of good jokes that he had heard while on the road. Despite his current father duties, Mr. Fox stood valiantly by Santa Claus throughout the night. Heavy weighs the crown of the king of the forest.

MILE MARKER 292.9
DEFEATING AGONY

Old Man again read internet research articles on sarcoptic mange for the second time in five months. He digested the hard facts which the articles shared. Imagine the most irritating itch ever and double the estimate. This is the agony of a fox with sarcoptic mange. The fox is too distracted to hunt or to sleep. Hunger and fatigue set in. The body's defenses are overrun, and the end begins. Old Man remembered these reading disease descriptions and admonitions and how they had scared him months before. Fold up to the fear or face it head on. No choice really—time to go to work.

Old Man knew it was possible, if all went well, to move his recovery out of the red zone within ten days. Two or three healing broths would stop the mites cold. With Santa's noticeable weight loss, clean organic calories were urgent, and he consumed plenty—quail, quail eggs, meat broth, chicken livers, boneless chicken thighs, bison meatballs, venison, elk, canned cat food, salmon, berries and manuka honey.

After meds and calories, sleep was the next healing balm. Mr. Fox watched over Santa Claus as he napped soundly for three hours each afternoon. Old Man had never seen a fox sleep this long in early afternoon. There was but one reason, and it is a magic healing ingredient called a friend. There is no better medicine in life than a best friend. Old Man watched as Santa Claus and Mr. Fox gekkered about life, their forest, moon rises, sunsets, and the good things to come. Old Man imagined there was no mention of illness, tragedy, or despair, as the noble Mr. Fox liked to drive on the high road of positivity. Old

Man did not speak gekker, but he was sure that Mr. Fox said, *I got your back, buddy. Get some rest.*

Santa drifted off to fox dreamland and, for a few hours, the agony subsided.

MILE MARKER 296.8
THE POWER OF A
FOX BUDDY

Old Man searched for Mr. Fox and his buddy, Santa Claus, and found them near the emerald-green Ireland moss mounds. There, the Christmas in August miracle was unfolding. Old Man hid and watched them silently. Mr. Fox and Santa Claus were now insepa-rable. Mr. Fox fed him mouth to mouth. He even shooed away the pups so Santa Claus could eat in peace. He sat near—always on guard. They exchanged yip barks and the occasional fox smile.

Buttons looked on from afar—with loving concern on her face. *Food and medicine will do what they can do. Angels and friends will do the rest*, she smiled.

Old Man's eyeball estimate was that Santa had lost thirty-five to forty percent of his body weight. He was now stabilizing and gaining back his Santa bulk. The high nutrient diet would continue for three to four more weeks. Old Man added kitten kibble, a source of beneficial taurine.

Old Man noted two positives. Santa's body was no longer hunched. Hunching is a sign of mange distress. Encouragingly, there was a glimpse of Santa's goofiness as he played with the pups and told them stories. The pups loved Santa's adventures and his big, good heart.

Santa interacted with Forever a lot when she sat alone; he walked close to her and barked softly. She looked at him as if to say, *are you talking to me? No one talks to me*. Santa smiled. *Yes, I will happily talk with you, Forever, but I am also here to listen to you*. Forever beamed. She had a friend, a friend who would listen to a lonely pup.

MILE MARKER 306.6
MR. FOX HAS A SURPRISE

Always believe in something with the quantum power of belief that a child has—full time, all heart in; not like an adult, who wedges fifteen minutes of believing in something halfheartedly between two errands in a packed day. Believing strongly with pure intentions is important to enjoying life. This was Mr. Fox's trail lesson on this day.

On the last day of August, Old Man and Smiling Wife returned to Fox World from Charleston, South Carolina. The trip was a nice mental break after months of hospital lobbies and waiting rooms. The week had passed swiftly with low-country boil dinners, putt-putt golf, seashell hunting with Bounce, and watching Beacon on his doggy surfboard. Hastened home by a molar abscess that needed an endodontist's attention, they passed the five hundred fifty miles north with college football season previews on sports talk radio and two stops for Carolina barbeque. One stop included banana pudding, and it was a righteous sugar experience. Beacon and Bounce licked the whipped cream topping from the plastic bowl and issued a four-paws up rating on PawGram.

Old Man and Smiling Wife did not speak about Santa Claus in the car—they worried silently. What would they find in Fox World? They had left one last dose of medicine for him a week ago. Did he get it? Did he take it? Did it help? Was it too late? There was a heat wave in Washington, DC—did the harsh meds and the heat hurt his stomach and do harm?

Back in Virginia, Old Man felt miserable with his swollen jaw, but he wanted to see Mr. Fox and check on Santa. So, he popped some pain relievers for his molar ache and headed into the forest. Mind racing, tooth throbbing, and scary storm clouds bunching in the dimming light, Old Man's belief that Santa was ok weakened with every step he took in the forest. No foxes came. The forest was still. Like a church on a Tuesday morning kind of still.

Whistle, whistle, whistle. No one. No answer. Had they walked up Fox Hill to safety with a flash flood warning blinking on the radar? Or worse, had Mr. Fox moved on? Had he and Santa given up because they stopped believing? Rolling thunder brought Old Man's mind to a creased focus. Danger coming, time to go. He placed the food bundle on high ground and turned. The incoming storm breezes picked up, but not quite enough yet to cover the sound, a yip. The human turned. There was Mr. Fox, standing tall, grinning, and believing.

Another little yip followed, and Santa Claus appeared, looking vibrant and healthy. His tail fur had noticeable gains and his weight was stable. Mr. Fox had obviously found and shared the farm egg caches that N. Oldman had placed around the woods before leaving for Charleston. Santa Claus was alive, a true Christmas miracle on the last day of August. Both foxes had an eye on the rapidly approaching cloudburst, but they wanted to say thanks—danger be damned (for a minute). Mr. Fox nudged Santa and the jolly fox tipped his invisible Santa hat—*thank you, N. Oldman, and merry Christmas (early)*. They grasped a big mouthful of chicken thighs—and in a flash, like Donner and Blitzen, they leaped Fox Creek and ran in tandem up Fox Hill as the thunder clapped.

Before going over the horizon, Mr. Fox turned. His look spoke paragraphs. *Two things were always coming back—his tail and you, because I believed. Do not ever stop believing, N. Oldman. It is our only currency in Fox World.*

MILE MARKER 312.7
ROAR

On a sunny Saturday afternoon in early September, Mr. Fox appeared, centered himself in a sun beam, and howled. It was a long howl, so authentic and graceful in its happiness that it filled every heart in the forest. The sun, reflecting fiery orange off his ancient head, backlit this courageous animal. First impression—this was a victory howl. But no, the modest Mr. Fox would not boast; it was not his style. But the howl when translated was existential in form—*I lived, and I live*. Roar, old lion, roar.

Around the perimeter of Fox World, one by one, little orange noses peeked around trees, over logs—a mate, four offspring, and a best buddy. Seven foxes (and a human) looked at the gentle king and replied, *you lived, and thus, we live*.

MILE MARKER 328.4
THE NEXT BEST THING

Old Man was soaked in perspiration when he reached Fox World. The heat index had been 105+ degrees for four days in mid-September. He found a stump seat in the shade and opened an ice water.

Fox World's animals are wild and only enjoy peace and prosperity when humans stay at a distance and Old Man respected that unequivocally. The wild must remain wild. And even though the barrier that separates human and wild animal is sometimes razor thin, it is impermeable under the principle of "do what's best for them and not what your heart longs to do." When an animal and a human bond on rare occasion, the rules hurt. Old Man knew this all too well. He would never be able to touch his fox buddy or pat his head or shake his paw or give him a warm hug. They had walked three hundred miles, survived every imaginable calamity, and known indescribable amounts of joy and adventure. Yet, they would never touch.

All that said, Old Man still had questions. What did Mr. Fox's coat feel like? Was it downy soft like a cat? Or was it coarse like a rough-coat terrier? Old Man was resigned to never knowing; it was part of a relationship with a wild animal. They were not a pet; they could not be petted.

Mr. Fox read his buddy's thoughts and approached a log near N. Oldman's stump perch in the shade by the sandy beach. He took a long draw on the proffered ice water. *Aaaaahh, that was good, N. Oldman – thank you.* Mr. Fox began rubbing his shoulder and flank against the bark. Back and forth. Up and down. Smooth strokes, then some vigorous scraping. Small clouds of fox fur caught the breeze and floated like fox bubbles to the grass nearby. Old Man smiled as he watched the weightless fluffs float in the summer air. No doubt the shedding brought relief to Mr. Fox in the sweltering weather. Months ago, his hair had fallen out due to illness. His coat was thick now—too thick for the sweltering late summer weather. The floating fur clouds were a sign of life—his armor was back.

Old Man walked to the "barber shop." He touched the thick clump of hair on the moss. It was not wiry or coarse—it was the opposite. It was softer than high thread-count Egyptian cotton. Aha, so patting Mr. Fox on the back would feel like this. His fur had hues of fresh cream, burnt sienna, smoke gray, sunset orange, and tumbleweed. Old Man gathered some to put in his fox keepsake box at home. It was filled with gifts from Mr. Fox—golf balls, sunglasses, cash, hawk feathers, a cigar lighter.

Across Fox River, Mr. Fox looked on. *Thank you for helping me get my coat back,* he telegraphed. *Now it is yours,* he nodded. He sipped a second drink from the ice water bowl. Then he turned, freshly coiffed, to Foxville to see what fun a spiffy-looking old fox might get into on a late summer evening.

MILE MARKER 333.1
POLLUTION CRISIS

As good as the forest walks were, the year had been a murderer's row of ills—injury, freezing cold, sweltering summer heat, flood conditions, poachers, partial loss of the forest's tree canopy. Cornered on the ropes, punch after punch found their mark and now this.

It was cool and sunny in Fox World in September. Mr. Fox was happy to see N. Oldman when he arrived for their walk. He shuffled his paws with glee and wagged his tail incessantly. Old Man's five-day stint in Corporate World was paused for the weekend. Old Man believed in doling out a full day's work for the paystub. His employer had been good to him, so it was late on Friday when he arrived in Fox World. He and Mr. Fox walked and talked. *Are you ok? How was your week? Are you feeling well?* Easy questions were exchanged as they walked and snacked.

Fire trucks sped past them in the paved parking lots adjacent to Fox World. Firefighters disembarked from the large red trucks and raced into the forest. Old Man looked for fire; there was none. Mr. Fox sniffed the air, he detected a bad smell, but it was not a forest fire. Frightened by the sirens and red bubble lights, he scurried deep into the forest. Old Man walked forward to investigate. As he approached Fox River, the problem was apparent, and it sickened him. The stream was a bowl of thick white cream. The spill had spread quickly to Fox Beach, Mr. Fox's favorite drinking area near a freshwater spring. Gallons and gallons of a milky white substance were pouring into Fox River from a parking lot culvert, the firefighters said. They worked efficiently to place pollution control netting in the stream. They were good at what they did, but it was like a small Band-Aid patch on an arterial wound. The thick, gelatinous substance bled out into Mr. Fox's precious stream.

Old Man shouted to Mr. Fox, "Don't cross the stream—even on Fox Bridge; it is dangerous!"

Mr. Fox circled. He paced furiously on the moss mounds in Fox World. He went from joyous to confused. Bewildered that his human would shout at him, he sensed danger. What had humans done to his pristine forest now? Old Man had no answers, and he certainly offered no excuses for his species. He and Mr. Fox would have to lead the animals to the other stream near Foxville and hope for the best. The water there was from a separate source. Mr. Fox talked to his clan. Old Man picked up a word or two of fox here and there, but he could not translate the message. But the stare was immediately decipherable. *You are our friend, and we care for you, but why do other humans hurt us?*

MILE MARKER 337.2
LIVE LONG AND
PROSPER, CAPTAIN

Old Man sat with Mr. Fox on a Thursday evening. He was leaving on a three-day, six-hundred-mile trip to rescue an elderly shelter dog and he told Mr. Fox about it as he munched bison burgers. Food sources were low in Fox World during the rainiest year on historical record. Old Man helped with occasional supplements, but he was cautious to not create dependency. Wild animals deserved the freedom of being wild. Old Man strongly believed that. Similarly, humans should not destroy wildlife habitat, Old Man thought; he had seen the hardship and consequences.

Old Man said goodbye and promised to bring the shelter dog for a visit to Fox World in three days. Ears pricked; Mr. Fox studied Old

Man closely. Then he did an odd thing. He waved with his back paw in a manner that looked like a Spock hand greeting on *Star Trek*. Old Man laughed—was that real or did he just imagine that? Or did the old warrior just bless the upcoming dog rescue trip with Vulcan energy? Mr. Fox continued to poke fun, *live long, and prosper, Captain; go where no one has gone before.*

Scotty, beam up Mr. Fox; he is too good (and funny) for this planet.

MILE MARKER 340.0
THE SCENT OF AN OLD
MAN AND AN AGING FOX

In the 1992, Al Pacino won the Academy Award for best actor in the movie *Scent of a Woman,* and many think that his poignant six-minute soliloquy about integrity and courage locked down the Oscar. At the crossroads in life, he said, we almost always know the right path, but often we do not take it because it is too darn hard. Old Man agreed. As stressed-out mortals, people often opt out of hard and settle on easy, and these opt-outs cast our destiny.

Old Man did not like the easy way. And it did not matter if he was fond of it or not, the easy way had never come and found him. When he had a tough or perplexing challenge, he did the same thing that he did when he was a young boy—he walked, and he walked a long time and a long way. Walking chased tough problems or decisions through the mind's mental mazes until the best possible answer came. Walking was the only mental coping tool he had.

Now he walked and talked in tandem with an old fox, and together, they lightened up the burdensome overthinking process by playing games. Mr. Fox enjoyed a game called "Touch." Old Man would place his palm on a tree trunk about eighteen inches off the ground and press it into the bark for ten seconds or so. Mr. Fox would follow and place his nose on the bark and sniff. He would scratch the bark with his front paw and sniff again. He would look at N. Oldman, sniff again, and smile. His engaging smile and soulful gaze delivered an unambiguous cipher: *Choose the right path, mark it for me, and I promise that you will never walk alone.* Old Man moved to the next tree, repeated the game, and responded, "Mr. Fox, the hard and right path is always an easy walk with you. Hoo-hah!"

MILE MARKER 344.4
GOOD BYE TO
CORPORATE WORLD

Old Man and Mr. Fox had been walking nine months when the call came, the telephone call that would unite them permanently. Old Man, as an executive, had made this type of call many times in his career and he was always saddened by making "the call." Old Man always thought of the person's children as he dialed the employee's phone number. Tonight, they would have to say at the family dinner table that Dad or Mom had lost their job. "No one wanted them anymore" being the sorrow-filled translation in the stunning dining room table quiet that followed. It was Old Man's turn; now he was the target.

The four-part process begins with "setting the bowling pins." The employer must make sure the employee is on notice that a phone call is coming. There is a set-up email or pre-call: "Hey, are you by your phone and laptop for a few minutes at 4:00 p.m.?" The second part of the process is "knocking down the bowling pins quickly with one roll." Words are formal and direct—e.g., your position has been eliminated. Thirdly, the hand-off occurs. There is an email notification chime on the laptop. The arrival of the email is synchronized with the rote phrase: "If you will open the email you received, HR will explain the executive package severance terms." Stage four in the process is numbness. A cherished job, and likely a career, are gone. It is like the girlfriend that you love dearly inviting you to coffee, and you arrive joyfully with red roses. Two minutes later, you never see them again. That kind of numbness.

Old Man had taken the call on a landline, affording clear audio to hear and write down the details. He listened and made notes for thirty seconds. The call ended with a perfunctory "wish you the best," and with that, a thirty-five-year career went poof. Old Man was too old, or maybe he was just too tired from his heart battle, to ask if there was another job he might fill. He printed and signed the release papers for his retirement. He would miss the excellent company that he worked for, the talented colleagues, and Corporate World. It had been a wonderful journey with incredibly pleasant people. He stared at the cold hard truth on the screen. He would be unemployed in a few months. Gone were friends and colleagues of decades. He was alone, very alone.

He did not tell his wife immediately, instead, Old Man grabbed his dash bag from the hook in the garage and walked out the door into Fox World. Mr. Fox would know what to do. He is wise, Old Man thought, he will have advice. Old Man did not really believe that. He was a sharp, focused business executive; there was not much a wild animal could offer an adult human at this point and he felt silly. Maybe it was time to let go of this silly fox stuff. Leave Fox World, find another job, and go back to normalcy.

But Old Man felt like running (defined more as a brisk walk with his health conditions), and Fox World was the only safe place he knew at this moment. So, he ran, and ran, and ran to find Mr. Fox, passing miles of autumn-tinged trees, white ripples of bubbly brooks, treetop bird calls, and bountiful serenity. Heart palpitations halted him. The galloping horses roared as his stress level red lined. "Take me," he shouted. "Darn weak heart, finish the job, I have had enough!"

The desperate ex-executive sat and pulled a bottle of water and emergency heart meds from the green backpack. The horses were galloping faster. Decision time. Take the meds or take his chances with the stallions. He cocked his arm to throw the meds in the creek. A stalwart image appeared in his peripheral vision, and it stopped Old Man cold. Mr. Fox was sitting on four-foot-high stump thirty feet away, his fire-orange fur catching the yellow shafts of sunlight descending through the trees. Mr. Fox turned his triangular-shaped head, eyes piercing Old Man.

Old Man returned a deep, examining look. The fox was nearly a decade old and had outlived his wild fox peers. He lived in a den with a cold dirt floor and hunted around the clock on diminishing lands to put food on his pups' table. He drank from a stream that an auto body shop had poisoned with paint and navigated floods from Virginia's rainiest year on record. Disease and enemies struck with no warning. Yet, Mr. Fox was steady in facing an unsteady and uncertain future. His bravery was admired by others but never acknowledged by him. *All in a fox's day*, he would say. Mr. Fox had no ego; he was a servant to others. Old Man had come to the forest to tell Mr. Fox how unfair the world was. What he saw before him was true inequity in fairness—an old fox with a hard life. Old Man swallowed his pettiness. He had no problems, at least not any of the magnitude of Mr. Fox's. With the next swallow, the emergency heart meds were consumed. The relief came instantly, the stallions slowed. Old Man took a long pull on the icy water and tossed Mr. Fox some protein biscuits. Munching on them, Mr. Fox gave N. Oldman a stern *don't-ever-scare-me-like-that-again-look*.

"Understood," Old Man apologized.

Mr. Fox surveyed the thick-treed forest with 180-degree neck turns to the left and to the right. Mr. Fox repeated the sweep, left and then right to doublecheck if he and Old Man were truly alone. Satisfied, he gave Old Man a *watch this* look. He raised his fox snout to the sky and sucked in two lungs' full of autumn forest air. When he exhaled, he let out a shrill, air-cutting squall. It echoed off the hard oaks but the softness of the holly and the pine, which ringed the forest, contained the sound in Fox World. In short, no one in Human World or Corporate World heard the guttural scream, but it was a clarion call to those lucky enough to be in the center of Fox World.

Mr. Fox gave him a second look— *I'm only going to show you one more time.* He followed with a longer, deeper, louder squall from atop the stump. The twelve-pound fox looked like a rare red wolf in full howl atop a hillside overlooking the prairie. Mr. Fox's howl resonated with something long lost inside Old Man—unexpressed pain.

When Mr. Fox tilted his nose skyward the third time, Old Man felt the pending cathartic purge well up inside him. On cue, he bellowed in unison with Mr. Fox. The air-piercing notes ranged in scale from hurt to angry to liberating to grateful to satiated. The primal scream dislodged and discarded three decades of Corporate World maladies and misgivings. He was free. No more one hundred hotel nights a year on the road existence. No more 6:00 a.m. flights. No more booth-jockey duty at trade shows on cement floors and threadbare carpet.

Old Man was thankful to the company in Corporate World that had provided bread for his table. He would forever miss his colleagues' intellect, creative problem-solving, abundant ideas for work-life balance, and smiles. When the last echoes of the fox/man cry ricocheted back, Old Man felt freedom of a magnitude and completeness he had never known. He was free. He was free AF (as a fox).

Mr. Fox smiled. *You may have been kicked out of the corporate jungle, but you are always welcome in our forest, N. Oldman.* The rejuvenated ex-executive looked over his shoulder to the tall office buildings of Corporate World and waved farewell with a tear in the corner of his eye; then he and Mr. Fox matched cadence and walked deeper into Fox World ... deeper and deeper ... until they disappeared.

MILE MARKER 346.1
FOX ARTHRITIS CURE

O ctober brought a light-switch weather event from scalding hot days to surprisingly chilly mornings, the official beginning of bone-broth season. Right on cue, Mr. Fox appeared to warm his snout in a piping hot bowl. The old boy was walking well, although his gait remained stiff with arthritis in his shoulder. The day's barometric pressure undoubtedly brought twinging pain. After the broth, he browsed a patch of flowered plants. He looked at Old Man, sniffed the pink and yellow flowers, and looked back again. *Pay attention, Old Man,* his eyes said.

Noted, Old Man acknowledged. He snapped pictures of the plants and ran them through a plant identification app. Oriental Lady's Thumb (pink) and Wreath Goldenrod (yellow) share a common property. When dried, the seed pods can be made into a tea and internet searches revealed that the tea soothes rheumatoid arthritis—allegedly.

Old Man picked the wildflowers and hung them to dry in his kitchen. Fox World's first pharmacy was officially open. Thank you, Dr. Fox.

MILE MARKER 350.5
1-2-3 FOR YOU & ME

It is unclear who started it.

Was it Mr. Fox with his unique back paw wave? Or was it Old Man who would thump the German-made pacemaker in his chest three times, say, "One-two-three," point at Mr. Fox, and finish with "for you and me"? 1-2-3 For You and Me! Whatever the origin, it always made the old lions feel better to do it. It was their fox/man secret code on the trail, and it warmed Mr. Fox's heart every time he saw N. Oldman do it.

MILE MARKER 359.5
ADORABLE UNDERFOX

The origin of the term underdog is quite literal and a bit barbaric. The underdog is a dog beaten in a fight. Conversely, the likely or actual winner is called the top dog. Later, the term "underdog" evolved to describe an entity that wins through luck, hidden strength, or concealed wisdom.

The longer the odds, the more of the emotional pull for Old Man. Maybe it was a character flaw—worry a bunch and invest a lot with no initial success or results and rationalize it as "belief." These days, Old Man laughed at his flaws (character or otherwise), a kindness he had not extended to himself often in life. Mr. Fox and his peaceful world had taught N. Oldman that life is cleaner, easier, and lighter when one laughs at their mistakes.

In the vulpes world, "Forever" would be the underdog—aka the "underfox." She was the smallest (by both height and weight) of the four fox pups. The other three fox pups treated her brusquely, chasing her away from food, and excluding her from fox games. Often, she was seen playing alone with human-provided fox toys or chasing butterflies. In her forced exile, she developed hidden strengths, ones that would make her a top dog someday.

Forever approached Old Man with a curious inquiry. *Will you be my friend?* Why was she not afraid? Possibly she thought that she was living on bonus time anyway, so why not take a chance? *Just trust. Timidity is a self-imposed death sentence in nature,* she had calculated. *Just trust.* With any underfox or underdog, the smallest is often the boldest and the toughest. Forever embraced both—with a smidge of hope sprinkled in.

Old Man grinned. Sounds like "belief."

MILE MARKER 366.7
"HERE" AND "NOW" ARE
HERE NOW ... AGAIN

Much joy filled Fox World on this afternoon. Here and Now, Mr. Fox's sons, were a rare sighting, so much so, that Old Man was not sure who they were at first look. There were two giveaways—the brothers are identical in physical appearance (like twins) and they are still inseparable, when one moved, the other matched the maneuver exactly. Here and Now moved through the forest with the fluidity an Olympic synchronized swimming team or a school of fish swimming in the sea. They played, napped, and cuddled as a chilly wind's nip ruffled their russet fur. Curious about the human with the camera, they bravely approached to the sound of Old Man's newly purchased fox whistle. The eight-month-old duo settled onto their soft green moss seats, turned their heads southwest, and watched the last glow of winter's setting sun. Buttons, their daily guardian now tucked them in with a squirrel snack. Across the forest, Mr. Fox did the same with the two girls.

Be, here, now, and forever in Fox World.

MILE MARKER 377.8
FOX WORLD IS AN
ORANGE STATE

Old Man eschewed politics. Spirited debate was once how people shared, learned, and grew. Today, political debate was a gateway to ad hominem attacks. So when politics surfaced, Old Man just clammed up, no one cared what an old man had to say anyway.

Election Day votes counted, people then fall into camps of either tepid dissonance or flame-throwing arguments. Math in, humans assess—do they live in a Red State or a Blue One? Or are the states' politics so intertwined that the state is a so-called Purple State? It was not a point of sufficient consternation for Old Man to ponder and thus, he did not waste energy on it. With that dismissive thought on politics, Old Man walked into the neutral, Switzerland-like Fox World, a politically agnostic Orange State. No mix of red or blue, Fox World was just orange—plain old orange like foxes!

Fox World is politics free. Its state flag is an hourglass with no sand in it and it reads: "Be Here Now." The state motto is: "If You're Alive, You've Won." It is a borderless country, llno need for them because humans would not respect animal boundaries anyway. The Orange State of Fox World has no Constitution, but if it did, the Articles would state:

1. Foxes share so that all can survive.
2. Foxes start no fights but reluctantly finish any fight that others bring.
3. Foxes forgive and have no long-term enemies.
4. Foxes listen quietly—for no fox ever learned much with his yap open.
5. Foxes pay no taxes; life is taxing enough.
6. Fox World has no exports other than cuteness and wisdom. Most humans never partake of these exports.
7. Foxes love unconditionally.
8. Fox World has no elections; leadership is a shared responsibility.

Old Man scanned the eight Articles that he had written on a brown paper lunch bag from his backpack. Oil spots had leaked from the wax paper-wrapped chicken salad sandwich in the bag but fortunately did not obscure the Constitution of Fox World. The document had multiple honorable cosignatories—Mr. Fox, Buttons, Be, Here, Now, Forever, Santa Claus, Favre, Bucky, Deja Blue, Colonel Hawk, Professor Owl, Russell Raccoon, and Julius Caesar (in memoriam). All were respected ambassadors of Fox World who stood for peace, patience, and fairness. "On second thought, maybe I am political," mused Old Man. "I plan to vote for the Orange State of Fox World in the next election."

MILE MARKER 383.6
ALL YOUR EGGS IN
ONE ONLINE BASKET

In the early '90s, about fifty paces from Fox World, one of the world's largest internet companies opened (or logged on) for business. Yep, right across from Fox Forest. The building is still there; the internet giant is not.

Old Man was on the verge of going stir crazy after three days in the house. His long overdue elective foot surgery was healing poorly, preventing his daily fox walks. He drove to the internet company's car park, rolled into a space in the empty lot, and limped to the edge of the forest. He lit a Cuban cigar, thinking fondly of his friend, Art, who had sent him the box of cigars from Florida. He missed Art, a man of magnanimous generosity and a gentle soul. They had been Corporate World warriors for three decades and walked the links of St. Andrews for a decade.

He did not expect to see Mr. Fox. Construction equipment in the east end of the forest had rattled the fox skulk, and they had moved deep into the forest. Old Man planned to find out more about the construction company's plans when his foot healed and he could walk to the construction site. The wind chill did its best to discourage ill-advised walking (aka limping). Who would be out on a stinging cold day like this?

Two old fools—apparently.

One in a surgical boot, the other nestled in a leaf bed under a holly tree. Separated for a few days, there was catching up to do—over coffee and bone broth, of course. Old Man walked back to the SUV and withdrew two insulated carafes—one coffee, one bone broth. This was not a coffee klatch; no enlightened social discourse ensued. Instead, it was just two old guys chewing snacks, slurping beverages, and grunting half sentences. Old Man caught him up on the Packers' chances for the playoffs. Mr. Fox replied that he had a new home in a hollow log. *Mr. Fox's Log Cabin*, he laughed. The rest was comfortable, buddy-style silence. Sometimes the need to say nothing says a lot. N. Oldman nodded it was time to go. Dark was dropping. "Did you get enough to eat?"

I'm just pleased to have your company. The food wasn't necessary, he replied with a warm fox smile.

Old Man left an extra boiled egg. Midnight snack, he winked. Mr. Fox nodded thanks and mouthed the egg. He trotted across the empty parking lot and up the sidewalk to the front door of the internet giant's building. Old Man pondered where he was going, so he wheeled the SUV around and pointed the headlights at the sidewalk. There was Mr. Fox near the door under a boxwood bush, which had collected a mound of leaves from the blowing wind. He was half buried in the leaf pile with his thick tail curled around his face. Nearby, steam exuded from a heater vent. The boiled egg was under his tummy where it would stay warm. He opened one eye and winked a silent message—*I'm ok, I am full, and I am toasty. Now go home and take care of that paw. Time for you to be a human being, not a human doing.*

As Old Man sat at the traffic light, left turn signal blinking, a cold reality chilled him far greater than the premature winter burst. Fox World, Human World, and Corporate World were colliding ever faster. The lone sentinel for hope was hunkered down in a bush on a teeth-rattling cold night outside a building where the Internet Age had been launched. Was it the sad vicissitudes of progress or acid reflux from strong coffee that formed a lump in Old Man's throat? Thumbing two antacids out of a foil, he knew the answer.

And there was no pill for it.

MILE MARKER 389.1
LONELINESS IS
NOT FOREVER

The fox family had scattered, as nature and season would have it. Nature is relentlessly rhythmic in its phases—winter birth, mom's nurturing in the den, frolicking in spring's sunshine, summertime play in the flowered fields, hone hunting skills in autumn, and then the harsh survival challenges of winter. Independence, craved as a teenage pup, is accompanied now by the realization that you are all on your own, little fox.

Mating season in January is a light-switch event. The calendar flips, and the new is in and the old is out, as Mr. Fox and Buttons would focus then on the next generation of Fox World. The couple would be busy with chores soon—new dens needed to be dug, old dens needed new escape hatches, encroaching threats needed to be scoped and assessed. Mr. Fox was so dawn-to-dusk busy that he needed a yellow construction helmet and a miner's lantern. What the storms and humans had taken, he must replace. He took stock; less available real estate in Fox World meant he must add more fox sweat equity to maintain stasis. He ignored his raw paws and arthritis pain and went back to digging.

The pups, once anxious for independence, had a revelation. Being on your own is not all it is cooked up to be. Parents will not bring food; they would have to forage alone in the bare winter forest now. And then there was the matter of lodging. They searched for an apartment in an abandoned log, hoping they could find one not taken, and even if it was available, the teenager's den would not be lined with fur-shed and scraps of cloth like Buttons' den had been. At nine months old, it was a spartan start to a life that textbooks state will last only five years.

On this Friday afternoon, Forever was alone in the middle of the forest. It was sunny but very cold. She felt the wind's chill, and loneliness added an extra chill. Forever agreed, the last week or two had been a light-switch event, and she was startled by the harshness. Every human heart has experienced the same, Old Man admitted, and watching the lonely young fox hurt his heart. Old Man felt the urge to call to her but was certain it would not work. He whistled. Her ears perked, her head turned, and her hope rose. She decided to be bold. She stirred with a downward dog stretch followed by upward facing dog. She approached. Thirty feet. Twenty feet. She paused at ten. She made three circles, corkscrewing down onto the moss. She made a chin pillow with her fluffy tail. Her look was certain and purposeful in its message: *Tell me a good story, Mr. Oldman. Today, I choose not to be alone.*

MILE MARKER 395.7
HAY BALE STRESS TEST

Virginia broke the historical annual rainfall record—forty-six days before year end. Old Man stood under his colorful Arnold Palmer umbrella and watched it rain. Three more inches of rain fell through the chilled "feels like thirty-nine degrees" atmosphere and delivered another battering deluge to Fox World. The foxes executed their survival checklist. Brace the fort. Gather supplies. Do lots of hard work in the cold and the rain.

After diligently consuming his bison and blueberries, Mr. Fox gathered the additional food cache of steamed chicken thighs in his mouth and began the long trek to high ground in Foxville. How many times he had hiked hurriedly to high ground in the past year, he could not remember. It was a long walk with a heavy load, but his fox radar told him fierce storm cells were coming. Onward. He looked right to his old den location on Fox Hill. It was, once upon a time, a safe dry spot, he remembered. Then a family had a child, and that child needed a swing set and jungle gym. So, Fox Hill was flattened by a bulldozer.

He kept walking, tiny feet gripping the mud, one paw in front of another. He felt his age and, deep down, the ceiling of his limitations. He was an old fox, an incredibly old fox. He stopped for a breather and dropped the meat to give his aching jaws a break. The trip to Foxville seemed longer and longer each time, but he was thankful for the provisions. The cagy fox had a plan. He called it the "help the kids without their knowledge" plan – like a father putting a secret five-dollar bill in a kid's school backpack for ice cream. The recently out-on-their-own fox pups would appreciate the nutritious meat—but they would not know that it was delivered by "fox father express". He knew their hideouts; a father always does. Furtively, father fox dropped meat parcels near the kids' log condos. He winked at Buttons—*remember, our lips are sealed.*

A father's good deeds achieved; Mr. Fox turned west to see the sun. There was no visible setting sun on this bleak day; instinct made him do it anyway. A hidden wavelength of solar energy broke through the dense clouds and charged his fox soul battery. He saw something else on the horizon and climbed on top of a log for a better look. Down the path was N. Oldman—huffing and puffing up Fox Trail with a bale of hay on his right shoulder. His cardiologist would frown on this. Mr. Fox grinned respect at the foolish Old Man. His best friend was delivering haybed hay by human express. Mr. Fox engaged fox four-paw drive and rushed to greet him. *Thank you, N. Oldman. You're nuts, but Fox World loves you.* Old Man freshened Mr. Fox and Button's haybed and, via specific compass headings, Mr. Fox directed Old Man to four haybed construction sites. On each, Old Man crafted a warm lair. The observant human noted the chicken cache near each pup's hollow log. Old Man shot Mr. Fox a "thought that the kids moved out on their own" look. *I said that they moved out of the house, not out of the neighborhood. I admit it, I am an old softie.* With that, Mr. Fox took up position behind Old Man as the human hiked a mile or so back to his "haybed." N. Oldman was one of them now, and the old softie was not going to let the human walk home alone.

MILE MARKER 399.0
SANTA CLAUS IS
KEEPING A LIST

"He is making a list and he is checking it twice; going to find out who is been naughty or nice."

Fox World was bright, sunny, and filled with animals on this winter day. An old friend, healed from illness, popped up—literally—to say hi today. Santa Claus decided to photobomb Mr. Fox's Thanksgiving portrait (and his nap). Santa Claus has returned to his former self by spreading pranks and laughter throughout Fox World. Encouragingly, Santa has gained weight also, and his white mane was thick and "Christmas fox fluffy". The look on Mr. Fox's face was priceless—*Is Santa ... uh ... like ... right behind me?*

"Yes, the photograph of you two should be in a polished wooden frame with a 'Friends for Life' brass nameplate," Old Man laughed. Later in the afternoon, "Be" assisted Santa Claus with assembling and scoring the try-outs for the reindeer team. Turnout was good; a line formed early.

MILE MARKER 404.2
BLUE WAGON

Old Man shut down his laptop at noon on Wednesday, his company was closing early for the Thanksgiving holiday. He changed his office voice mail for the holiday, walked into the office lunchroom, and rinsed his coffee thermos. He was three weeks from "retiring." He was going to miss the game. The competition was keen and his colleagues were winners. Corporate World's regimen would dissolve in three weeks. Then Old Man would find out how much of his identity was composed of, and wrapped around, a thirty-year career.

He rode the subway train home. Passenger load was light due to the holiday, and he chose a window seat on the left side of the train car for the twenty-five-minute ride. Office towers, condo buildings, and superhighways choked with get-out-of-town traffic whirled by. His thoughts whizzed by similarly. One year ago today, he was spending several days in the hospital for heart failure complications. Now, he was fox-healed, and he smiled fondly at that thought.

And then it appeared, off the right side of the train. It was not green, given the season, but it was nevertheless an oasis. Fox World, a human healing nirvana, was four blocks away. He needed a Fox World fix.

Old Man walked to his house, changed into comfortable sneakers, and traded his overcoat for a goose-down parka. He pulled the blue utility wagon from the back of the garage. The wagon was affectionately known as the "Fox World food truck" and it was time to do a food run. The weather forecast predicted one of the most bitter cold Thanksgivings in decades. Another polarizing extreme in a calendar year of wacky weather swings. Meals on Wheels decided to depart a day early due to the forecasted bitter temps and take lots of warming calories to everyone—birds, deer, and foxes. Seeds, nuts, apples, bison jerky, and peanut butter cups filled the cart. There was even a secret hideaway compartment with a Snickers bar (for emergency use only). Old Man consulted his survival manual. Temps below thirty-five degrees are potentially dangerous. He ate the candy bar and replenished the hideaway pocket with a fresh reload. Better safe than sorry and there was no need to suffer.

Old Man pulled the squeaky cart to the forest. The wheel's squeaks announced his arrival in advance, like the jack-in-the-box tune from an ice cream truck. Mr. Fox was happy; he knew that on board the cart was an emergency stash of cherry candies. With a grin, he implored N. Oldman to break the emergency glass and retrieve the cherries. Old Man did. *Double tragedy averted in the same day*, the two old lions laughed.

Old Man distributed the snacks and sat down for a holiday cigar and a one ounce shot of Blanton's bourbon—sshhh, don't tell Smiling Wife. Foxes, deer, raccoons, chipmunks, owls, hawks, and heron gathered and feasted. Old Man breathed in the eternal calmness of Fox World which had lightened his burden in the most frightening year of his life. He was more than alive now; the center of his soul was aglow.

Old Man sipped his single barrel bourbon shot and drew on the cigar until the tip glowed like his soul. Home was here and he was home.

Later, Mr. Fox listened to the squeaky wheels of the empty cart leaving Fox World, and watched the shrinking flashlight beam in the darkness. *Thanks for the giving,* he fox-whispered.

MILE MARKER 407.8
GRATEFUL FOR A
PLATEFUL—ONCE MORE

It was Thanksgiving Day. Soon the turkey and pumpkin pie would slide in the oven to bake and fill the house with scents redolent of family gatherings. Cranberries (and cherries if you knew a fox) would be ladled. Arguments would ensue about the best way to make green-bean casserole (with or without crispy onion rings) and the best recipe for stuffing (oyster, cornbread, etc.). Prayers would be said and maybe there would be a moment or two to let minds relax and drift away to grateful blessings. Old Man jotted a list of his blessings in his orange journal.

- friends, true blue ones.
- adversaries, they make you stronger.
- adversity, for you never know who you truly are without it.

- adventure, the kind where fear is vanquished and serendipity rules.
- good jokes (and the occasional bad one).
- belly laughs, the kind that make you cough and cry.

After dinner, Old Man watched the old fox atop Lincoln Logs on a windy evening. Mr. Fox summed up everything best with a smile that said, *I am grateful for a plateful.* Turkey-laced bone broth and a slice of warm pumpkin pie with a mound of whipped cream capped Mr. Fox's Day. He had no television; but he was excited to watch the "live" football games of children in nearby backyards. Mr. Fox reclined his lounger on the log and awaited his favorite show of all—the full moon rising on Thanksgiving night.

What a plateful.

MILE MARKER 411.2
THE WIND IS
YOUR FRIEND

Thirty-five mph gusts blew dust, leaves, and debris through Fox World on this afternoon. Its frosty bite scattered the timid and unprotected. There he sat. Face into the wind. Not only brave, but also wise. He knew that a strong wind, when faced, blows your ills and troubles behind you. Walk into it. Let it ruffle your hair and pin back your ears, for it is cleansing.

Most of us want the wind at our back. *Nope,* says Mr. Fox, *it only blows your troubles into your path. Brace up and face up. Walk into the wind and watch it blow your troubles behind you.*

MILE MARKER 414.3
FOX WIFI

Old Man walked along the edge of the forest, not in a hurry, not lingering either. It was a thinking walk. His mind rolled through the miles of the past months. The walkabout was nearing its five-hundred-mile endpoint. Would it stop there? If so, what would be next? He loved the forest, the lake, the pond, the streams, the small mountain - all props in this wonderful odyssey with Mr. Fox. He sat by the creek and thought about the elderly fox whose eye was closed again with irritation. The canine needed a bit of help. On a still day when the water's surface is calm, sound travels easily across the lake. What one says on one side of the lake can be heard on the far shore. Is the same true in the atmosphere? Can a helpful thought made with intent travel across the ether and arrive where it is needed? Is it "heard"? Old Man had been pondering the presence and power of the spiritual world's Wi-Fi since his near-death experience.

Mr. Fox emerged from the thicket in the Lincoln Logs section of Fox World. And climbed atop Lincoln Logs. Why was Mr. Fox there? He had three or four other favorite places. Then Old Man remembered—he had been thinking about this place as he mixed an eye poultice earlier. Mr. Fox had incurred another storm-related eye injury and Old Man had an idea for treatment. Had thought and intent sent a telegraph to Mr. Fox in Fox World?

Mr. Fox curled up at one end of the tumbled logs and nibbled at two honey-laced hamburger balls—one with a baby aspirin nougat and the other with an amoxicillin filling. The meds were for an eye infection, his second in a year. Would the plan work? Well, Old Man thought—only if intent travels over the ethernet. He was banking on Mr. Fox's injured eye being itchy and the amoxicillin-infused honey being on the fox's paw after eating. What a big if. Old Man needed the med-covered paw and painful eye to connect and deliver the poultice. And they did—three times. Paw to eye. Paw to eye. Paw to eye. Like Dorothy's heels clicking in Oz. There is no place like home; there is no place like home.

Mr. Fox rested his chin on his paws. His eyes, on their way to healing hopefully, closed slowly. Sleep approached. *Watch over me, please,* he begged. Old Man read him holiday messages from friends in Utah, Mississippi, the Carolinas, upstate NY, Canada, Cape Cod, Florida, downtown DC—places so far away that he knew them not. Mr. Fox reflected, *there are many kind humans out there.* Then, as a content dog will do, his chest inflated with air and slowly released in an audible, cathartic sigh.

Old Man held his sentry post for an hour, maybe more. The overcast winter afternoon framed a familiar picture. The king of the forest and the once-successful executive were again just a guy and a baby fox—nine years hence. They were nestled safe in the escapism of a silent Fox World. Accepting ethernet calls only.

There is no place like home.

MILE MARKER 427.5
PANCAKE HOPES

Old Man and Mr. Fox met for breakfast flapjacks. *I've never had a blueberry pancake that did not make me smile,* Mr. Fox grinned. He was correct. Pancakes lift spirits. Pancakes unite people. Problems are discussed, understood, and resolved over pancakes.

In his career, Old Man had moved to new cities nine times. When he arrived in a new town, he would take a Saturday morning drive through the rural countryside and look for a firehouse sign that read, "Pancake Breakfast Today." He had two motivations. First, he was a hungry bachelor. And secondly, as a single guy back then, he was lonely in a new town. Pancakes and syrup fixed that. At the firehouse's picnic tables, he would pour molten maple goodness over a steaming hot flapjack, strike up a conversation with a volunteer firefighter, tap into the local gossip, tell a story about his faraway home in southwest Virginia, and take the first awkward steps into a new community. All over hot pancakes.

Stomach full, spirits lifted, and with invitations from newly made friends to a Saturday afternoon golf foursome or a secret fly-fishing hole, he would go home and unpack the mover's boxes. Hope renewed. All because of pancakes.

Now, he lived near Fox World and had not relocated in fifteen years, so he had not done "firehouse hunting" in years. For old time's sake, he decided to share a pancake or two with his old fox buddy. Silver-dollar sized, lots of maple syrup, sprinkled with blueberries. "Eat up, old fox ... and let me tell you a story ... uh ... about the time

I got lost in northwest New Jersey ... yep ... I was looking for a secret brown trout fishing spot."

Mr. Fox listened with rapt focus. Maybe he was just waiting for a pause in Old Man's run-on story to ask him to pass the whipped cream. Mr. Fox would never be impolite, especially while eating pancakes. He listened to N. Oldman's incessant chirping with a big fox smile.

Pancakes and syrup once again did their trick. The syrup-driven gratification bonded the two hungry buddies on a crispy cold winter day and their hopes for the future glowed.

MILE MARKER 432.1
SPIDER-FOX

Snapped off at the seven-foot vertical mark by a windstorm, the trunk of the tree was horizontal to the ground like a hockey stick with its toe in the dirt. The sixty-five-foot-long balance beam, elevated by seven feet, formed a fox observation tower for the forest's leader.

Mr. Fox walked to the tree and sized up the raised beam. He did the calculations of an athlete and a scientist. F= MA. Force = mass times acceleration. *Should he downsize his launch factor because of his arthritic hip? With an injured eye matted slightly closed with drainage, was his depth perception still spot on?* His sat and looked up. His tail wiggled left to right, right to left, across the crunchy leaves. His healthy eye was locked in on the beam.

Old Man wanted to shout, "Nooooo!". But he too had been there mentally. There comes a day when you just want to know. You just need to know: "Have I recovered? Am I better? Do I still have what it takes?" The answer was waiting ... pretty or ugly ... with no in-between. Mr. Fox shot up in a beautiful, slow-motion arc. It seemed like it took minutes to cover the seven vertical feet. Up and up and up he flew, like an orange arrow shot into the heavens.

Ninety percent of the way there, it became apparent that he was going to come up a few inches short. He hit the horizontal part of the log chest first. Air escaped his lungs with an audible grunt. Head, front paws, and right shoulder made it to the top of the log; his hind-quarters and long, fluffy tail dangled. Old Man almost ran to catch him. The fox's claws dug into the bark, his chin rotated to the far side of the log for leverage, and his tail came up and lassoed the tree limb and he leveraged himself atop the beam like Spider-Man.

Yay! A new vertical leap record in Fox World! Of course, the Russian judge deducted 0.1 point for the landing. Go figure. Old Man froze as he watched this wonderful spectacle. The feat was not the leap; it was summoning the courage to try. Mr. Fox exuded confidence in his pose atop the log. Even though the leap made his legs tremble and his heart race, he knew concretely the answer that he sought. *He still had it. He was still strong. He was still atop his world.*

MILE MARKER 440.1
SEVEN FOXES, ONE
TREE, INFINITE HOPE

Gathered in the forest with the fox family,
For a Christmas we thought, he may not see.
Paws intertwine, eyes sparkle with glee,
In awe of Fox World, lit by the tiny holiday tree.

Full fox bellies sing their joy out loud,
Humans look on with souls tingling proud.
Bucky and the reindeer munch molasses and corn,
A blessed year rejoiced, as dreams are reborn.

Pass the cherries,
And, to the chicken, add blueberries.
Mugs of hot chocolate and rock bowls of broth
Will warm our innards and keep our hopes aloft.

With friends, bow humbly and break holiday bread.
Forget for now the troubles ahead.
It is Christmas season, that's the reason
Cheer be to all, 'cause we all need some.

MILE MARKER 448.2
MOST RAIN IN
VIRGINIA HISTORY

Two weeks before year end, 4.32" of rain fell, further breaking the 1889 annual rainfall total of 61.33". Thus, Mr. Fox and his ability to survive all, made history again. The fox born in the largest snowstorm in Virginia history had now officially survived Virginia's rainiest season a decade later.

The stress was in Mr. Fox's face, though. The ups and downs of this year had been a psychological amusement park ride. Old Man knew that look, the stare bespoke permeating despondency and there were only two possible outcomes—give up or keep trying. Does one dare to turn the cards over and read fate's declaration? The old fox would reject the premise of that question categorically. *Life is not the turn of a card,* he would say. *Luck is made, not revealed.*

He shook the moisture from his burnt-orange fur and looked to the sky with respect for the raw power of Earth. He was humbled by it, but he allowed himself a fleeting moment of pride. It was a measured moment—the type that acknowledged victory without gloating. He and his family had survived the worst storms in the history of Virginia. It had been deep-to-the-bone hard, but Mr. Fox and Fox World had won.

MILE MARKER 455.7
A GREAT LAST DAY IS A
PERFECT FIRST DAY

Old Man and Smiling Wife made a list and titled it "Last Day in Washington". It was retirement day for N. Oldman, and he slept little overnight. The last day of your career (like birth and death) only comes once and Old Man did not know whether to feel sad, excited, or simply resigned to what was. The acid growled loudly in his stomach. Thinking it generated by the coffee, he placed his coffee cup back in the car's console. The stomach agitation triggered a memory, the same taste from a coffee on a flight from San Diego over a year ago. Except this morning, he did not think, *work hard, run fast, do more.* He accepted the end, the end of an era as it was always referred to tritely. Old Man laughed at his wry mood. Would he reach for the golf clubs or flyfishing rod next? Unlikely. He was addicted to fox wisdom and if the old fox would have him, Old Man was good for another five hundred miles.

The weather started sunny and moderate for mid-December. Old Man tuned the satellite radio to a holiday music station, and he and Smiling Wife drove into town at 8:30 a.m., taking the long route down the George Washington Parkway. It was his last day in Corporate World (and downtown D.C.), and he had many good-byes to share. On the last day of his career, he savored the scenic byway, the roaring Potomac River, iconic Georgetown University on the hill (the stone steps of which he had climbed many winter mornings). How many spring and summer mornings had he sat, windows down and sunroof open, in George Washington Parkway traffic and relished every moment of the blooming trees above him, he wondered. Not enough, he concluded.

N. Oldman and Smiling Wife crossed the Key Bridge and turned right into Georgetown. A film of their love life rolled in his head. They looked down on the C&O Canal and reminisced about their Jack Russell terrier walks and ice cream cart purchases there. The bar where they had their first date was on the left; the restaurant where they were engaged appeared on the right. Straight ahead was the Hay Adams Hotel, the site of their rooftop wedding. Smiling Wife winked as they passed Camelot, where he may or may not have had a bachelor party libation. They laughed like teenagers and the melancholy was broken.

N. Oldman parked at the garage that he had parked at for seventeen years and gave his keys to the parking garage manager. Then he gave the man a bear hug. He had become a dear and solid friend over a decade. N. Oldman admired his courageous immigration story from Ethiopia to America.

As they walked south on Connecticut Avenue, Smiling Wife pulled the "last day list" from her purse—have coffee at the Hay Adams, buy a White House holiday ornament, see The White House Christmas tree, share a drink at the legendary Round Robin Bar, nibble a steak salad at The Palm, visit cigar buddies at JR's, procure a dozen white-chocolate-covered Oreos from the Chocolate Mousse, window-shop on Connecticut Avenue, and enjoy the annual staff holiday party at Otello's Bistro. Handholding was scheduled throughout and surprises (including an Omega retirement watch and a St. Andrews Old Course plaque) were interspersed in the day by the ever clever Smiling Wife.

They finished the goodbye bucket list at 3:00 p.m. The weather downshifted and brought a romantic surprise. Snowflakes fell and dotted their knit caps and wool coats as they cupped their hot chocolate by The White House Christmas Tree. Smiling Wife's eyes reflected the multi-color lights of the holiday tree. Old Man toasted her, the tree, and the day.

"Not a perfect career, but a perfect last day."

They returned north on the George Washington Parkway. For old time's sake, they turned up the heater and rolled down the windows. To their right, the engorged Potomac raged, un-calmed by the blanket of snow falling gently.

"Was it truly the perfect day? Did you do everything that you wanted to do?" she asked.

"Are you thinking what I'm thinking?" he replied. "I am tired, and I am sad about the end of my career, but for five hundred miles and one year, I have found solace on the toughest days in one place. Let's check off one last box today. Onward to Fox World!" Her smile lit up the car as she slid across the seat, put her arm around his neck, and hugged him. Time rolled back two decades; they were two scared but excited lovers on their first date—driving home from a dinner and a cobblestone walk in Georgetown. Time in the mind is what one wills it to be. Snow crystals blew in the open car windows, dusting Smiling Wife's brunette hair with an ice tierra. *Perfect last day*, Old Man smiled back.

Mr. Fox, Buttons, Bucky, Colonel Hawk and Professor Owl squirmed with hard-to-maintain patience in Fox World. It was quiet, snow quiet. The sun sank inch by inch in the Winter Solstice sky, as did their spirits. *Maybe it was snowing too much for him to come,* they surmised. *But it is his special day; he always comes to tell us stories on special days.* Mr. Fox pawed at the snow dust, passing the time, scrolling back through a year's worth of adventures on the trail. Most of their feats were secret; people would not believe their story anyway. *Buddies never lose faith. N. Oldman is my best friend; he will come.* Buttons put her right paw around her mate's neck and hugged the forest legend tightly. Professor Owl perked up and jumped to a higher branch. In the wind, the tree-top branch rocked. She swayed side to side in the towering oak. "It's them. They're coming!", the owl screamed. Mr. Fox dashed with excitement to the forest's edge. Bucky ran in closer, snorting ice clouds through his nostrils in excitement.

Old Man and Smiling Wife parked their car and walked into the edge of Fox World. The seven of them walked, talked, and laughed as wispy snowflakes fell on their shoulders. Smiling Wife had one more surprise—she had hidden animal treats in the car. Blueberries, cherries, jerky, and peanuts were distributed and enjoyed. How exquisite, an animal party extraordinaire on Old Man's retirement day. The warmth of love glowed inside them and countered the frost on their fingers, paws, and hooves.

The duo of humans and the quintet of loyal animals were snow-covered when the impromptu soiree ended. N. Oldman and his wife said goodbye, leaving a second helping of treats as they left. Calories make heat, and heat means survival on night like this. Mr. Fox watched their car until the taillights disappeared on the horizon. He looked at Buttons and Bucky beside him and at Professor Owl and Colonel Hawk above him and whispered words heard loudly in their hearts: *Perfect first day.*

MILE MARKER 460.5
MOON WATCHER

O n his first day of unemployment, Old Man walked the edge of the forest to find an ideal viewing venue for the full moon rise. Buttons had already claimed her spot and she was absorbed in the spectacle of the skies settling and the moon popping above the horizon on cue. She affirmed Old Man's conclusion that animals know more about the sky's timetable than humans. They depend on it; they are connected to it. Observing her, Old Man admired how animals have no wasted motions. They do only important and vital things. Watch what they watch, and you will know life, Native Americans believed.

Buttons' eyes sparkled in the moon's glow. Clear skies meant safety—the storm no longer threatened her family. Winter Solstice brings longer days in which to forage and spruce up the den. Food and warmth are the most important survival staples. While Old Man's fancy retirement watch read 5:17 p.m., he had no clue what time it really was in the universe. Buttons did. She examined the sky and the moon, and she declared with exacting accuracy that Fox World time is *be here now and forever.* Old Man looked at his new Omega Globemaster watch, admired the quality, and thought of the three and a half decades of road miles that earned it. The timepiece was beautiful, but it was what he did next that made Old Man treasure it. He set the watch's hands to Button's prescribed time zone of *be here now and forever.* He felt better already.

Do not watch the watch; watch the fox.

MILE MARKER 469.7
SANTA'S WORK IS DONE

Santa Claus looked down across Foxville and measured his success in orchestrating a perfect Christmas. After all, he was Santa Claus, and it was his job to make happiness.

In the valley, there was a Charlie Brown-sized tree (selected by Forever) with sparkly lights. Ornaments, compliments of Smiling Wife, with the names of all the foxes adorned the tree. Toy balls, bouncy and squeaky, for the pups were scattered around the festive tree. Animals, except for the occasional a crow coveting a shiny trinket, do not care for human toys. Foxes do, and he never grew tired of watching the pups race through the woods with flashing light ball toys after dark. N. Oldman had supplied an abundance of Christmas Eve snacks; Buttons' maternal instinct kicked in and she wrapped a portion for tomorrow and buried them in the forest fridge. Old Man was fascinated with how foxes buried their food caches in hideaway spots around the woods and were able to find the "fridge" later. How did they do it? Fox GPS? With the bounty, there would be a Christmas Day banquet on the moss mounds tomorrow. With his final scan, Santa Claus watched Mr. Fox and Buttons exchange holiday "I'm-in-love" looks; Santa was happy for his buddy and his wife. He had lived the bachelor life to the fullest, but he secretly wanted to come off the road, meet a mate like Buttons, and settle into a nice hollow log home.

Santa Claus made one last Christmas wish. With Fox World arranged in the perfect holiday setting in the valley below, his wish was for another world, Human World. Santa Claus, being a traveler, had seen many humans in many places. Humans always seemed stressed, hurried—just like N. Oldman was a year ago. Santa's wish was that the inhabitants of Human World slow down a bit, be troubled less, and love animals more—even if for one day.

Lastly, he bowed his head and said a grateful prayer of thanks. Death came for him last August, but his best friend, Mr. Fox, had summoned Mr. Oldman to help, and they had given him the best of early Christmas gifts: life, precious ole life. Santa Claus was alive to see one more Christmas in Fox World *which made him the luckiest fox in the world*, Santa thought, *and this made him feel joyous because there was no place more beautiful than Fox World at Christmastime.*

MILE MARKER 474.2
ORDINARINESS IS THE
GREATEST GRAVITY

Their destiny walks were winding down; their destiny was not. The calendar read one year elapsed, and the pocket-clipped pedometer neared the one million step mark. Old Man's cardiac rehab quest, drawn up on a legal pad the day after he left the hospital, was near its formal end, but the old lions were trail (and trial, if their scars were evidence) bonded, and their destinies were forever threaded. They were grounded—like gravity. Sir Isaac Newton researched and postulated the law of gravity and within the world of physics, it stated simply that beings are bound to the spinning blue marble called Earth by centrifugal force. Gravity is a law that can be neither disobeyed nor broken. Gravity binds.

Old Man agreed—partially. But he believed that there was a second gravitational law, one which applied to the soul. Ordinariness, i.e., following the mundane, was an egregious form of gravity to the spirit. Repeated rituals and habits dig the crevasses which become life-long ruts. These trenches become hope's confines and they cage the soul.

Old Man studied Mr. Fox, asleep at his feet. For a year, the teacher taught; the guide guided. His fox wisdom was always straight-line cause and effect logic—*bust the rut and do the un-normal. In his mind, he seemed to know that the law of (emotional) gravity had an escape clause and he pursued it religiously. His daily list was long: find a log, hop up, look up to the gigantic blue sky, count airplanes, smell flowers, walk with a trusted human, take chances, be fair in an unfair world, love all, watch the sun set and be grateful for a bowl of bone broth on an icy morning. Most of all, dare to be a friend to someone quite different from you.*

Escape gravity's clutches. Be an extraordinary fox.

MILE MARKER 478.5
THE PRODIGAL
BROTHER RETURNS

Old Man had learned a skyscraper full of knowledge in the year of walks. Mr. Fox was selfless, magnanimous, and liked by all. The fox asked for nothing but gave his all for others. Old Man always felt small in Mr. Fox's presence, like a person who strives to do good versus one who has achieved great goodness. Old Man felt the world (whether it be Fox, Human, or Corporate) owed the old fox a blessing or two.

Mr. Fox never requested anything from others, but he silently wanted two things and Old Man studied the fox's heart until he knew his inner desires. The last thing that Mr. Fox's heart could endure was to outlive his beautiful forest. His wish was that Fox World never be destroyed, and unfortunately, the bulldozers were at the front gate.

He might be a brave fox, but he knew that he was no equal for the heavy, crushing steel treads of the bulldozers and backhoes. No one in Fox World was, not even his bulked-up buddy, Bucky. Help, if it came, would have to come from humans. Mr. Fox pawed the dirt in front of him, processed a painful thought, and swallowed hard. Betrayal tasted sour. Mr. Fox pondered whether humans would save his beautiful, ancient wilderness. Would they step up or stand down? He could count on Old Man; he did not know about the rest.

Old Man read the fox's mind adroitly. Mr. Fox had taught him how to do so—just another trail secret shared between two buddies. Beyond the forest's salvation, Mr. Fox had a second longing. He was a father, a grandfather, a devoted mate, a good friend. He was also an orphan, having lost his father and mother early in life. By the laws of nature, he should have perished that first winter. Yet here he was a decade later; he had lived a long arc.

Mr. Fox was also one other thing—he was a brother. He missed his lone brother. *Was he still alive? If so, where was he? Mr. Fox's brother had walked west through a dark, scary tunnel under the wide expressway a decade ago. What was on the other side of the wide superhighway? Was there another beautiful forest with less Human World intrusion?* Old Man smiled. He might have good news for Mr. Fox. He had seen an odd (and old) fox recently in the western end of the forest near the big, dark, scary tunnel.

As for the rogue bulldozers and how to save Fox World, Old Man had an idea—one that had worked many times in Corporate World. He needed a plan, a team of caring people, and some money. And a lot of luck.

A few days later, Old Man spotted the new-on-the scene fox stranger at a previously scouted location. He was asleep atop a weathered bench nicknamed "the Favre bench" by Old Man years ago. The bench was smashed at one end by a fallen tree. When it rained, the fox slept under it. He was shy, but not skittish. He was fearful of humans, but not scared of Old Man, as if he had known the human from long ago. Life on this side of the highway had not been good for Favre since he returned to Fox World. He was very hungry and needed sustenance on this icy cold January day. After a life alone, he now decided to go paw forward and trust a little bit. Mr. Fox's brother approached the human—not real close but close enough to study the old man. Old Man shared bison strips, a staple in his backpack. The old fox accepted the meat gratefully. *I know you*, the fox thought.

Old Man studied the fox and compared him to the fox photograph archive in his smartphone. This fox was stoutly framed with a large head and thick mane like a lion or a bear. The fox was old—not ancient old—but there was a I've-been-around-the-block look on his experience-crevassed face. Some of the facial lines looked hurt-etched. He was a fox with a "missing piece"—like the surviving half of a life-long couple experiencing a first gray winter alone. Purposeless, he scrounged up a meal daily and walked around aimlessly. There was no need to hurry home to an empty den. He was no different than a human in his twilight years sitting down at a one-chair dinner table before a hot plate warmed bowl of soup and a framed 8x10 of his beloved on the wall. This fox was sad. Plaintive looks from his sunken eyes called out.

Old Man's walk home from the Favre bench was a snow-crunching cake batter of frost-chilled toes in his hiking boots and worrisome thoughts in his head. If the eternal human question is "Who am I?" then Old Man was fixated on the existential interrogative close to home: "Who is this fox?"

N. Oldman had the answer at home, he was sure of it.

MILE MARKER 481.3
OLD PHOTOGRAPHS
UNITE TWO BROTHERS

At home that evening, Old Man paged through his fox photo-graph e-archives, but he eventually realized that he did not have what he needed in his smartphone or his e-cloud storage. He climbed the stairs to his loft office on the fourth floor of the brownstone—what he needed was under the spare bed in the loft bedroom and there he found his old laptop and its hard drive of several hundred photographs from a decade ago. Most had been taken with pocket cameras and downloaded by his wife. He was looking for a handful of photographs of Buttercup's two sons, which he had taken ten years ago. He found the e-folder marked Buttercup's Boys. In the file, he found Mr. Fox's brother.

Mr. Fox's brother was the larger of the two brothers—even back then. The appearance of "larger" was mostly due to his fluffy thick coat and large head. The brother looked like a fat bear cub. The fox coat around his neck was golden yellow like a lion's mane. And there was a thin black ring on his tail between the orange fur and the white tip. The old fox's markings were exact matches with the smartphone photograph that he had snapped earlier that day. Proof!

This new-to-fox-world-forest strange fox was Mr. Fox's brother! And after nearly a decade, he had returned to Fox World.

Old Man expended hours on several afternoons and exhausted his arsenal of human tricks, but eventually Old Man led Mr. Fox to the Favre bench and his brother was there, enticed by a rotisserie chicken left for him. Old Man watched the two foxes' eyes lock. Ten years of mental fog melted, and they lifted their noses and activated their nostrils. Scent, the most powerful sense in a canine, began the rewiring of their past. Stunned by their eyes, they sniffed incessantly and tilted their heads quizzically. The recognition confirmation sequence proceeded to the final stages—staccato high-range squeaks, dancing feet, and tail wags.

Separated by a decade of time and an eight-lane highway, Buttercup's boys had come full circle. Old Man managed a swallow around the lump in his throat. In human-years terms, it was akin to two brothers reuniting on their seventieth birthday party. Mr. Fox and Favre did what reunion partygoers do—they posed for a photograph, they shared cake (chicken), and had a coffee (bone broth). They started walking west to the big scary tunnel, the fox brother portal. Old Man gave them "brother space" and did not intrude. Maybe they talked about building side-by-side retirement condos on Fox River. Or maybe they shared family photos. Or maybe they told war stories about Fox World and The Other Side of the Expressway World perils. Maybe they just said, "Good to see you, brother," and set their fox clock on the "be here now" dial and strolled silently.

Old Man smiled in admiration as they faded over the horizon. Old Man mouthed the words, "Buttercup would be proud, boys."

MILE MARKER 485.3
HOW FAVRE GOT HIS NAME

For days, Old Man watched the fox brothers get reacquainted. Mr. Fox showed his brother the parts of Fox World that he had never seen. Favre, ever shy, hung back, and took it all in. Favre scouted brushy areas and concealed shadowy spots where he could hide in the future. His favorite hangout remained the broken wooden bench near The Great Fallen Oak. There was tall heather grass near there which would camouflage him.

Old Man was fond of the bench; he sat there often until it was broken. Years ago, he would walk to the bench in the forest on his lunch break during work-at-home days. He would nibble on a chicken salad sandwich and ripple-cut potato chips and listen to sports talk radio. The bench was old back then, but sturdy and comfortable.

Old Man laughed as he remembered the last time that he sat on the bench. Per habit, he had unwrapped his lunch sandwich and tuned into satellite radio. A sports channel issued a sports alert at noon. As an avid Green Bay Packers fan, Old Man shushed himself and listened raptly when he heard the words "Brett Favre" and "star quarterback" in the alert. Brett Favre had un-retired (kind of) and joined the Minnesota Vikings, an oak stake through any Packers fan's heart. Old Man recalled what happened next and laughed harder. Angry with the news, Old Man packed his unfinished lunch and stormed out of the forest, only to return an hour later to get a candy bar and cigar which he had left on the bench seat. What he saw stopped him cold. A midday thunderstorm had uprooted a sizeable maple tree and deposited it on top of the bench and the tree trunk split the wooden bench in two pieces. Right down the middle. Old Man was rattled by the sight, having been on the bench one hour ago. The morale to the story: if Brett Favre had not "un-retired" and gone to the Minnesota Vikings, Old Man would be dead. Thusly, the smashed bench became known as "Favre's Bench", and years later, the old fox, who liked to sleep under it and play near it, was given affectionately the moniker of Favre.

Old Man laughed a third time. A fox named after a bench named after a football player. The only other possible choice for the bench's name would have been "Viking." But no self-respecting Green Bay Packers would name a fox "Viking." Favre and his brother, Mr. Fox, both Packers fans, breathed a sigh of relief as they nibbled their blueberries nearby. Apparently, they had narrowly escaped being named Viking I and Viking II, which would have constituted the greatest tragedy in Fox World history.

MILE MARKER 488.3
THE THREE
HERMITS CLUB

The Hermit Thrush is an odd little (slightly smaller than a Robin) bird with a spotted belly and cute pink feet. It is a loner bird, thus the name, and makes a coffee cup nest on the ground in a bed of leaves—like a furled fox on a frosty morning. The muted melody of its flute-like songs cannot be heard from afar. The bird's song originates from deep in the woods—giving the Hermit Thrush the reputation of "the bird that sings alone."

The Hermit Thrush breeds north of Virginia. Infrequently a migrating, heading-south hermit thrush will stop in the Mid-Atlantic states in late autumn and stay. This year, Fox World was blessed with such a treat. As this little feathered marvel danced on the tree branch and fluttered its tail before the zoom lens, another hermit appeared—under the tree where the thrush was perched.

It was Favre. He was limping a bit—most likely his paws were sore from digging his winter den. He issued his customary salute; he stuck out his tongue at Old Man, and thus his ID credentials were verified. "My oh my, Favre, where have you been? It has been a few days."

He responded with a shy, aw-shucks dip of the head. It translated as, *you know, just around—here and there. My bivouac is wherever my bedroll unfurls. I walk and camp alone. I'm a hermit.*

Favre wore the hermit's name tag with pride for he knew the highest meaning of the word. A hermit is a person (or animal) who lives in solitude in pursuit of a spiritual quest. Speckles looked down at Favre and telegraphed his thoughts: *Hear that, friend. We may be alone, but we are enlightened. Or, at least, we are on our path to enlightment.*

Chili soup was on slow simmer on the gas range back home, so Old Man said goodbye to the Fox World hermits. Packers game time was a half hour away. Walking briskly, Old Man hope to make it back for kick-off. Exciting today, the forecast was for snow at Lambeau Field. A bowl of chili with crushed corn chips sprinkled on top and a snowy Lambeau on television—no better Sunday ritual. He paused and looked back to the forest. He smiled, truth be known, he had become a hermit, too, over the last year, a hermit human who walked with the animals. That would get a hearty laugh in Corporate World and maybe it should. If N. Oldman wanted to "un-retire" and go back to the playing field in Corporate World, it was time to leave the animals and turn in his hermit gear. Maybe this five-hundred-mile jaunt was just a silly long walk to pass time until he healed, he semi-concluded.

Old Man recoiled at his momentary betrayal of Fox World. Then, he did what he would have avoided in the past: he leaned into the issue and challenged himself with ego-cracking questions. Was Fox World real? Or, was it mostly imaginary? Did he care what other humans thought? Where was he the happiest and why? Surely, he knew himself better after five hundred miles with this fox in the forest, but (and here was the defining question) had he learned to love himself? Did he accept himself? There is no road to redemption or path to self-acceptance in an unexamined mind. With this burning self-questioning, light poured into his thinking along with its twin flame, clarity. Old Man had his answers, distilled wonderfully by the purity and clarity of Fox World.

Old Man turned back to the path to Fox World. He and Favre boiled bone broth on a camp stove and streamed the Packers game on his smartphone and N. Oldman told Favre about his football player namesake. Favre looked up from his soup, puffed out his furry lion's mane chest, and asked: *is my brother, Mr. Fox, a legend in Fox World?*

Old Man sized up his answer and replied, "You both are, Favre, and someday your legend will travel far beyond these trees."

MILE MARKER 491.1
PIZZA DIPLOMACY

Trees began to fall in the east end and the glaring holes in the tree canopy would take one hundred years to fill in again. Light from the sky poured into the once dark secluded corners of Fox World. This is where the animals went to rest in the daytime and their sanctuary was evaporating, tree by tree. Old Man was worried about the bulldozers in Fox World; land clearing was the next phase. Whenever a threat this powerful materialized, the politicking, the planning, and the financing were already done. The opposition was large and organized, and the die was cast. Mr. Fox and he were grabbing a tiger by the tail if they initiated a forest-saving venture, but long odds were their emerging specialty. concluded. Old Man pulled a small wooden golf-scoring pencil and a palm-sized notebook from his backpack. He wrote "Saving Fox World Game Plan" at the top of the page. He drew a vertical line down the middle of the page and labeled the two columns: "Liabilities" and "Assets." Before any mission, an inventory must be taken to know what you have and what you need. Mr. Fox, relaxing under a pine tree, wanted to laugh at his friend. He was doing that human thing again by making lists on paper and doing analysis. But Mr. Fox bit his lip and checked his criticism; Old Man knew what he was doing. Lists and analysis had been a presage to many victories in the past year. Mr. Fox let Old Man do his magic. At this point, magic is what they needed.

"Fox World Liabilities": no or little time, the competition had a huge head start, the competition had massive amounts of money, the competition had pages and pages of technical plans, and the animals had no political constituency or advocates.

"Fox World Assets ": hundreds of miles of experience, the perspective of having faced victoriously the ultimate challenge (death), a beautiful forest to motivate them, and lovable wildlife citizens.

Old Man turned to a fresh page and wrote an outline for a six-point plan: (a) put a cute face on the project's cover page to illicit empathy, (b) codify an emotional appeal i.e., do not let Mr. Fox outlive his forest, (c) get the word out on social media, (d) build a support network of influencers, (e) launch an epic call-to-action event town hall meeting, (f) leverage the animals' underdog status.

And so, the plan began. The deadline was seventeen days. Old Man set up a bank account for the project and tapped his financial reserves. Working with the local community, he built a protect-the-animal's-forest team and expert opinions were enlisted and incorporated. Coalitions were explored and assembled. High ranking local officials and decisionmakers were invited and prepped. Press interviews were arranged and conducted. An informative (but basic due to time constraints) website was launched. Save-The-Wildlife flyers were crafted and hung with colorful balloons on tree trunks. A town hall meeting site was secured and decorated with photo collages of Fox World's residents and the bulldozers that threatened them.

If chicken soup is good for the soul, Old Man had learned in thirty-five years in Corporate World that lots of piping hot pizza is the elixir for a successful meeting. Pizza is business meeting comfort food. Old Man ordered dozens of pies, and a town hall pizza and soft drinks bar was set up with fox plates, fox napkins, and call-to-action brochures. People came for the cause, and they were comforted by toasty pizza, chilled Peppermint Patties for dessert, and a go-cup of hot coffee for the walk home in the windy, twenty-degree night. Parking was limited, forcing attendees to walk three to four blocks in the icy wind to the Fox World Town Hall. The steaming hot takeaway coffees were a nice way to say: "Thank you, thanks for coming; thanks for caring, and stay warm on the walk home."

The Town Hall attendance was overflow—a lean up against the wall, standing room only type of squeeze-in. Those who had no seats were "VIP'd" with pizza and cola service by Smiling Wife. The officials with the bulldozers explained their plans. The citizens bristled and countered. The well-meaning bulldozer team looked at their tense faces. The next move broke the tension—they asked for ideas. Negotiations began. Maybe hearts were warmed by hot pizza on a frigid night, maybe a bit of Fox World magic dust drifted in via the vents. Compromises emerged and humans agreed that the centuries-old forest should be preserved with care. Plans were altered and enhanced to preserve the tree canopy and the wildlife's habitat as much as possible.

Afterwards, Old Man stacked empty pizza boxes, cleaned up soda cans and swept the floors. His wife put the Fox World animal photo collages in protective plastic and folded the tripod easels. The giant animal (fox, owl, deer) balloons would go home tomorrow—too windy tonight. He poured a coffee for his wife. They toasted paper cups. "Worried or happy?" she asked.

"It is not fair. Our house will always be safe and provide warmth and security for us. Their home is on the brink of destruction and time is running out. We fail and their home is destroyed forever. Yes, I am worried. I have walked five hundred miles with that old fox in this forest oasis. If not for the walks with him and the calming serenity of the forest,

I doubt that I would be here. So, I guess I am a bit overinvested in all this. Who would have thought that a former business executive would now be retired and throwing a pizza party to save a fox?"

In a row of boxwoods several feet outside the town hall site, Mr. Fox sat alone. *I did,* he replied to N. Oldman. Then he turned into the icy wind and walked the two miles back to Foxville. During his hike, he stopped twice to shiver. He was cold and the forest would be even colder if the trees were gone.

MILE MARKER 495.2
THE GATHERING

The animals sent their best emissary—the elder statesman Mr. Fox. Buttons combed his hair and brushed out his tail. *You must look your best,* she said. Mr. Fox obliged her. Everyone needs a task or two to attend to in worrisome times. Doing things—even menial things—burns off nervous energy and helps with the waiting. The waiting was agony.

Mr. Fox left Foxville two hours early. He did not want to be late for his meeting with N. Oldman. *Hmmm, well groomed,* he noted as he passed the stream and looked at his reflection in the glassy surface. Buttons had done a fine barber's job. His heart twinged; *he loved Buttons and he was so lucky,* he mused.

Mr. Fox walked deliberately. Not slow, not fast—just an even pace. When you think the woods might disappear soon, you walk mindfully and cherish it. He carried nothing with him. No valise with important documents inside. No fountain pens with which to sign treaties. Onboard the little fox was the simplest of protective armors—a life lived right and a hopeful heart. *Would that be enough? Well, for 9.9 years, it had been,* Mr. Fox whispered to himself.

Mr. Fox staked out a wait spot with clear visibility to Human World. This brought risk. With a clean sight line came the reciprocal—he too could be easily spotted. Always wise and strategic, Mr. Fox was never one to roll the casino dice. Today he did, and he stood boldly on the cart path from Human World. He would have been embarrassed if the descriptor "stoic" was used by onlookers—but those who saw him on this day would use no other word. Stoic and brave he was.

Meanwhile, a mile away, Old Man fiddled with his backpack. Freshly washed, it smelled like the fluffy goodness of a dryer sheet. He filled the backpack for his hike. Fox World map, camera, batteries, SD cards, dried cherries, turkey jerky, coffee thermos, med kit, and pocketknife. A micro-sized, torch-flamed cigar lighter brought home from a Scotland golf adventure went in the backpack next, as well as his beloved cigar cutter—long lost but found and returned by Mr. Fox. Wool cap and gloves, needed as the windchill was in the teens, were added. The piece de resistance came last. It was a special cigar—deemed special because he selected it at the Fox Cigar Bar in Scottsdale, Arizona for a special day and this was a day of destiny. Lightly smoked and not inhaled, one cigar per week had no contraindication to his arrhythmia. He fired up the My Father Garcia & Garcia. A blue-gray ring of smoke rose from the fiery orange tip. He began walking, puffing, and smiling.

Down the trail, Mr. Fox smelled his buddy before he saw him. Fire and smoke are not a forest's friend, but this was the sweetest smell that Mr. Fox's nostrils had ever detected. The smoke was a best buddy alert; his old friend was coming. N. Oldman rounded the last bend on the paved walking path, and Mr. Fox's tail twitched back and forth. Old Man signed their secret one-two-three-for-you-and-me greeting to him. The old fox nodded *back at ya* with a signature warm grin. There is a time and place for small talk, and this was not one of those times. The fate and balance of Fox World hung in the air. It was a "get right to it" moment. N. Oldman cleared his throat twice and began a raspy soliloquy to Mr. Fox, who signaled for N. Oldman to stop. *Something this important ... well, we should tell them together.*

They departed the edge of Human World, rustling through the forest's crunchy leaves. They crossed the first of Fox River's dual forks on Helping Hands bridge—Mr. Fox did so adroitly. Old Man followed clumsily and prayed that Smiling Wife would not learn of his disobedience. They vectored across Fox Island and forded the second branch of the river. The tall heather grasses and fallen hollow logs surrounding Foxville came into focus on the distant horizon.

Professor Owl followed, tree to tree, flying low across the treetops. Colonel Hawk flew a higher arc in the robin's-egg blue sky—circling, protecting. The animals begged for advance info, wanting to know the verdict. The raptors replied, *all we can tell you is that they're coming.* The foxes gathered and grabbed a sit spot, all the family members— Buttons, Be, Here, Now, Forever. The itinerant Santa Claus and the seldom-seen Favre joined in—waiting, watching. Russell Raccoon and Deja Blue paced nervously in the background. Mr. Fox and N. Oldman arrived in a clearing, the town square of Foxville, both blowing vapor clouds into the chilled air. They rested a moment and Old Man poured a coffee to warm his vocal cords. Mr. Fox hopped atop a log and began: *We are here to give you an update on the fate of Fox World.*

Old Man and Mr. Fox unrolled the color map. The animals bunched over each other's shoulders for a bird's eye view. Anxious looks lined their faces. Mr. Fox scanned the crowd, met eye to eye with all, and gave them an it-is-going-to-be-ok nod. They had confidence in Mr. Fox. As a forest animal team, they had faced many troubles. Floods. Pollution. Hunters. Drones. Subway trains. Apathy of humans. And now, a road grader was at their door. All the animals drew in a deep breath, shaking with fear on the inside but with determined-to-survive looks on their faces. *Let's have it,* their eyes spoke. They looked down proudly at the Map of Fox World on the stump. It was their home, their secret world. To any that believed, it was a magical place, an oasis of serenity, but only if one dared to believe.

My, my—what a beautiful map, they reflected. It had every detail of their homeland. N. Oldman had walked hundreds of miles with Mr. Fox here. The trusted human had shared their paw scribblings with an artist—a wonderful lady in Canada. All agreed, it was their treasure map. It captured forever the luster and magic of Fox World. No bulldozer would ever dismantle the magic even if it did take the trees. The human explained what he had heard at the Big Meeting in Human World. He divided the discussion into three parts—Left, Center, Right.

"Center is the heart of Fox World and home to Foxville. It has been decided that no harm will come to this land. The largest and most pristine part of Fox World is safe.

"Left (east). The stream will be fixed and restored here. It will eliminate the raging floods. The work will take nine months. Old, sick trees will be removed. Some are as big as The Great Fallen Oak. New thick grass and small young trees will be replanted. All this comes at a big price—over one hundred majestic oaks have been targeted, including my Heart Attack Tree. The trail to Fox Mountain will be closed for a while."

Our cousins there are displaced, Mr. Fox added. *They need our comfort. Territorial instincts aside, we need to open our homes and welcome them.*

"Right (west). This is a future construction area, but there is great news. The bicycle bridge at Snapping Turtle Pond will be repaired. Human World has rallied to protect the animals here. No large trees will fall where Professor Owl and her family dwell."

Q&A followed. Paws were raised and recognized. Mr. Fox handled the questions aptly and warmly. The animals nodded their assent to the plan. None were jaded, as in, *what choice did we have? Previously, the only deal ever handed to them was a raw one. This was an honest deal negotiated by a fair man and other humans,* they all agreed. The animal meeting in Foxville broke up quickly. Humans like small talk;

animals have no time for it. Everyone resumed the essential chores of tomorrow's pass-fail survival.

Mr. Fox walked N. Oldman back to Human World. Halfway, Old Man stopped. He turned to Mr. Fox. "Head on back home, little buddy. I can make it home from here. I have my flashlight. I hope that you are happy with the land deal. We did our best."

Mr. Fox smiled—one part happiness, one part resignation from accepting fate's path. *Human World can take our land; they cannot take Fox World. It is not a place; it is a state of mind. You know that now, N. Oldman. Go tell the others. Write it down.*

After a year of walking with the forest sage, Old Man understood that. Fox World was more than a place; it was a corner of his soul forever.

MILE 500
THE INDESTRUCTIBLE
TRIO

It is said that animals can read auras and thus, they know if you are good or bad; happy or sad; ill or healthy. Maybe the prescient Mr. Fox knew the outcome of their walk before it began; possibly he did not. One thing was for darn certain: Old Man needed the full five hundred miles to collect and learn the right answers for his soul-deep changes. One fox lesson echoed in Old Man's mind: one must be tough to survive, no doubt, but only the kind and gentle can thrive. Mr. Fox epitomized this way of life, and the fox's lessons were mixed into the trail dust and the mud caked on Old Man's hiking boots. Life is equal measures of pleasant, tingly experiences, like the gold butterflies that lifted him when he (nearly) died, and ache-producing, gut-checking challenges. There is no secret sauce in the bone broth; the solution is to just keep walking, and walking, and walking until you find peace and balance.

Every story has both a happy and a sad ending, depending on where it stops. This was the happiest of days; it was mile five hundred and it held a special surprise for Mr. Fox (and N. Oldman).

Outside, it was not raining. It was doing whatever you call "water pouring out of the sky like a broken fire hydrant." More aptly described, it was like standing under a waterfall, looking up, and darn near drowning. It was that brand of rain. Ten degrees colder, and Fox World would have been receiving the largest snowfall in a decade. "Fitting", Old Man mumbled to himself, "not one mile of this walkabout has been easy." The snowstorm of the century had come a decade ago when Mr. Fox was born and now today on Mr. Fox's tenth birthday, there was a horrific northeaster overhead. *Full circle*, Old Man and Mr. Fox concurred telepathically.

One year into their healing, five-hundred-mile Fox World journey, Old Man and Mr. Fox were meeting for a birthday party. Rain be damned. They had survived a royal flush of life's ills and ailments—grave sickness, hobbling injury, betrayal, freezing ice, sweltering heat, pollution/poison, ravaging floods, falling trees, interlopers, backstabbing enemies, and loneliness. Paw on shoulder, they had emerged with matching limps, and two great big beaming smiles. And today, they were going to party hearty in Fox World. Gone was the struggling and the quiet frustration. Their penance was paid up in full. They had faced, they had dealt, they had cried, they had recovered, they had rejoiced, and best of all, they had just kept walking.

Weather aside, it was time for a birthday party. Old Man was excited to celebrate the life of Mr. Fox—one decade in Human World time, 1,200 full moons and 3,652 sunsets in Fox World time. N. Oldman peered out the fourth-floor loft window of his brownstone. The gray mess of cloud cover outside the glass said one thing—wear your warmest and driest storm gear. He studied his closet and selected a pair of warm, flannel-lined khakis. Good choice, especially when paired with his knee-length Irish-green boot socks. He added a Mountain Hardwear silk undershirt as a base layer, then a downy-soft, blue-checked flannel shirt and an Orvis wool sweater—all topped by a navy-blue Barbour Beaufort waxed jacket. The Beaufort, two- and one-half inches longer than the sporty Bedale, was his choice for purchase years ago for a very practical reason. With the extra its length, the Beaufort could be worn over a business suit jacket. Thus, the coat had been a travel mate on business trips to the rain-clogged streets of London, the nippy mist of Edinburgh, and the fog of Germany's Bavaria. Now, retired and discarded, he was dressing for a walk in the pouring rain with an old fox. How far he had fallen, Corporate World's old guard would think (but politely not say).

Yes, his fall had been jarring—thankfully hard enough to crack the confining encasement of self-limited thinking and self-shorted horizons that had ruled fifty years of his life. He did not care for the opinions of others any longer. For one year and for five hundred miles, he had walked and talked with a fox. And he had never felt better, never more sane, never more alive. Old Man was free. A heart-sparked smile spread wide across his weathered face. His fall into Fox World was neither harsh nor unwelcomed. If his fall had cracked through anything, then the thing was pleasant and savory, like a crunchy, flaky bite of beef en croute. Fox World was no rabbit hole, Alice. Instead, it was a portal to a life enhancing, soul expanding world if accepted wholly and unabashedly. The noble canine, Mr. Fox, had mentored that acceptance.

The last articles of clothing Old Man donned were his tread-worn-thin-by-the-trail, rabbit brown in color, water-repellent thankfully, hiking boots and a navy-blue waterproof baseball hat that he had seen in a shop window on North Street (Rt. A917) in St. Andrews, Scotland many years ago. The Scotland souvenir might well save him from drowning today, he chuckled.

Gone were the heart operation-derived blood clots in his legs and chest, but not the semi-permanent stiffness they bequeathed him. His calves ached as he wiggled his socked toes into the boots. He moaned under his breath and then told himself to shut up. "Man up," he said, then he paused and said on second thought, "Fox up." He was amused at that line; Mr. Fox would smile when he heard it later. He finished his Noah's Flood ensemble by tying his boots and guffawed when he glanced in the mirror and saw "a birdwatcher headed to the golf course via the Appalachian Trail."

Downstairs, Old Man warmed a Cornish hen in a steam tray. In a small saucepan, he heated homemade no-salt bone broth while pinching small strips of bison into the pot. He added a teaspoon of Manuka honey, a pinch of taurine supplement and dried organic blueberries and cherries to the broth. When the stew was hot, he poured it into his black Yeti thermos and stowed the aluminum bottle in the snazzy avocado green Tumi backpack. In addition to the food supplies in the pack, he added heavy-gauge plastic tarps. He had a nostalgic, but nutty, idea, and he was not sure it would work (again), but he added the tarps to the backpack hopefully. When the hen was warmed, he stuffed speckled quail eggs, sourced at a gourmet shop, into the belly cavity of the meaty bird. He wrapped the hen several times in aluminum foil to preserve the cooked heat.

The last party preparation was the most important. The birthday cherry pie was made by a local baker who was once a pastry chef at The White House. Old Man cut two generous hunks of the cherry-laden pie and put the slices plastic snap-top sandwich containers. He opened the refrigerator, rummaged for the whipped cream, and added it to the backpack with a grin. After all. Mr. Fox was a whipped cream kind of guy.

When he opened the garage door, the choice was before him. Walk or drive? Driving would cut off a mile. And, if by chance Mr. Fox was not out in this gale, having the SUV nearby would allow Old Man to retreat to warmth and cover. Old Man studied the question. He knew the answer. Mr. Fox was always waiting—in snow, in howling winds, in jungle heat, even in pelting rain during the rainiest season recorded in Virginia history.

Puzzle solved; if Mr. Fox was out there walking in this monsoon, then so would Old Man. With that, he grabbed his whittled walking staff, hit the CLOSE button on the garage-door switch, and stepped into the beating rain. As the door descended, he saw his fifteen-year-old Jack Russell terrier, Beacon, appear and look at him sadly. Old Man and Beacon often sat in the garage with the big door retracted and enjoyed a rainstorm. Beacon loved to snuggle on Old Man's lap during storms, wrapped in a fleece jacket. But today, he wanted more. Mr. Fox was Beacon's friend, too. Old Man smacked his forehead and cursed himself. How could he even consider leaving Beacon behind on Mr. Fox's tenth birthday? Senility was his best guess.

He fitted a fleece sweater over Beacon's head and connected the Velcro toothy strips on the dog's Ferrari-red rain jacket. Old Man put the dog sling apparatus over Beacon's neck and tucked it and the fifteen-pound, tri-colored terrier inside his Barbour. Beacon nestled into his dad's chest and sighed. The odometer dial read five hundred, the stars were aligning.

Old Man often had a spatial epiphany in Fox World, and he was chewing on it as he headed out for the final installment of what was once called a "simple rehab walk". When challenged by infirmity, danger, or even just harsh inclement weather like today, everything slows down, appears bigger, and takes longer. Time is suspended; senses are heightened. The forest becomes towering and daunting, and an adult becomes a kid again and sees the forest through a child's eyes where adventure is simultaneously magical, scary, and mysterious. The canopy towers above feeble, once bright-eyed mortals who look to the sky for hope, the treasure of wonderment, and mindfulness in the quietness of the animal's forest. Mr. Fox walked his philosophy—*we all desire to see the world as a child again.*

Old Man and Beacon dove into the rain and navigated Fox World's guide stones—the Green Moss Mounds, the Cherry Candies Rock, Mr. Fox's Haybed, Fox Stream, Fox River, Helping Hands Bridge, Fox Bridges I and II, Secret Garden, and the Secret Oasis at Fox Beach. Finally, in what seemed like hours later, Beacon and Old Man crossed under Foxville Gate and stepped into the center of Fox World. The tree trunks wore their muted winter coats—tumbleweed brown, faded copper, almond paste, raw sienna. Many say winter is harshly drab. Old Man differed; he felt winter's rawness purified the soul.

Amongst the gray tones, there was a sparkly jewel in the forest, a glowing, fiery-orange ruby. Mr. Fox hovered under a waxy-leafed bush, water dripping from his orange nose. Despite the February's wet, arctic punches, Mr. Fox was faithful to his human friend. Old Man's thoughts rolled back. It had rained this hard the day that he had collapsed with sudden cardiac arrest and lay unconscious on the forest floor. Talk about coming full circle—this was it.

Old Man built two sturdy rain shelters with the heavy gauge plastic tarps. The tents, suspended from low-hanging limbs, blocked the deluge of falling rain. Each tarp covered one end of a forty-foot fallen log. On top of the log on each end, he put a dog blanket with rubber padding underneath, broke open chemical-activated handwarmer packs, and placed them under the blanket. The winter air ignited the heat elements in the packs and warmed the blanket. He placed Mr. Fox's rock bowl near the blanket and poured the steaming bison broth into the bowl.

Near the bone broth bowl, Old Man placed the piece de resistance, fresh baked pie made with organic cherries. He reached deeper into the backpack and removed a maple sugar "1" and "0," placed them atop the gorgeous-looking cherry pie, and then sprayed a dollop of whipped cream. Mr. Fox nodded approval from a few feet away. Birthday pie for an old fox is silly, some would say. Old Man had long ago eschewed what "some" would say; "some" were not here.

Old Man, respecting wild animal-human space boundaries, moved down the log and made a camp for Beacon. Beacon snuggled into the handwarmer-fueled blanket. He whined softly at Mr. Fox; Mr. Fox yipped back, but he was reluctant to jump atop the log. Old Man unpacked more picnic goodies and the fox's temptation red-lined; he wanted to join the soiree. Old Man and Mr. Fox had learned certain hand-paw signals from each other. Old Man made a swipe upward with his palm, from waist to chin, and Mr. Fox reacted instantly and jumped up onto the log. He looked up quizzically as if to inquire, *where did the rain go?* He saw the protective tarp, smiled, and shook vigorously, sending rain pellets flying, and then corkscrewed himself down into the toasty blanket just as he had seen Beacon do. He sniffed the bone broth's aroma. He smacked his lips in approval, but he did not eat yet. He was courteous—after all, he was a gentleman, a refined fox. When someone invites you to afternoon tea on your birthday, you do not gulp down your food with no mind to etiquette.

"Happy birthday, Mr. Fox. This is your special day. You are one decade old." The timeframe did not register with the fox. When N. Oldman switched scales, Mr. Fox perked up. "You have seen one hundred and twenty full moons. That's incredible, you made it, buddy. I am so proud of you," Old Man exclaimed.

Mr. Fox hung his head modestly. *Just another day in Fox World, and birthdays are a human concept, he thought, but he had to admit that seeing his human buddy and terrier friend, Beacon made him very happy.* Old Man countered, "Hey, if it wasn't a day of immense celebration, you, Beacon, and I would not be out in this crazy storm." Mr. Fox paused for a bison bite swallow and acknowledged his assent. *We certainly are a skulk of old fools out in a storm. There's no denying that.*

All three grinned, the trail buddies of a decade duration were together again.

Old Man poured a cup of fresh-roasted blueberry coffee. The coffee's steam rose to his nostrils and woke him from the rain's rhythm. His soul's awakening had been marinating for months. Old Man had changed, and he knew it. The former Wall Streeter, who had once bragged about dining at forty-one of the Zagat Guide's top fifty restaurants in New York City in a single year, looked around and realized that he was viscerally joyed in every fiber of his being. This makeshift bivouac in a rainy forest was better than the chef's table at the best restaurant in any city. Best of all, he was huddled with his best friends, Mr. Fox and Beacon, in a rainstorm on the elderly fox's birthday.

Old lions gather, and sooner or later, the storytelling starts. They recanted hundreds of miles of travel tales and laughed at their mishaps and travails, slapping their paws on their knees in rhythm as they guffawed. They became uncomfortably quiet, as men do, when the storytelling swerved into the stories of dangerous times. The sad days from their trail walking were acknowledged with a throaty gulp and awkward silence. A wry grimace and a distant stare often tell a painful story best.

The meaty broth and the warm blanket had a desired result. Mr. Fox grew sleepy, and Old Man watched over him as he rested. It was the richest gift that he could give to a wild fox. With Old Man nearby, the aging fox could sleep without fear. Beacon curled and dropped into a slumber too. Chests rose and fell, and the nose whistles of two drowsy canines synchronized into a relaxing forest melody. Old Man felt complete; he had no missing pieces. He had no pining ache for something else somewhere else. Old Man breathed in a smile. This was the apex, the apogee, of his life.

Sadly, the afternoon, unlike the rain, began to fade, and the skies turned wolf gray. Old Man reached into his frayed, well-traveled, avocado-green backpack and removed Mr. Fox's gifts—a steamed hen stuffed with quail eggs and spiked bouncy rubber balls dipped in organic peanut butter and rolled in freeze-dried blueberries.

"Mr. Fox, the Cornish hen is for your birthday dinner. Take it back to your den tonight and share it with Buttons. The peanut butter-blueberry chew toys will be a nice midnight snack until the stormfront dissipates. Thank you for being my friend, Mr. Fox. If the boundaries of animal and man allowed it, I'd give you the biggest, warmest hug ever. Thank you for being my guide and thank you for sharing your amazing life with me. I see life differently now; I am free."

Mr. Fox looked appreciatively at the gifts. It was a bounty for an old fox on a sure-to-be-icy night. He and Buttons would not have to hunt for a couple of days. The blueberries would give them a midwinter vitamin C boost. More than anything, he appreciated Old Man's words.

N. Oldman, we have walked and talked for many sunsets, and I have a secret to tell you. After you became sick, I always doubled back on our walks and followed you home to make sure that you made it there safely. I did so because you cared enough to become a part of us. You helped us, you protected us, you fought for us. You shared our story, and many came to help. Our future is bright because we have one for the time being, and that is all we can ask for.

The citizens of Fox World—Bucky, Deja Blue, Professor Owl, Colonel Hawk, Russell Raccoon, and my fellow foxes—have decided to give you a different name. With it, you will be with us forever. Our walks may have healed your illness, but you were never old, N. Oldman. Well, maybe all of us in Fox World are a wee bit ancient, but you were never truly an old man. As such, you can no longer be known as Old Man or N. Oldman. You have accepted a new life in the forest with us. Your new name in Fox World is A. Newman.

N. Oldman smiled acknowledgement and acceptance. Yes, he was a new man, one with the newly gifted name of A. Newman. It took a little fox to make him realize it, or put simply, to walk him to it.

A. Newman do not forget us and our forest and ask others to do the same. Our numbers are dwindling. When we are gone, Fox World is no longer.

Mr. Fox took one last draw on his bone broth, finished his cherry pie, mouthed the Cornish hen, and jumped catlike to another dry spot under the tarp. He peered out and up at the rain. His wise eyes scanned the skies. He would have to swim a swollen Fox River to get back to Buttons. *Never easy*, he agonized. He turned his head to look straight into A. Newman's hazel eyes and into the coffee-brown eyes of Beacon. His amber fox eyes with their hypnotic black vertical pupils were warmly intense. Silence, broken only by raindrops on the plastic tarps, accentuated their eye lock until on cue and in unison, the indestructible trio shouted, "If you are alive, you have won." And into the rain, Mr. Fox dashed.

A. Newman lit his portable camp stove, warmed his hands, and prepared a coffee pod. Beacon, swirled in the depths of a fleece blanket, eagerly accepted a beef jerky stick. A. Newman swallowed a bite of cherry pie as he brewed the coffee. Tears misted in his eyes. The tough business executive of old would have blamed the biting wind or the steam rising from the java. He knew better. Ultimate acceptance of one's vulnerability is life's best healing balm.

A. Newman sat in the damp forest and reflected on his life and year-long journey. Fox World had given him much. He had healed here. He and Mr. Fox had bled here. He had peeled away an unhealthy façade and become real here. He danced here with his mother to an Elvis song and returned to his father's cabin porch here. Best of all, he had found a best friend here. Another tear dripped on his cheek, rendered by a heartfelt admiration for the little fox who had led the way on this odyssey. Their journey was complete, and then again, maybe it wasn't. Once a portal to love, admiration, respect, learning, and courage is opened, discovery never ceases. Circles close, yes, they do, but they also loop a balanced mind and a softened heart forward with steady momentum. A. Newman felt the slingshot effect. Redemption is not a trail; it is simply the absence of regret. Choose the right trails, walk them with good beings, and redemption becomes a state of mind (maybe with a country & western soundtrack, he laughed). No one would believe his fox story even if he told it. A Corporate World dropout and an aging wild fox had walked five hundred miles together. He stared into the pounding rain, let the emotion well up, wiped a third tear with his jacket sleeve, and grinned with pride. "Darn right, we did."

Darkness ensued and wrapped the man and the little dog in its veil. They did not want to depart Fox World, but Smiling Wife would be worried. A. Newman pulled a flashlight and a pocketknife from his backpack. The father-gifted knife was perfect for what he did next. *Full circle*, Mr. Fox would call it. He opened the utility knife and began to whittle on the log by the flashlight's beam. The carved words, "500m. If you are alive, you've won" remain there to this day.

On the Great Fallen Oak.

In Fox World.

AUTHOR'S NOTES

As this book heads to the printing press, Mr. Fox is eleven and a half years old. He is remarkably healthy, and still leads Fox World with wisdom and compassion. Since the summer of Be, Here, Now, and Forever, Mr. Fox has raised seven more fox pups: Madison, Jefferson, Monroe, Chance, Faith, Lupie, and Lavin. He also adopted and mentored an orphan fox named Friendly. Sadly, his beloved mate, Buttons, passed away several months ago. His brother, Favre, still patrols Fox World and watches his brother's back. Favre has fathered three pups – Eternity, Kady, and Wyoming. Santa Claus, Mr. Fox's friend, continues to take unexpected faraway trips and returns with jokes and stories to make Mr. Fox laugh.

Mr. Fox's forest friends, Bucky the deer, Russell Raccoon, Colonel Hawk, Professor Owl, and Deja Blue the heron, are doing exceptionally well. Bucky fathered triplets last year. Professor Owl has mothered four broods of owlets, nine in all. Colonel Hawk has hatched three hawk broods. Deja Blue brought her adorable daughter to Beaver Lake for a visit last summer. Fox World's denizens wake daily to a thinning tree canopy as their wooded oasis becomes further imperiled.

A. Newman enjoys his fox-inspired outlook and remains a faithful, ever-pursuing student of Fox World's wisdom. Due to heart arrythmia, A. Newman never returned to Corporate World. He still hits duck hooks off life's first tee, literally and metaphorically, but he laughs and enjoys the humble hunt for both the golf ball and life's meaning.

Smiling Wife began an exciting new job in a Corporate World building adjacent to Fox World. On her first day of work, Mr. Fox and A. Newman walked her to the front door.office.

A. Newman and Smiling Wife visit Mr. Fox with a sliver of organic cherry pie. They are joined on their woodland strolls by their Jack Russell terriers, twelve-year-old Bounce, and seventeen-year-old Beacon. Beacon, no longer able to walk long distances, rides in a spiffy red carriage that he refers to as "his Ferrari."

Local officials and volunteers continue their diligent leadership to preserve the forest and wildlife habitat. It is a difficult and challenging pursuit. All worthy things in life are. If you have ideas on how Fox World might be preserved as a protected wildlife habitat area, please send a note to foxworldnow@gmail.com or visit www.foxworldnow. com. Any thoughts are greatly appreciated.

ABOUT THE AUTHOR

Jack Russell is the author of **"Fox World, 500 Miles of Walks and Talks with an Old Fox"**, the story of a man and a fox united on a series of long walks over the course of a year. Both survive dire challenges on the journey, and the man learns invaluable lessons of resiliency and mindfulness from the wild fox. Drawn in by the fox's courage, the man joins the fight to save the fox's forest and his animal friends. **Fox World** is based on true events.

Jack traveled North America and Europe for three decades to assist Fortune 1000 companies with building distribution channels, developing new products, and launching start-ups. His efforts were instrumental in building a pet health insurance company in America and he underwrote over one hundred fifty affinity programs in his career. Jack studied economics at Virginia Commonwealth University and many years later, attended executive programs at The University of Pennsylvania and Georgetown University. Jack lives in Lake Frederick, Virginia with his wife, Susan, and their Jack Russell terriers. As well as fighting for Mr. Fox's forest to be declared a nature preserve, Jack and Susan enjoy giving freedom rides to shelter dogs and assisting with their shelter medical bills. He is a beginner at photography, an ever-learning birdwatcher, a football fan when Green Bay is on television and an enthusiastic golfer of diminishing skills.

Contact Info:
foxworldnow@gmail.com
www.foxworldnow.com
@foxworldnow on Instagram and Facebook

CPSIA information can be obtained
at www.ICGtesting.com
Printed in the USA
LVHW011548241022
731425LV00009B/889